TRANSISTOR IGNITION SYSTEMS

No. 882
$8.95

TRANSISTOR IGNITION SYSTEMS
By Carroll A. Brant

TAB BOOKS
Blue Ridge Summit, Pa. 17214

FIRST EDITION

FIRST PRINTING—SEPTEMBER 1976

Copyright © 1976 by TAB BOOKS

Printed in the United States
of America

Reproduction or publication of the content in any manner. without express permission of the publisher. is prohibited. No liability is assumed with respect to the use of the information herein.

Hardbound Edition: International Standard Book No. 0-8306-6882-9

Paperbound Edition: International Standard Book No. 0-8306-5882-3

Library of Congress Card Number: 76-43635

Preface

Transistor ignition is not a new idea; it has actually been around for over 20 years. With the aid of heavy advertising that promised super performance for the large-cubic-inch engines of the 1950s, many aftermarket transistor ignition systems were sold and installed. Car makers sold transistor ignitions as optional equipment on some of their more expensive models. Transistor ignition was the vogue for the fast cars of the time.

The glamour of transistor ignition soon faded for a number of reasons. The transistors and diodes then available were designed primarily for radio communications use, and they proved somewhat unreliable when used under the extreme temperature variations encountered in auto engine compartments. Many systems were installed with great expectations of great improvements in speed and performance but met with disappointment because of incomplete ignition overhaul when the system was installed, or because of other engine problems not found and corrected at that time. Servicing of installed systems was often unsatisfactory because many mechanics lacked knowledge of how the systems worked.

In the 1960s great progress was made in the design and manufacture of solid-state devices that multiplied their reliability and possible uses, and improved manufacturing methods brought the prices for these improved products within the range of the experimenter's purse. This sudden availability of reasonably priced transistors and diodes that could be relied upon to serve many purposes encouraged new research into transistor ignition circuits.

The late 1960s and early 1970s saw the passage of laws regulating the amount of pollution emitted by gasoline-powered engines. The public was also made aware of the fact that gasoline supplies were not limitless, and that autos must be made with provisions for economy of operation as well as for strict control of exhaust emissions.

These events served to bring transistor ignition to the attention of the public again, and also to the attention of the car makers. The car makers reasoned that if ignition systems could be built to make engines to perform better, they should also be an aid in raising engine efficiency (emission control) and operating economy (gasoline mileage).

Transistor ignition is becoming more prevalent on the modern auto engine with each new model. Many excellent replacement systems are now available for car models not originally so equipped.

This book will explore the original-equipment systems as well as some of the many types of replacement systems available. It will not attempt to explain the engineering theory of operation of the many systems, but it will explain components and systems as an aid to professional and do-it-yourself mechanics in the installation, troubleshooting, and repair of transistor ignitions.

A book such as this would be an impossibility without the cooperation of many firms and individuals. I gratefully acknowledge the assistance given by:

Accel-Weber
Allison Automotive Company
Beckman Instruments, Inc.
Borg-Warner Automotive Division
Champion Spark Plug Company
Delco Remy Division of General Motors Corporation
Chrysler Corporation
Delta Products, Inc.
Essex International
Ford Motor Company
General Electric Company

Ignition Systems, Inc.
Judson Research and Manufacturing Company
Motorola, Inc.
Nisonger Corporation—Piranha Ignition Ltd.
RCA Corporation
Speedatron
Sorensen Manufacturing Company
Stevens Associates
Mr. C. R. Stevens
Mr. L. M. Jennings

I also wish to express my appreciation to Thomas R. Powell for many suggestions incorporated in this book and for the many hours of valuable assistance given. I most want to thank him for the lovely granddaughter to whom this book is dedicated, Lynn Marie Powell.

Carroll A. Brant

Contents

1 Functions of An Ignition System   11
Ignition Advance—Fundamentals of Electricity—Conventional Ignition System—Ignition Coil—Typical Ignition System—Capacitor—Ballast Resistor—Basic Maintenance Problems—Dwell—Extending Dwell—Construction of High-Voltage Components

2 Maintenance of Conventional Ignition Systems   34
Test Equipment—Checking Primary Resistance—Ballast Resistance—Starting Voltage—Distributor Checks—Points and Capacitor Checks—Coil Testing—Checking Suppressor Cables—Checking Other Suppression Devices—Spark Plug Maintenance—Engine Troubleshooting—Ignition System Troubleshooting Chart

3 Semiconductor Devices for Automobiles   57
Rectifying Devices—Transistors

4 Transistor Circuits   67
Amplifier Configurations—Bias Stabilization—Coupling—Timing Circuits—Sensing and Control Circuits—Voltage Regulation Circuit

5 Transistor Ignition   80
Problems of Conventional Ignitions—Advantages of Transistor Ignitions—Ford Contact-Controlled Ignition—Capacitive-Discharge Ignition—Pointless Ignitions

6 Auto Manufacturers' Transistor Ignitions — 92
Chrysler Magnetically Triggered Ignition—Troubleshooting the Chrysler Ignition—General Motors Delcotronic Ignition—Troubleshooting—Delco Remy High-Energy Ignition—Ford Magnetically Triggered Ignition

7 Replacement Transistor Ignition Systems — 143
Judson Electronic Magneto—Delta Mark Ten Capacitive-Discharge Ignition—Delta Mark Ten B—Mark Ten Test Procedures—Tri-Star Tiger 500 CD Ignition System—Stevens Ignition System—Accel Breakerless Electronic Ignition System—Megaspark Optoelectronic Breakerless Ignition—Piranha Electronic Ignition—Borg-Warner Electronic Ignition—Allison Optoelectronic System—Essex Elightronic Ignition—Sorensen Magnition Ignition System

8 Electronic Ignition — 207
Dwell Extender—Point-Triggered Capacitive-Discharge Ignition

9 Scope Testing of Transistor Ignitions — 221
Basic Ignition Patterns—Advanced Ignition Testing—Obtaining and Interpreting Patterns

Glossary — 244

Index — 249

Chapter 1

Functions of An Ignition System

For an internal-combustion engine to operate, some means of igniting the compressed air/fuel mixture must be an integral part of the complete engine assembly. This process of igniting the mixture—or as the process is more simply named, *ignition*—has evolved through four distinct systems to the jump-spark system in present use.

These four distinct system types are: (1) the *hot-wire* ignition used nearly 100 years ago, (2) *break-spark* ignition used extensively on single-cylinder, slow-speed stationary engines for over 50 years now, (3) *trembler-coil* (vibrating points) ignition, used on Model T Ford engines, and (4) *jump-spark* ignition which has been in use for some 70 years and of which there are two kinds, battery-coil and high-tension magneto systems.

One reason for the four major stages of system evolution has been a search for more reliable ignition. A reason for many refinements of the presently used jump-spark ignition has been the increasing need for reliable spark control as compression ratios have increased, better fuels have become available, engine speeds have increased and, correspondingly, torque and horsepower for a given displacement have increased.

Another reason for recent refinements of ignition systems is the enactment of legislation setting standards of permissible emissions by motor vehicle engines. Transistor ignition, with its reliability and ease of control, provides a large advantage in control of exhaust emissions from engines.

To gain the greatest efficiency in an engine, ignition of the mixture must take place in each cylinder near the end of the compression stroke so that the mixture will be completely, or almost completely, burned by the time the piston has been forced to the bottom of its stroke by the expanding hot gases. This time for complete combustion varies with different brands of fuel of the same octane rating and, of course, with different grades of fuel.

The combustion time varies also with the air/fuel ratio, which, in turn, is affected by atmospheric pressure, temperature, and humidity. This explains why your car does not run well in Denver on a cold snowy day when it was tuned properly at Sacramento in 80°-plus dry weather. An engine should be tuned for its operating environment.

Correct ignition timing of an engine is done at an idle speed to specifications set by the manufacturer. These specifications take into consideration such factors as compression, carburetion, recommended fuel, and valve timing. At best they represent compromise settings for various geographic areas, driver habits, and driving conditions. As the engine is operated over varying speed ranges and load conditions, the critical time of ignition of mixture varies considerably for two reasons. (1) The actual time taken for the piston to complete its power stroke, and hence the time available for complete combustion, is much less at high speed than it is at low or idling speed. (2) The mixture entering the chamber varies from rich to lean with changing engine speed, and the actual compression of the mixture changes with RPM.

IGNITION ADVANCE

To provide the necessary change in spark timing with changes in engine speed, two methods of advance or retard of timing are used in the conventional ignition distributor. (On some late-model cars, a third retard device may be found that operates as a part of the emission control system and is called a *vacuum modulator*.)

Centrifugal Advance

The first advance device is the *centrifugal* advance, or as it is sometimes called, the *mechanical* advance. This mechanism is operated by two weights, loosely pinned at one end. The centrifugal force developed by the rotating distributor shaft tends to throw the weights outward against the tension of the springs, holding their unpinned ends toward the center of the distributor, or "closed." As the speed of the distributor shaft increases, the centrifugal force increases, and the farther the weights move out toward the maximum possible movement. This movement of the weights is transmitted to the breaker cam so that the cam is advanced as the weights move outward. Thus, the centrifugal device advances the timing as engine speed increases.

Vacuum Advance

Another advance mechanism, which operates independently of the centrifugal advance, is the *vacuum* advance. This unit is designed to provide additional advance over and above that which the mechanical advance is capable of providing.

The conventional vacuum advance uses the vacuum in the intake manifold to provide the additional spark advance required under part-throttle operation, and it has a spring-loaded diaphragm connected by linkage to the distributor advance plate, or as it is called, the *breaker* plate. The spring-loaded side of the vacuum unit is airtight and is connected by tubing to a point on the atmospheric side of the carburetor throttle valve when the throttle is in the *idle* position. When the throttle is in the idle position, there is usually almost zero vacuum at the point where the vacuum control connection is made. (This is not true on all engines. On engines having vacuum present in the line at idle speed, the line must be disconnected and the vacuum side plugged when setting the initial ignition timing.) When the throttle is opened, the valve swings past the opening of the vacuum passage, and the vacuum can then act on the diaphragm of the spark advance mechanism. This causes the diaphragm to deflect, and its motion, through the linkage, advances the breaker plate. The amount of movement of the diaphragm is proportional to the amount of vacuum present, and so the amount of advance is controlled by the amount of vacuum.

For a better understanding of how an ignition system operates, and to enable a mechanic to logically locate a problem in any auto electrical system, it is necessary to know the meaning of the basic electrical terms used in the automotive industry.

FUNDAMENTALS OF ELECTRICITY

Electricity, from whatever source, is considered to be the controlled flow or movement of electrons. *Electron* is the name given to negatively charged particles of atoms. It then follows that the flow of electrons, or electricity, is *from negative to positive*.

Electromotive force, the pressure that will cause a current to flow, is measured in volts and is commonly called *voltage* (symbolized by the letter V). Nearly all vehicles today use the 12V, negative-ground system. If the system voltage is substantially increased, as by the alternator regulator being set too high, serious damage can result. Voltage higher than that for which the system is designed can increase the current in the circuit to a value that will overheat wiring, and components may be permanently damaged or destroyed.

Amperage is a term given to the amount of current flowing in a circuit. Each circuit in an auto is designed to draw a certain amount of current, or a certain number of *amperes*. If the voltage applied to a given circuit is raised or lowered, the current symbolized by I, will rise or fall accordingly.

Resistance (R) is opposition to the flow of current in a circuit. Resistance is measured in *ohms* (Ω). All electrical circuits have a predetermined resistance built into them. This resistance enables the circuit to accomplish the purpose for which it was designed. Unwanted resistance, however, such as that caused by loose connections or faulty components, is a major source of trouble and failure of auto electrical systems.

The *power* (P), or rate at which work is accomplished in an electrical circuit, is measured in *watts*. The number of watts is the product of volts times amps. For example, if a certain automotive coil operates at 12 volts (12V) and allows 3 amps (3A) of current to pass through it, the coil must use 36 watts (36W) of electrical power (12V $\times$ 3A = 36W).

The electrical terms explained above are stated as Ohm's law ($I = ER$) and Watt's law ($P = E \times I$). They can be easily remembered and used in troubleshooting when stated in the following manner: *volts = amps $\times$ ohms, amps = volts/ohms, ohms = volts/amps*, and *watts = volts $\times$ amps*.

CONVENTIONAL IGNITION SYSTEM

The conventional ignition system, as shown by the drawing in Fig. 1-1, is made up of two basic circuits. The *primary* circuit consists of the battery, ignition switch, ballast resistor, primary winding of the coil, contact set or points, and capacitor (condenser). The points and capacitor are housed in the distributor. The wiring connecting these parts is shown as a solid line.

The *secondary* circuit consists of the secondary winding of the coil, distributor cap, rotor, spark plug wires or cables, and spark plugs. The wiring connecting these parts is shown as a dashed line. The common return for each of these circuits is the engine block and car frame, called the *ground*.

The battery is the heart of an ignition system, supplying all power necessary for its operation. The negative terminal is connected to the engine block and car frame by a large cable. The positive terminal is connected by an insulated cable to the starter solenoid, and from there to the ignition switch.

Primary Circuit

The ignition switch serves as an ON−OFF switch to complete the circuit between the battery and coil and, usually, the radio, heater motor, and so forth. When turned to the maximum clockwise, or START, position, the switch activates the starter relay, engaging the starter motor. It also bypasses the ballast resistor by a wire from the START contact in the switch to the coil or through a separate set of contacts in the starter relay.

The ballast resistor in the primary circuit is designed to control the coil current for all driving conditions and engine speeds. It is always bypassed during starting because the battery voltage may drop to less than 10V during cranking and thus leave insufficient coil voltage.

The ignition coil, by induction, steps up the low battery voltage to a level sufficient to jump the gap of the spark plug in the combustion chamber.

The breaker points are located on the breaker plate inside the distributor housing. These points open and close the primary circuit as they make and break contact with the action of the distributor cam. The cam has the same number of lobes as there are cylinders in the engine so that the initiation of ignition is controlled by the rotation of the cam.

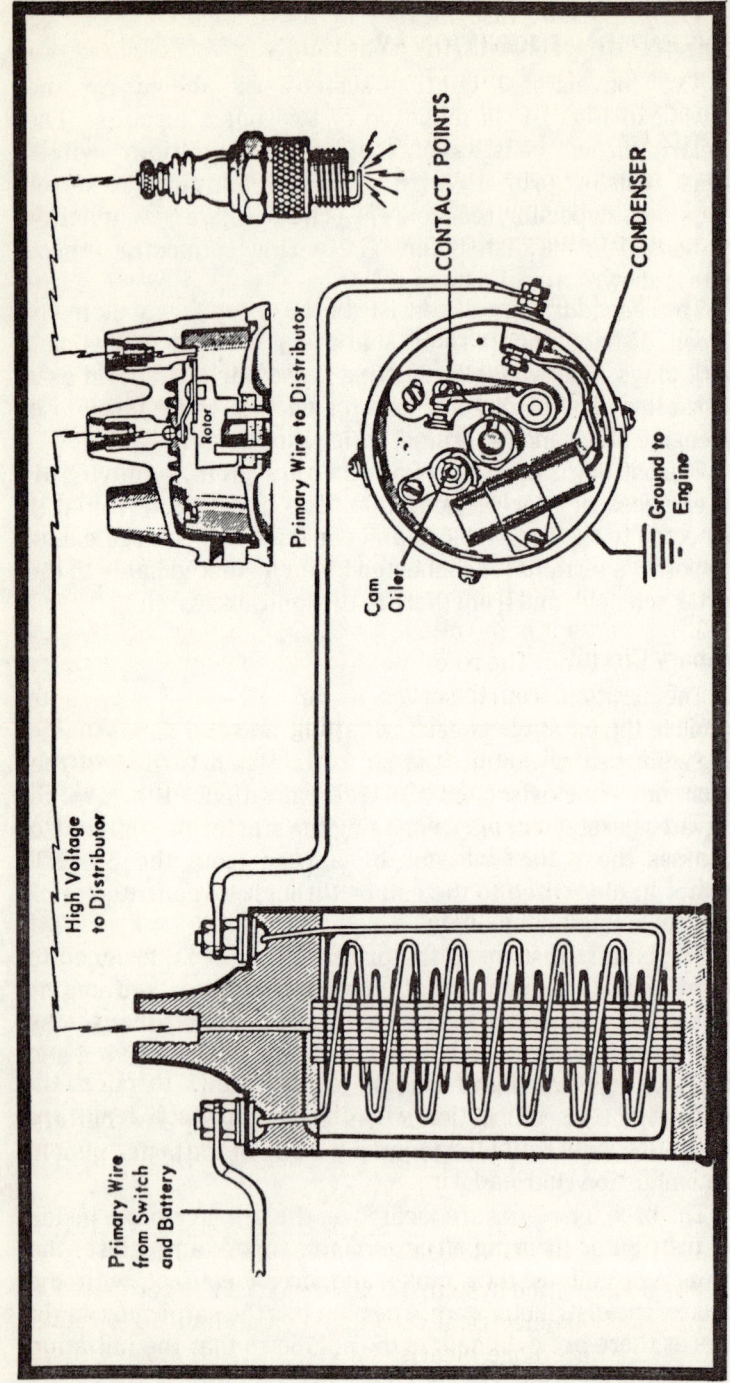

Fig. 1-1. Block diagram of conventional ignition system.

The capacitor, also located in the distributor body, is connected in parallel with the points and affords a place for the electrons from the primary winding to go when the points are open and the primary circuit is incomplete.

The primary circuit is completed through the ground return circuit, consisting of the grounded-point contact, distributor body, engine block, car frame, and ground strap to the negative battery post.

Secondary Circuit

The high voltage necessary to jump a spark plug gap is developed in the secondary winding of the coil when the points open. A high-voltage wire or cable serves as the path from the high-voltage tower of the coil to the center tower of the distributor cap.

The cap serves as the distribution center, directing the high voltage to the proper spark plug tower in the cap. This distribution is accomplished by the action of the rotor, which is mounted on the distributor cam and indexed to provide a small-gap path for high-voltage current to the spark plug at its proper firing time. The rotor makes a rubbing contact with the high-voltage lead from the coil.

The high-voltage leads, or plug leads, conduct the high-voltage from the distributor cap's spark plug towers to each spark plug in the engine, in the proper firing order.

The spark plugs provide a spark gap in the combustion chamber. When the high voltage jumps across this gap, the air/fuel mixture is ignited.

The complete path of the high-voltage current, or secondary circuit, is from the grounded terminal of the battery through the ground strap, through the car frame and engine block, through the shell of the spark plug that is firing, across the plug lead to the distributor cap, through the rotor and coil lead to the secondary winding of the coil, through the secondary to its connection with the primary-coil lead, and back to the positive battery post through the ballast resistor, ignition switch, and lead wires.

COMPARISON OF IGNITION AND LIGHTING CIRCUITS

When an ignition system's primary circuit is compared to other automobile electrical circuits, such as lighting circuits, one notable difference clearly stands out. Automotive lights are either *on* with a complete circuit, or *off* with an open circuit, as controlled by an ON—OFF switch. Turn-signal lights are *off* or *on* as controlled by the turn-signal switch; but when they are *on*, the circuit is periodically interrupted at a rate determined by the design of the flasher unit and the load presented by the lamps in the circuit. An ignition system is either *off* or *on* as controlled by the ignition switch; but when it is *on*, the circuit is interrupted by the points in the circuit. The number of interruptions per revolution of the distributor shaft is controlled by the number of lobes on the cam, which corresponds to the number of cylinders in the engine. The number of interruptions per second or per minute is thus controlled by the RPM of the engine, which drives the distributor shaft at one-half engine speed (in 4-stroke-cycle engines). This controlled circuit interruption is necessary for the timing of ignition as well as for the actual operation of the ignition coil.

IGNITION COIL

The ignition coil consists of two windings. One end of each winding is connected to the negative (—) terminal of the coil. (A coil of this type is referred to as an *autotransformer*.) The

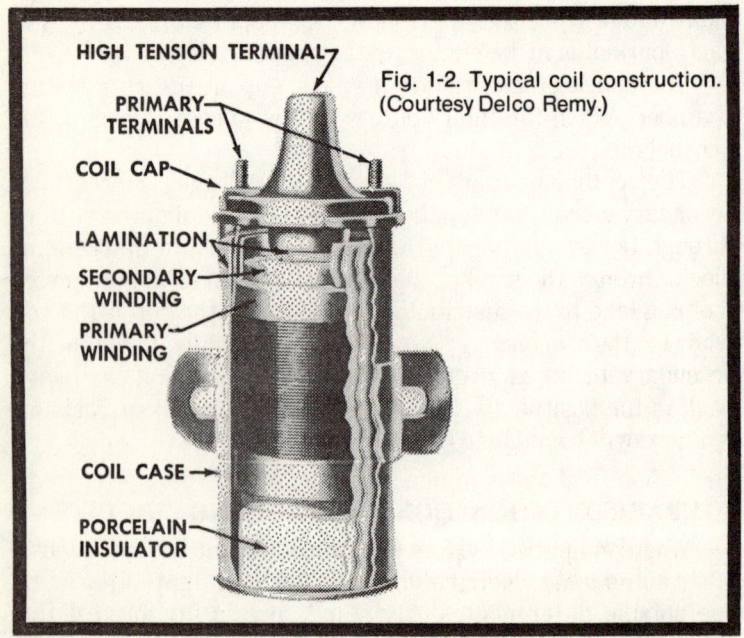

Fig. 1-2. Typical coil construction. (Courtesy Delco Remy.)

primary, or low-voltage, winding consists of 200-plus turns of relatively heavy wire; and the secondary, or high-voltage, winding consists of 20,000-plus turns of fine wire. All turns are insulated from each other, and both windings are on the same core. The core is made up of a number of small iron rods to concentrate the magnetic lines of force. The secondary is wound first, and the primary is wound on the outside of the secondary. This assembly is immersed in an insulating compound or oil and sealed in a metal can. The top of the coil is made of an insulating material so that leads from the windings may be brought out without danger of shorting (see Fig. 1-2).

The coil operates on the same electrical principle as an alternator or generator: *induction*. When a relative motion exists between a magnetic field and a conductor, a voltage is induced in the conductor, and current will flow in the conductor if the circuit is complete. Also, any conductor will have a magnetic field around it when a current is flowing in it. An alternator generates its output by moving a magnetic field over loops of wire (conductors). A generator produces its output by passing loops of wire through a stationary magnetic field. A coil (transformer) gets its output by a changing current flow through the primary, causing alternate buildups and collapses of magnetic lines over the secondary winding, which, in turn, induces a voltage across the terminals.

TYPICAL IGNITION SYSTEM

Figure 1-3 is a pictorial schematic of a typical ignition system. Note that the ballast resistor in this circuit is a calibrated resistance wire used as the connection from the ignition switch to the positive coil connection. The shorting of the ballast resistor during starting is accomplished by a set of contacts on the starter solenoid.

When the contact points in the distributor close with the ignition switch turned on, current can flow from the negative battery terminal to ground, through the contact points, through the primary winding of the coil, through the resistance wire and ignition switch, and back to the positive battery terminal through the common connection point on the solenoid.

This flow of current in the ignition coil's primary winding produces a magnetic field in the coil as indicated by the thin lines surrounding the two windings. The current and thus the magnetic field, however, does not reach its maximum value

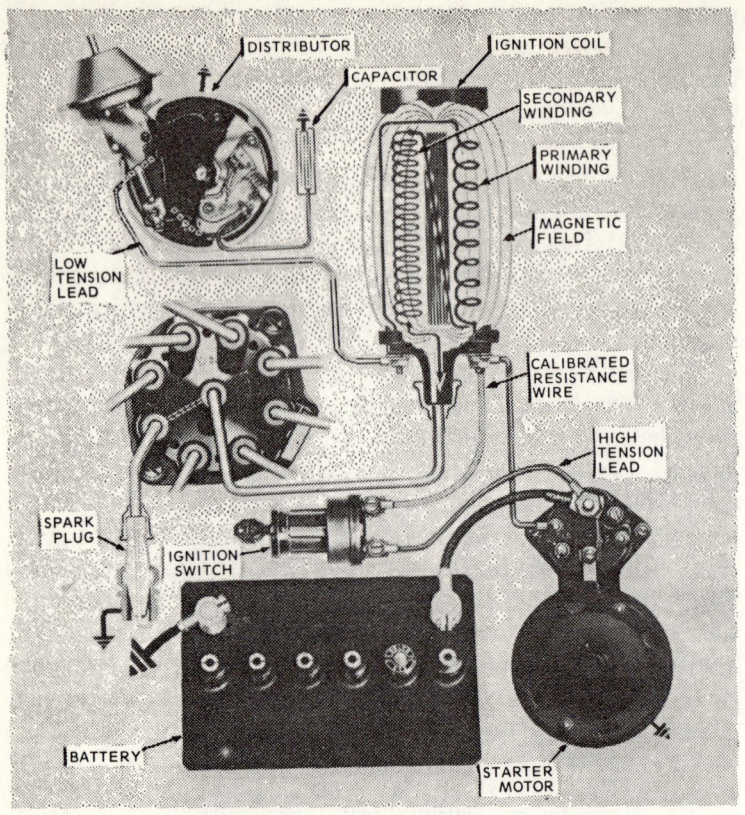

Fig. 1-3. Typical ignition system. (Courtesy Delco Remy.)

instantly. A small fraction of a second, a buildup time, is required for this to occur.

This is true of any coil because of the *self-induction* that occurs as current starts to flow through the coil. Self-induction produces a momentary countervoltage in the coil which opposes any change in the amount of current flowing. This countervoltage must be overcome by the battery voltage so that the value of current can increase to its maximum as determined by the resistance of the primary winding and circuit.

While the buildup time is short, it is a factor in ignition performance, particularly at high engine speeds. At high speeds the time that the contact points remain closed is so short that the current, and thus the magnetic field, cannot increase to its maximum value. Any ignition system must be designed so that adequate voltage will be available from the ignition coil under all conditions of engine operation.

During the time that the distributor contact points remain closed and the flow of current is increasing, energy in the form of magnetic flux is being stored in the coil. That is, the strength of the magnetic field continues to increase to a maximum, called *saturation*. This maximum may be reached at low engine speeds but not at high speeds. Further rotation of the breaker cam brings the next cam lobe around to where it strikes the breaker lever's rubbing block, thus causing the contact points to break or open.

Current tends to continue to flow across the separating contacts because of the self-induction of the ignition coil. Self-induction opposes *any* change in the amount of current flowing in a winding. Thus the primary winding attempts to keep the current flowing in the primary circuit. If it were not for the ignition capacitor connected across the contact points, current would continue to flow between the separating points. This current would form an arc, which would burn the points quickly and drain away most of the energy stored in the coil. There would be insufficient energy left in the coil to produce the necessary high-voltage surge in the secondary winding.

CAPACITOR

The ignition capacitor provides a place where the current can flow during the instant that the points begin to separate. The current flows into the capacitor instead of forming an arc between the separating points. The amount of current that the capacitor can accept is very limited, so it becomes charged very quickly. The capacitor thus acts as a storage chamber for the electrical energy, which quickly brings the flow of current in the primary circuit to a stop. As the flow of current is halted, the magnetic field, which depends on this flow of current, decreases rapidly in concentration. The rapid change in the concentration of the magnetic field causes a high voltage to be induced in both the primary and secondary windings. In the primary winding the voltage may reach 200V or so, resulting in further charging of the capacitor. In the secondary winding, which may contain up to 100 times as many turns of wire as the primary, the voltage could go as high as 25,000V (primary voltage times turns ratio).

Normally, however, the voltage does not increase to this high value. It increases only to an amount sufficient to produce a spark at the spark plug gap. This voltage is usually somewhere between 6,000V and 20,000V. The actual value depends upon such variables as engine compression, speed, mixture ratios, width of spark plug gap, spark plug temperatures, and so forth.

As the spark appears at the spark plug gap, the energy in the coil (stored in the form of magnetic lines, or flux) begins to drain from the coil through the secondary circuit, thus sustaining the spark for a small fraction of a second, or for several degrees of crankshaft rotation. During this interval, the charged capacitor discharges back through the primary circuit, producing an oscillation of the current flow in the primary circuit during the brief interval that is required for the primary circuit to return to a state of equilibrium. Note particularly that the ignition capacitor does not discharge until after the spark has occurred at the spark plug gap.

The above sequence of action is repeated as each lobe of the breaker cam moves under and past the rubbing block on the breaker level to cause the contact points to close and open.

BALLAST RESISTOR

The ballast resistor appears in several different physical forms, such as a resistance wire lead or resistance wire enclosed in a ceramic block or within the coil. Regardless of the physical appearance, each ballast resistor performs the same function—maintaining the current flow in the coil primary at a value sufficient to cause coil saturation and prevent excessive current flow that would damage the coil and contact points. Most ignition coils using resistors and starter bypass circuits are really 9V coils. The ballast resistor is designed to maintain coil voltage near this value and is bypassed during starting, when the battery voltage may fall to nearly 9V.

The ballast resistor is a special heat-sensitive resistor that has a *positive temperature coefficient.* That is, the resistance increases as the temperature of the resistor increases. When the engine is idling, the contact points are in the closed position longer, causing the resistor to get hot and increase in value. By Ohm's law, the greater the resistance, the greater the voltage drop across it. Hence less voltage is applied across the coil.

When the engine speed is increased, the contact points are closed for a shorter time. This allows the resistor to operate at a cooler temperature; and the cooler the resistor, the less resistance it has. Thus the voltage in the primary will vary from approximately 9V to as much as 12V, depending on engine speed. At higher engine speeds, it is necessary to have less resistance because the contact points are closed for a very short time. The extra voltage across the coil is needed to provide current for magnetic saturation of the coil at high engine speeds.

BASIC MAINTENANCE PROBLEMS

Ballast resistors are not all of the same ohmic value, nor do they have exactly the same temperature coefficient. They are designed for a certain coil and circuit application. Care must be taken when replacing only the coil or the resistor to be sure that it is compatible with the unit not replaced.

Ignition capacitors are not all of the same physical size nor of the same capacitance value. They are designed to load and unload in the proper time with a certain coil. Even a perfectly good capacitor of the wrong value will result in poor ignition and rapid deterioration of the points. Figure 1-4A shows metal transfer from the negative to the positive breaker point, caused by a capacitor of less than the required capacity. Figure 1-4B shows metal transfer from the positive to the negative point, caused by a capacitor of excess value.

Proper point installation, alignment, and adjustment are very important to the operation of an ignition system. Dirt or oil on the points may prevent the engine from starting or cause it to run erratically at high speeds. Another cause of high point resistance is misalignment of the points at installation (see Fig. 1-5). Rapid point wear or burning is often caused by dirty or misaligned points.

Point *adjustment* can also be very critical for high-speed engines. There is a direct relationship between the maximum distance the points open (point *clearance*), the degrees of cam rotation during which the points remain closed (*cam angle* or *dwell*), available saturation time, and ignition timing.

DWELL

Dwell angle, or simply dwell, is the number of degrees the distributor cam turns while the contact points are closed. During the dwell period, a magnetic field is built up in the primary winding of the coil. However, time is required to build

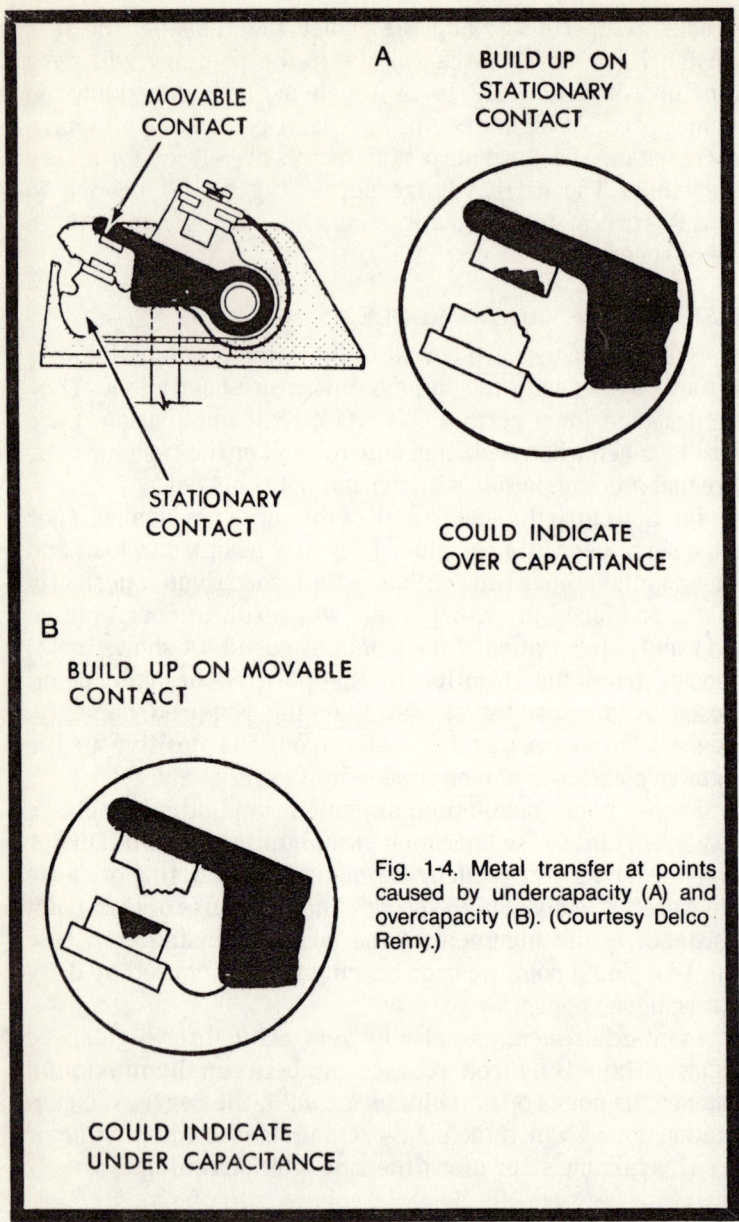

Fig. 1-4. Metal transfer at points caused by undercapacity (A) and overcapacity (B). (Courtesy Delco Remy.)

up a full-strength magnetic field. When a full-strength magnetic field is produced, the coil is said to be saturated. Coil saturation at low engine speeds presents no problem because of the relatively slow rotation of the distributor cam. At high

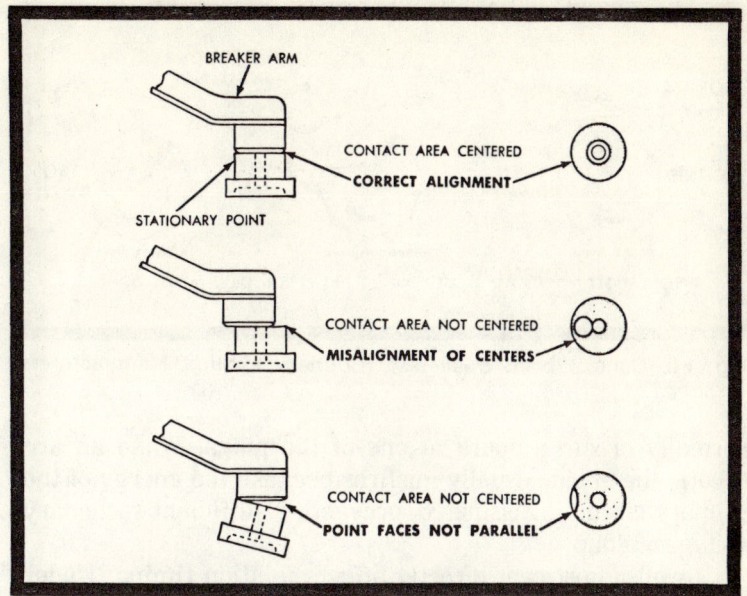

Fig. 1-5. Contact breaker point alignment.

speeds, however, unless the contact points are adjusted to provide a sufficient dwell period, coil saturation cannot be reached.

In an 8-cylinder engine running at idle speed of 400 RPM, the ignition system must produce 30 sparks per second to fire all the cylinders. With an engine operating at this speed, dwell angle is not very critical, because more than sufficient coil saturation time is available. However, with the engine running at 4000 RPM, 300 sparks per second would be required to fire all cylinders. This is the speed at which dwell becomes very critical. If the dwell were reduced only slightly from the required amount, the engine would begin to misfire at high speeds because the coil would not have time to become saturated. Figure 1-6 is an illustration of dwell and its relation to point gap.

Although dwell is not critical at low speeds, point gap becomes very important. With the engine cranking, there must be sufficient point gap or the points will arc excessively and the engine will not start readily. Also, if an engine is operated with too little gap at low speeds, the points will wear rapidly. If the points open slowly and do not open wide enough, an arc will continue across the contact points, using energy that would

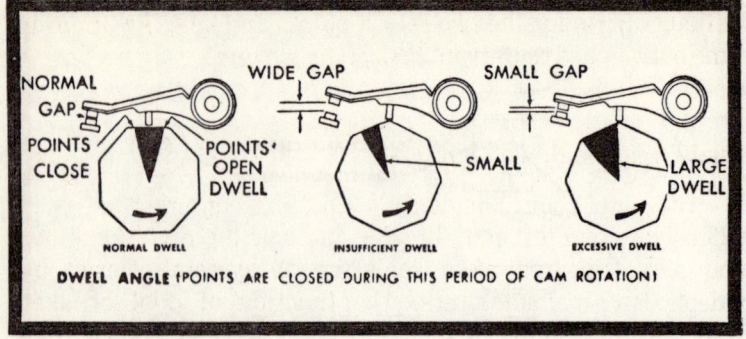

Fig. 1-6. Contact point dwell test. (Courtesy Ignition Manufacturers Institute.)

normally create a spark at one of the plugs. When an arc occurs, the engine usually misfires because the energy of the primary circuit is dissipated, preventing sufficient secondary voltage buildup.

Dwell adjustment directly affects ignition timing. Under certain conditions, the rubbing block on the movable contact arm may wear. As a result the dwell angle increases, which, in turn, causes the ignition timing to be late. Also, if dwell is decreased, timing is advanced.

EXTENDING DWELL

For some very high-RPM engines, the time necessary to mechanically open the contact points plus the time for the spring to close them decreases the available dwell time to the point where the engine would misfire at top speed. To cure this problem, two types of distributors were developed. These types are the dual-point, dual-coil system, which never became popular, and the dual-point, single-coil system, used by Ford and Chrysler on their large, high-RPM engines.

Dual-Point, Dual-Coil Ignition

In the dual-point, dual-coil distributor system, each coil supplies the voltage necessary to fire four cylinders. Each se of contact points is independent of the other, and each controls the primary circuit of only one coil. Distribution to the spark plugs is made by a rotor that provides a high-voltage path from each coil to the four spark plugs fired by the coil. The available dwell time, with each point set and coil firing half of the eight cylinders, is an advantage of this ignition system at very high engine speeds. However, the difficulty in timing the two sets of points and keeping them in time outweighed the advantages of the system.

Dual-Point, Single-Coil Ignition

The dual-point, single-coil ignition system was used extensively by Ford and Chrysler for their high-RPM engines and also appeared as a replacement system offered by independent manufacturers. The function of dual breaker points in this system is to provide a longer dwell period at high speed than is possible with a single breaker set. The longer dwell period permits greater coil saturation and thus greater secondary-voltage output.

One set of the dual points (Fig. 1-7) is called the *make* set, and its function is to close the primary circuit and begin the dwell period. The other point set is called the *break* set, and its function is to open the primary circuit, which induces the high voltage in the coil's secondary winding. The point sets are connected in parallel with each other and in series with the lead between the coil and the distributor. One capacitor is in parallel with the points.

Each point set is adjusted for a normal dwell period of 26° to 28°. But since the dwell periods overlap each other slightly, the total dwell of both sets may be 36° to 40°. It would be impossible to adjust a single point set to 40° dwell because the point gap would be so small that sparking across the gap would occur constantly. If the engine did run with such a small point gap, the points would quickly pit or burn, resulting in an extremely short point life.

In the dual-point distributor shown in Fig. 1-7, an insulated jumper strap connects the two point sets in parallel. With the point sets connected in parallel, primary current can flow through either point set or through both point sets at the same time.

The action of dual points can be understood by studying the illustrations of Fig. 1-7. The point set on the left of the cam is the *make* set. The point set on the right of the cam is the *break* set. Cam rotation is clockwise.

In position 1, the *make* set is closed, while the *break* set is still open. The primary circuit has just been completed and the dwell period begins.

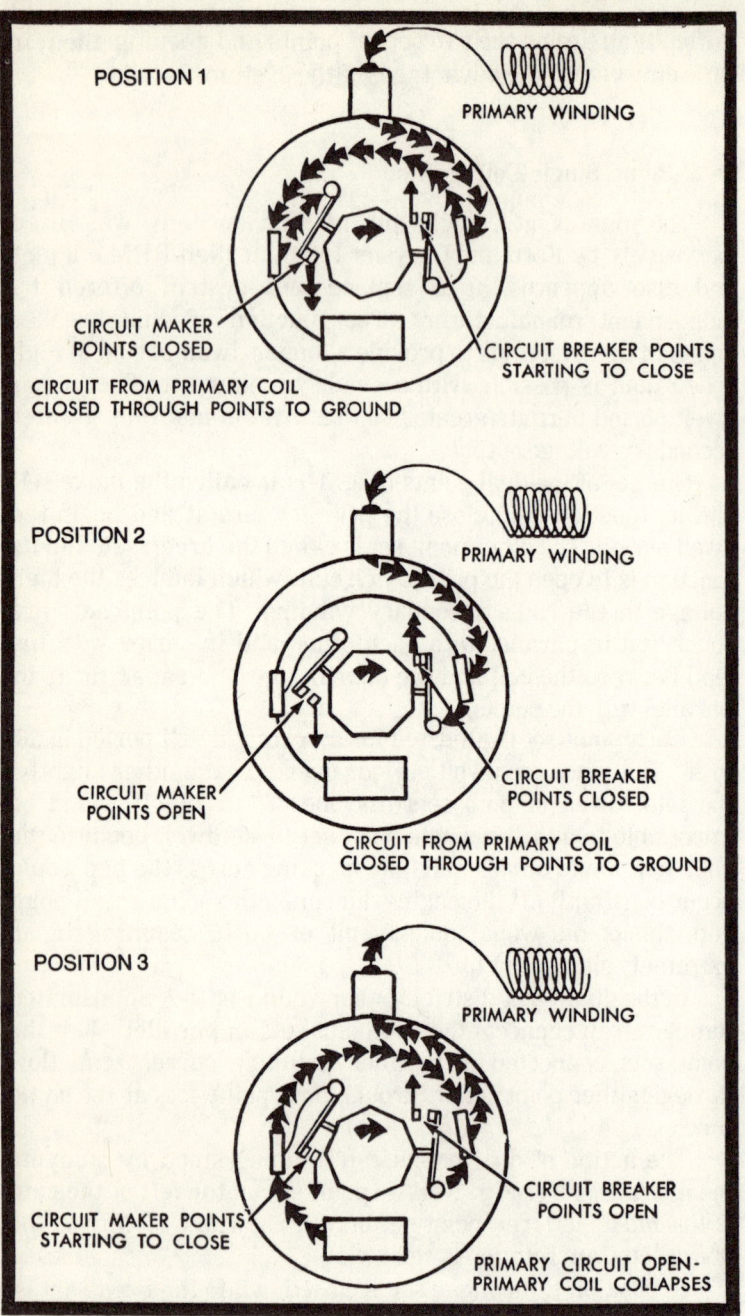

Fig. 1-7. Illustration of dual breaker points. (Courtesy Ignition Manufacturers Institute.)

Position 2 shows the *make* set just starting to open. The primary circuit is not interrupted, however, because the *break* points are still closed.

In position 3, the *break* set has opened. Both sets are now open, and the primary circuit is interrupted. The opening of the *break* set is quickly followed by the closing of the *make* set, and another extended dwell period begins.

CONSTRUCTION OF HIGH-VOLTAGE COMPONENTS

The major parts of the high-voltage side of the ignition system are the high-voltage winding of the coil, which has been discussed, the rotor, the distributor cap, the spark plug cables, and the spark plugs.

Distributor Construction

Figure 1-8 shows a cutaway view of an Oldsmobile distributor cap and rotor. The cap is of a molded Bakelite material whose insulating qualities are such that leakage of the high voltage between the terminals is prevented. The terminals are usually of brass and designed to hold the coil and plug wires tightly to prevent arcing at the connections. The rotor is made of molded Bakelite and is key located on the distributor shaft for timed rotation. A spring connector rides against the bottom of the center-tower coil terminal and is

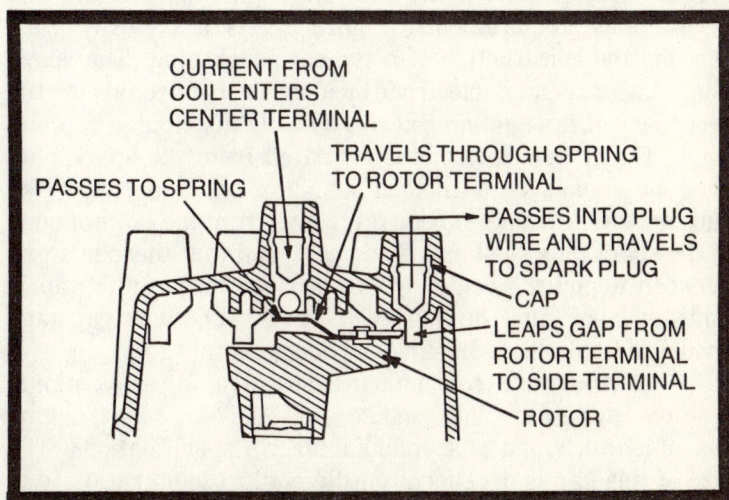

Fig. 1-8. Cutaway view of Oldsmobile distributor cap and rotor. (Courtesy General Motors Corporation.)

attached to a brass bar at the end of the rotor. The high-voltage surge from the coil leaps the gap from the end of this brass bar to the spark plug cable nearest to it during its rotation. Rotors can develop a short to the distributor shaft and cause misfiring or complete ignition failure. Excessive pitting, or filing off, of the end of the brass bar may also cause ignition misfiring or failure.

Modern spark plug cable is of the radio suppressor type. The conductor in the cable is made of a cord impregnated with a carbon solution and is designed to have a certain resistance per foot of cable. The conductor can develop breaks in the carbon from rough handling or heat from the engine manifold, so take care in the installation or reinstallation of these cables. Purchase cables for the particular engine on which they are to be used so that each cable will have approximately the same resistance. While the suppressor cable was designed to eliminate radio noise caused by oscillating high voltages, other benefits accrue. The damping of the high-voltage oscillations by dissipation across a resistance results in a more reliable spark and longer life for the spark plugs, points, and capacitor.

Spark Plug Construction

A spark plug is made up of three major parts: the electrodes, insulator, and shell. The actual construction of the plug is engineered for many different engine applications and performance requirements. Figure 1-9 is a cutaway view showing the construction of a typical spark plug. The spark plug has a center electrode which is connected to the secondary of the ignition coil through the distributor cap and rotor. The center electrode is insulated from the spark plug shell by means of a molded insulator of a porcelainlike substance. The side electrode protrudes from the bottom edge of the spark plug shell and is so positioned that there is a gap between it and the center electrode. The size of the gap is adjusted by bending the side electrode. A round-wire gap gage should be used when adjusting and checking this gap.

Plug gaps range from 0.020 in. to 0.040 in. for conventional ignition systems, and should be set to the engine manufacturer's and plug manufacturer's specifications. The size of this gap is dependent on the compression ratio of the engine, the characteristics of the combustion chamber, and the design of the ignition system. The present trend is toward a wider gap, made possible by improved ignition systems. The advantage of a wider gap is that it holds more of the mixture than a narrow gap, and consequently there is better opportunity to ignite the mixture.

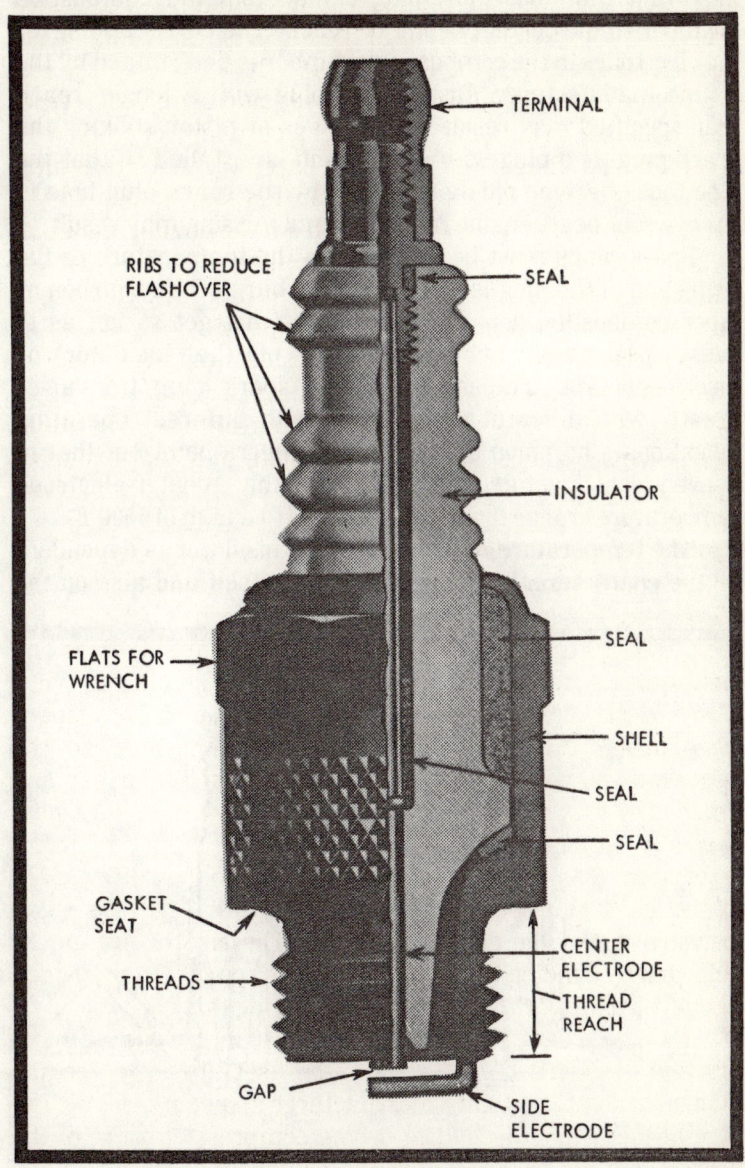

Fig. 1-9. Cutaway view of typical spark plug. (Courtesy Champion Spark Plug Company.)

The shell of the spark plug is threaded so the plug can be easily replaced. The commonly used thread sizes in modern automotive engines are 14 and 18 mm.

In addition to having the correct thread size, it is important that the spark plug extend into the combustion chamber to the correct depth, or reach. The correct point for the electrodes in the combustion chamber is determined by the engine manufacturer. Installing a plug with a longer reach than specified may result in the valves or piston striking the spark plug. If a plug with short reach is installed so that the electrodes become partly sheltered by the spark plug hole in the cylinder head, engine roughness and missing may result.

Spark plugs must be designed so the temperature of the firing end of the plug is high enough to burn off any carbon or other combustion deposits. But it must not get so hot as to cause preignition or deterioration of the insulator or electrodes. The temperature of the spark plug tip varies greatly with different engines and with different operating conditions. Champion Spark Plug engineers point out that in conventional automotive service the center-electrode temperatures range from a low of 500°F to a high of 1500°F.

The temperature of the spark plug insulator is dependent on the characteristics of the spark plug itself and also on the

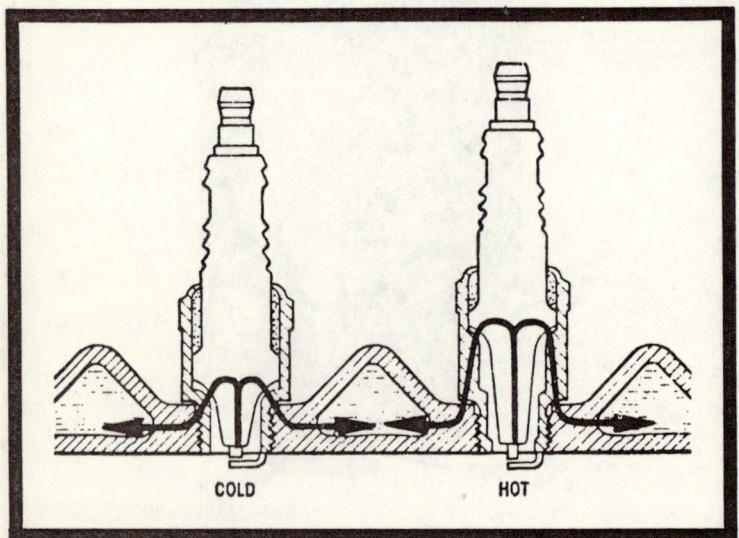

Fig. 1-10. Porcelain lengths for various heat ranges of spark plugs. (Courtesy Champion Spark Plug Company.)

burning fuel in the combustion chamber. The latter temperature will vary with the design of the engine, compression ratios, cooling system, and air/fuel ratio.

As the tip of the spark plug absorbs heat from the burning fuel, the heat travels up the insulator to the spark plug shell, to the cylinder head, and then to the water jacket. The heat absorbed by the insulator increases as the temperature in the combustion chamber increases. More heat will be absorbed as the area of the insulator exposed to the hot gases is increased. If the path the heat must follow to reach the cooling system is short, the tip will have a lower temperature than if the path is long. Plugs with long paths for the heat to follow (long lower porcelain) are known as "hot" plugs, while plugs with short paths (short lower porcelain) are known as "cold" plugs (Fig. 1-10).

Spark plug design engineers have made some design changes to extend the heat range of a given plug and to provide better sparking under adverse conditions.

To provide effective sparking and prevent erosion of the side electrode, the center electrode of the spark plug must be of negative polarity. Negative polarity at the center terminal considerably decreases the voltage required for ignition. This effect is due to the higher operating temperature of the center electrode. Electrons will leave the hotter surface at a lower voltage. Most coils have the primary leads marked either + and −, or BAT and DIST. Connecting the − (or DIST) terminal of the coil to the distributor coil will insure the proper polarity.

Chapter 2

Maintenance of Conventional Ignition Systems

Most automobile owner complaints of loss of power, sluggishness, hard starting, or missing are blamed on the ignition system. This placement of blame is valid in many instances because of the normal lowering of ignition efficiency through use over a period of time. This is the reason for performing periodic maintenance and tuneups. However, many complaints of "ignition failure" or "poor ignition" are not the result of a faulty ignition part or the adjustment of ignition parts as such, but the malfunction of parts related to the ignition system proper. This is the reason for checking the battery, alternator output, and wiring before performing maintenance, adjustment, or replacement in the ignition system itself.

TEST EQUIPMENT

To do a proper job of ignition maintenance or tuneup, certain items of test equipment and a knowledge of how to use them are essential. A list of such equipment ranging from "most needed" to the "highly desired" might be as follows:

- 12V test lamp
- Voltmeter with 0V–10V scale readable to 0.1V, plus 0V–20V scale
- Ammeters, 0A–50A and 0A–300A
- Ohmmeter with 0 to 100, 1000, 10,000 and 100,000-ohm ranges

- Tachometer
- Dwell meter
- Battery—alternator tester
- Oscilloscope

There is now on the market an oscilloscope that will perform nearly all the functions performed by the named test equipments manufactured by Beckman Instruments, Inc., Fullerton, California. Complete information on how to use the oscilloscope for tuneup, troubleshooting, and maintenance of ignition systems as well as for location of other engine problems is given in Chapter 9.

The inductive ammeter referred to is a clampon type, which does not require a circuit to be broken to get a current reading. To begin routine maintenance or a complete ignition tuneup, the battery should be given a voltage check. A voltmeter across the battery terminals should indicate 12V. If the reading taken is less than 12V, start the engine, and while it is running at a fast idle, again take a reading across the terminals. If the reading taken is 13V or more but again falls to less than 12V when the engine is stopped, the battery must be charged or replaced before proceeding with ignition maintenance or tuneup.

CHECKING PRIMARY RESISTANCE

Many cases of poor ignition are traceable to high resistance in the primary circuit caused by poor connections. Unwanted resistance too low in value to be detected by the average ohmmeter can be located by the use of Ohm's law, a voltmeter, and the voltage drop method. This method of locating unwanted resistance is accomplished with the motor off but the ignition switch on. *Caution: Do not leave ignition switch on with points closed longer than is necessary to perform these tests.* Pure DC (uninterrupted) flowing through a coil will eventually overheat and damage the coil, as there is no countervoltage developed by inductance when nonpulsating or uninterrupted current is applied.

With the ignition switch in the ON position, place the voltmeter leads or test lamp leads at the coil—distributor lead connection and ground. If a voltage reading approaching battery voltage is obtained or the lamp lights, the points are open. Rock the engine until the voltage reading approaches

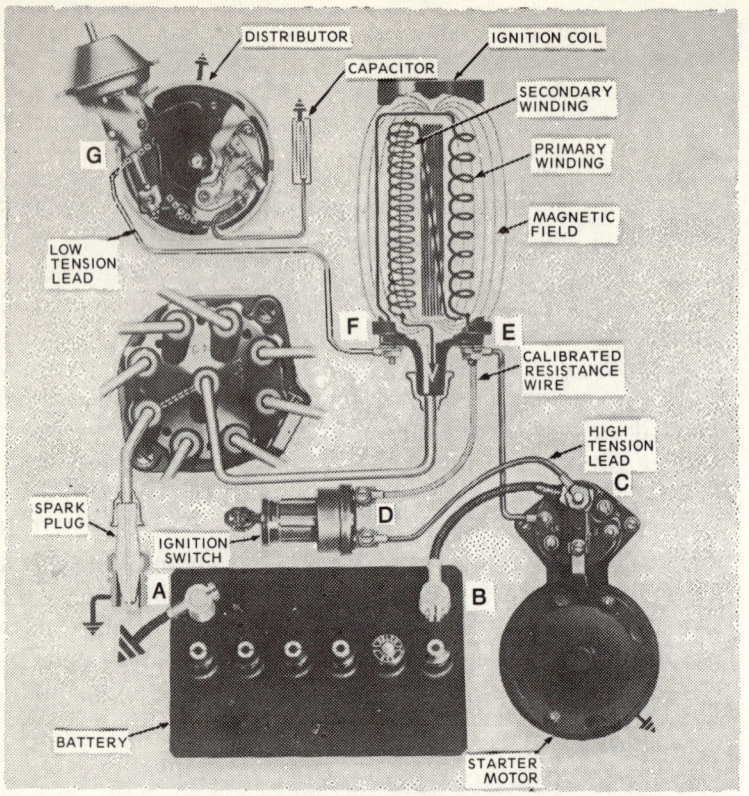

Fig. 2-1. Voltage measurement points in primary circuit.

zero or the lamp goes out. The points are now closed, and current is flowing in the primary circuit.

For the voltage checks that follow, refer to Fig. 2-1 for check points and write down the readings taken so they may be referred to when analyzing the results. Battery voltage between points A and B (battery posts) with ignition current flowing in the circuit should be recorded and should be a minimum of 12V.

Take a voltage reading between point A (negative battery post) and a good ground contact on the engine block. If *any* reading is obtained, resistance in the ground strap or at the negative-post connection is indicated. Check and repair (or replace) grounding components as necessary.

With the negative voltmeter lead on the engine block, place the positive lead at point C on the starter solenoid. The reading obtained should be the same as the battery voltage (A to B). A reading lower than battery voltage indicates a voltage drop due to resistance in the positive battery cable or its connections. Recheck any voltage drop so indicated by placing the voltmeter leads on battery *post B* and starter contact *post C* (do not touch leads to *cable ends*). A reading of as much as 0.1V would indicate poor cable connections.

Place the voltmeter leads at points C and G. (You will have to remove the switch to gain access to the terminals.) Any reading, even less than 0.1V, would indicate resistance in either the ignition switch or its leads. The ignition switch may be turned off and on a few times, and the wires under the dash that are attached to it may be shaken to verify the location of the trouble.

Place the negative voltmeter lead on a good engine block ground. Place the positive lead first at point D and note the reading, and then at point E and note the reading. The difference in these two readings is the voltage drop across the ballast resistor. The system shown employs a resistance wire; if a ballast resistor is used, connect the meter between negative, or distributor, side of the resistor and point E. Any difference between this reading and that obtained at point E indicates resistance in the ballast-to-coil lead.

With the negative lead of the voltmeter still on engine ground, place the positive lead at point F, the distributor-to-coil connection. A reading of more than 0.2V indicates too much point resistance, but this reading does include any possible resistance in the distributor-to-block circuit. As a check to isolate actual point resistance from distributor-to-engine-block resistance, place the negative lead of the voltmeter on the body of the distributor and compare the voltage with that found from point F to engine ground.

BALLAST RESISTANCE

Before turning the ignition switch to OFF, place the low-reading inductive ammeter on the lead between C and F, and not the current reading.

Caution: If you use an ordinary ammeter with metal test probes instead of one with a clampon attachment, insert it in series with the ignition components. Ammeters with test leads must be connected in series, never in parallel.

From the readings taken, the resistance value of the ballast resistor can now be found. Use Ohm's law (ohms = volts/amps). Divide the voltage drop across the resistor by the current in the circuit to find the resistance in ohms. Compare this value with the specification of the manufacturer for that particular coil-ballast combination. This method of checking the resistance of a ballast resistor is usually more accurate than using an ohmmeter, as the correct value may be less than 1.0 ohm and difficult to read on the usual ohmmeter. *Caution: If you do use an ohmmeter, use it with the ignition turned off, or you will damage the ohmmeter.*

The DC resistance of the coil and its operating voltage can be found by using the voltage and current readings taken and applying Ohm's law. The coil voltage and resistance values can then be compared to the manufacturer's specification to determine if the correct coil and ballast resistor have been installed and are operating within proper limits.

STARTING VOLTAGE

Another DC test that should be performed at this time is checking the available starting voltage at the coil. The high-voltage lead should be removed from the distributor center tower and shorted to the engine block to prevent the engine from starting. *Caution: Do not leave this cable ungrounded, as the high voltage developed may puncture the cable or short across the distributor cap, damaging the cap, cable, or coil secondary.*

With the negative lead of the voltmeter placed on engine ground, place the positive lead on the coil side of the ballast resistor. Turn the ignition switch to ON and note the reading on the voltmeter. Hold the ignition switch in the START position and again note the voltmeter reading. This voltage at the coil-ballast connection should rise to at least 9V for efficient starting.

DISTRIBUTOR CHECKS

Figure 2-2 is an illustration of a typical external-adjustment type of distributor (Delco Remy). Dwell on this type of distributor is adjusted through a window with the engine running.

Visual inspection should be made for a worn gear, excessive side play of the shaft due to worn bushings, binding

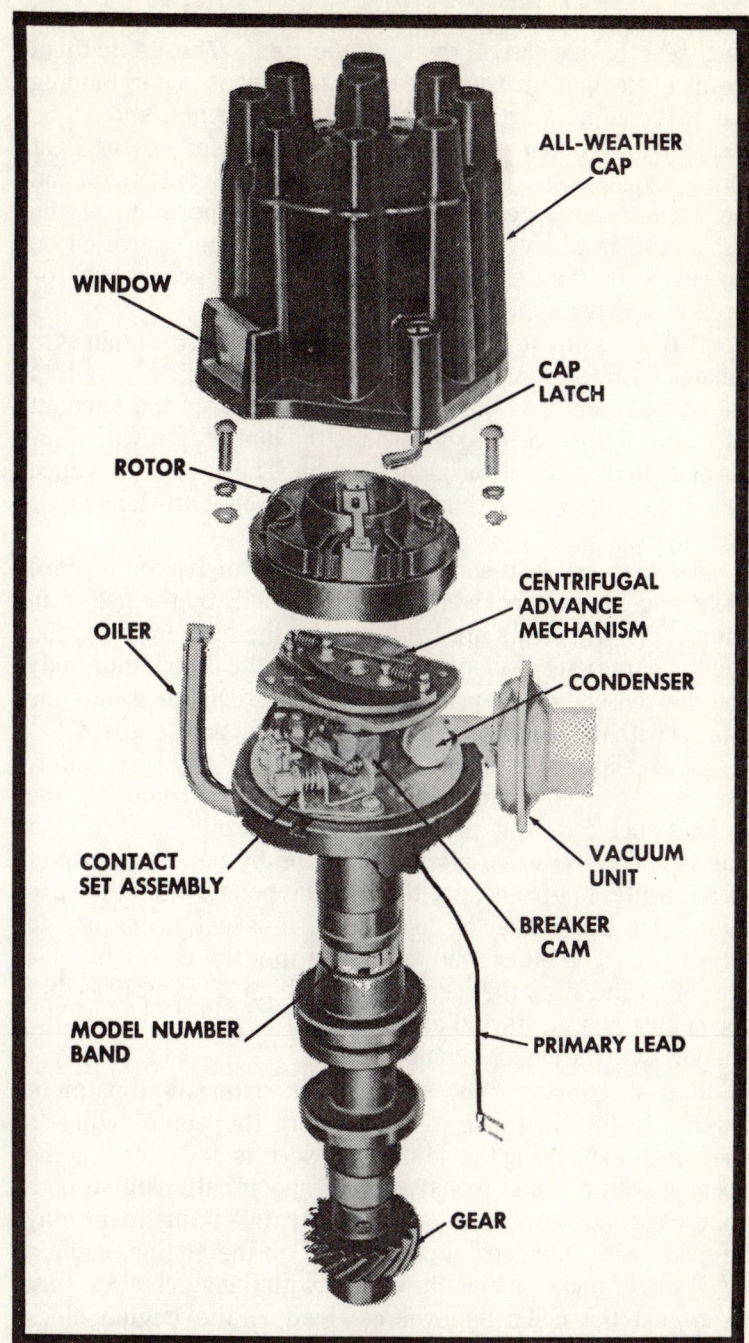

Fig. 2-2. External-adjustment distributor. (Courtesy Delco Remy.)

of the shaft due to a bent shaft or cracked housing, and roughness or excessive wear of the cam. The centrifugal advance mechanism should be visually checked for binding due to bent or worn posts or weights. Springs should be checked for broken or obviously stretched springs or bent spring hanger posts. The advance action of the centrifugal and the vacuum advances can be checked by operation of the distributor on a distributor-testing machine, in operation on the engine by the use of a timing light and degree wheel, or directly on some oscilloscopes.

The vacuum advance may be checked for diaphragm leakage by rotating the distributor plate, forcing the arm into the vacuum unit and then placing a finger over the vacuum inlet. Any leakage around or through the diaphragm will allow the plate to return to its original position. The vacuum advance cannot be repaired and thus must be replaced if any leakage is present.

The primary lead should be inspected for frayed or bare spots, and can be checked for unseen grounds by the use of an ohmmeter. The points are held open by the cam for this test, and the ohmmeter leads are connected to the distributor body and the coil end of the primary lead. The resistance must be infinity with the points open and zero with the points closed.

When replacing contact points on this or any distributor, use care to keep fingers or any oily or dirty tools off the contact surfaces. New points may have an oily surface, and this should be removed after installation by pulling a strip of clean, white, lint-free paper through the points when they are closed. On this model of distributor, it is not necessary to adjust point gap other than to be sure that the cam will open the points and allow the spring to close them. This assures that the engine can be started and the dwell adjusted through the window with the engine running.

For distributors not having the external-adjustment window, point clearance may be set to the manufacturer's specification by using the adjustment screws and checking the opening with a round feeler gage. If specifications give both point clearance and dwell, or dwell only, this adjustment may be made with the distributor installed on the engine, using a dwell meter and cranking the engine with the starter. Be sure to ground the coil's high-voltage lead to the engine block during this adjustment.

The distributor shown in Fig. 2-2 has an oiler tube, and this tube should be filled with SAE No. 20 oil when the distributor is serviced or at regular vehicle lubrication periods. Some distributors are equipped with a cam lubricator wick. This wick should be replaced at the time the contact set is replaced. Do not attempt to oil this wick, but replace it as necessary. On distributors having neither an oil cup nor wick, place only a small amount of cam lubricant on the cam when replacing points, or if the rubbing block and cam are found to be dry and wearing.

The rotor should be inspected for cracks and a bent, broken, or exessively worn center-spring contact. The end contact of the rotor can be wiped clean, but if it shows excessive wear from pitting, it must be replaced. Do not file the end of a rotor.

The distributor cap may be cleaned with a cloth and should be thoroughly inspected for cracks, carbon tracks, and burned or corroded upper and lower terminals. The upper terminals may be cleaned with a brass brush that will fit into the holes.

POINTS AND CAPACITOR CHECKS

It is impossible to make repairs to a capacitor or coil. If either proves to be faulty, it must be replaced. In the absence of a capacitor checker, an observation of buildup on the contact points will indicate the condition of the capacitor. Contact points, after a few thousand miles of operation, will normally have a gray color. They will be rough and pitted, with small indentations. Such points show a satisfactory capacitor value and will provide satisfactory service for many additional miles. If the points show a metal transfer, with metal buildup of 0.020 in. or more, this condition indicates a leaky capacitor or a capacitor of incorrect value. A transfer of metal from the negative point to the positive point indicates a capacitor of insufficient capacity. Over capacity is indicated by a transfer from the positive (movable) point to the negative (stationary) point. Either condition indicates replacement of both the contact set and the capacitor. Care must be taken when replacing these items to prevent the pigtail lead of the capacitor from interfering with the closing spring of the movable contact arm or with the arm itself. Be sure the contact points are in alignment and making full contact with each other. Bend *only* the stationary contact to align the point contacts.

COIL TESTING

A coil is best tested off the engine by a coil tester. This type of coil testing heats the coil, and thus can detect a coil that operates okay when cold but breaks down when hot. Some coil testers check the output voltage and current; thus the output high voltage and current can be checked against a master coil or against the manufacturer's specifications. A bad coil must be replaced by one having the same polarity of high voltage.

If a coil tester is not available, an ohmmeter can be used to determine if the coil is usable. The coil must be disconnected from the circuit. Using the low-resistance scale of the ohmmeter, place each lead on a primary terminal. If the reading is less than 4 ohms, the primary is probably okay. High resistance indicates an open primary, and low resistance (1 ohm or less) indicates a shorted primary.

The resistance of the secondary winding is checked by placing one ohmmeter lead in the high-voltage secondary terminal and the other lead on either primary terminal. A good secondary winding will read less than 10,000 ohms. An open secondary will show infinity on the ohmmeter. A few shorted secondary turns will not show in this test, because of the high resistance of the secondary winding.

CHECKING SUPPRESSOR CABLES

Modern spark plug wires are of the suppressor type. The core of the cable is usually made of a carbon-impregnated nylon cord or a synthetic, rubberlike conductor. The end terminals are crimped on, with a tang extending into the conductor for contact. They are usually replaced every 30,000 miles or less, as heat and vibration from the engine makes them deteriorate. They are also subject to damage during removal or installation. Looseness between the end terminals and the distributor or spark plug terminals may result in arcing and corrosion in the cable contacts.

Suppressor cables may be tested with an ohmmeter, and the readings obtained then compared with the engine manufacturer's specifications. To avoid damage to good cables, the distributor cap should be removed with the cables still in place, and the ohmmeter leads should be applied to each contact in the cap, in turn, and the corresponding spark plug terminal at the other end of the cable. If the resistance of a cable is far too great, move the cable in the cap to check for loose contact, or remove the cable from the cap and check the end-to-end resistance. Cables should also be checked visually for cracks, pinholes, or burned spots where they may be shorting to the manifold or engine or to one another (crossfiring). It is usually better to replace cables in sets if only one or two bad ones are found. A set is made for a particular engine, and it is good practice to check the resistance of each cable before installing.

CHECKING OTHER SUPPRESSION DEVICES

Some ignition systems used a distributor rotor containing a built-in resistor. Such rotors are easily recognized, as the resistor is on the top of the rotor, between the center-contact spring or carbon and the gap contact end. This rotor can be checked for resistance value and checked against the manufacturer's specifications. With the ohmmeter in the $R \times 10,000$ range, place one lead on the spring or carbon contact and the other at the gap end contact.

The distributor cap with built-in resistance is now rarely used, but it is easily recognized by the higher-than-normal towers. The resistance in this case can be measured with an ohmmeter by placing one lead on the contact inside the cap and the other lead inside the tower. Again, the resistance reading can be checked against specifications. The cap must be replaced if the resistance is less than half or more than twice its specified value.

Another method of radio noise suppression is the use of resistor spark plugs (Fig. 2-3). The value of the resistor in the plug may be measured by placing one ohmmeter lead on the plug terminal and the other on the center electrode at the firing end of the plug. Most spark plugs of the resistor type will show about 20,000 ohms resistance. Many late-model General Motors engines use both resistance plug cable and resistor spark plugs. Thus the resistance of the plug and the resistance of its associated cable must be added together to find the total circuit resistance.

The operation of any engine is dependent upon its ignition system. The efficiency of an ignition system and hence of the engine's operation is directly dependent upon one component that has no moving parts. That important component is the spark plug.

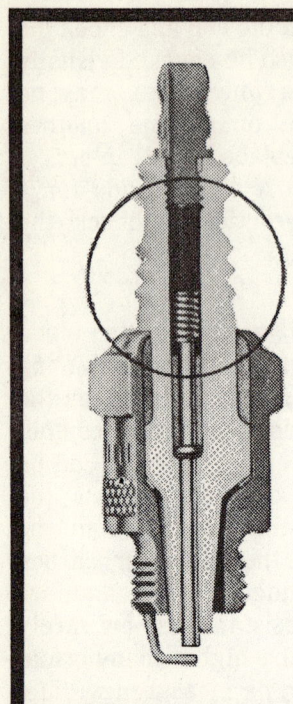

Fig. 2-3. Resistor-type spark plug. (Courtesy Champion Spark Plug Company.)

SPARK PLUG MAINTENANCE

Spark plugs are exposed to more stress than any other part of the engine. They must conduct several thousand volts of electricity into the combustion chamber. The terminal end of the plug may be ice cold, while its firing tip 3 in. away is exposed to flame temperatures of over 3000°F. However, when the correct plugs for a particular engine and its type of operation are installed, there are only four possible defects of ignition attributable to the plugs. They are: wearing out; fouling, caused by accumulations of carbon; wrong gap; and a cracked, leaking, or loose insulator. The first secret of long plug life is the same as that for most efficient operation: Select the correct plug for the job.

Spark Plug Sizes

Spark plugs are made in various physical sizes to exactly match the requirements of the cylinder heads in which they are installed. Present automotive spark plugs use either 14 or 18 mm diameter threads. They may be installed with a gasket or designed with a taper seat. Some manufacturers of plugs requiring gaskets have them attached to the plug. This makes the plug easier to install and remove.

Engine designers may use any one of four different thread reaches in the 14 mm plugs: $3/8$, $7/16$, $1/2$, or $3/4$ in. (Fig. 2-4). All of these plugs use gaskets. The tapered-seat and 18 mm plugs are made for automotive applications, with a standard reach for each type.

Heat Ranges Available

Figure 2-5 shows the five standard heat ranges of plugs and the numbers assigned to each by Champion Spark Plug Company. Not shown are the special heat ranges made for racing or other special automotive applications. Another type of spark plug, differing slightly from the conventional plugs and also made by Champion, is the *Turbo-Action* plug.

A modern high-performance automotive engine requires relatively cold-running plugs during full-power operation. Yet the same engine develops only a small part of its potential power for slow-speed operation; for this service relatively hot-running plugs are needed. To cope with this problem of extending the heat range, Champion designed the *Turbo-Action* with the insulator nose and electrodes deeper into the combustion chamber (Fig. 2-6).

These plugs, identified by Champion with the suffix letter Y, are used in practically all overhead-valve passenger car engines and in many truck and tractor OHV engines where space is adequate for their installation.

Turbo-Action designs take advantage of charge cooling at higher engine speeds. As shown in Fig. 2-7, the cool fuel charges drawn in at a high speed lower the temperaure of both the firing tip and the electrodes. Thus, with more protection against overheating at high speeds, the plug can be designed to give more fouling protection at low speeds and idle. The *Turbo-Action* plug runs hotter at low speeds but cooler at high speeds than the conventional plug.

Replacing Plugs

Spark plug manufacturers recommend that plugs be replaced at intervals of 10,000 miles to avoid loss of engine operating economy due to worn plugs. Plugs should be checked, cleaned, and regapped with each tuneup if replacement is unnecessary.

Champion letter prefix "H" (such as H-10, H-11)

7/16"

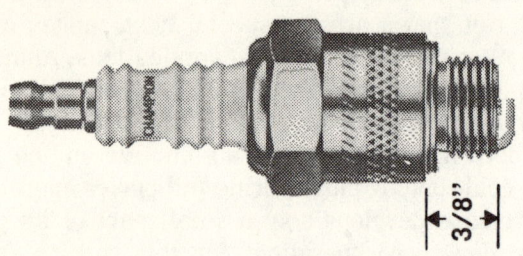

Champion letter prefix "J" (such as J-8, J-11, etc.)

3/8"

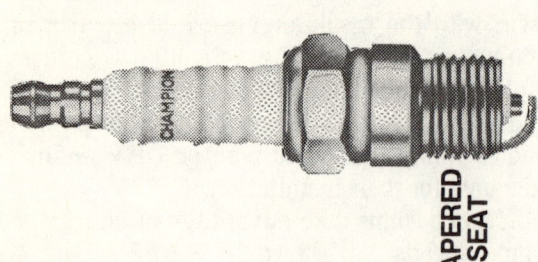

TAPERED SEAT

Champion letter prefix "BL", "BN" or "F" (such as BL-13Y, BN-9Y, F-9Y)

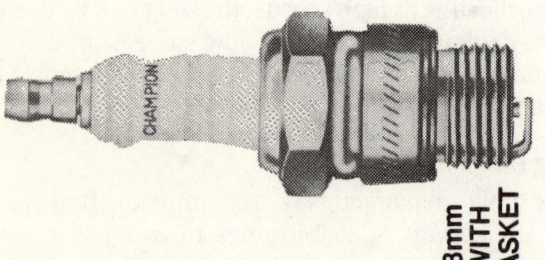

18mm WITH GASKET

Champion letter prefix "D" (such as D-10, D-16, etc.)

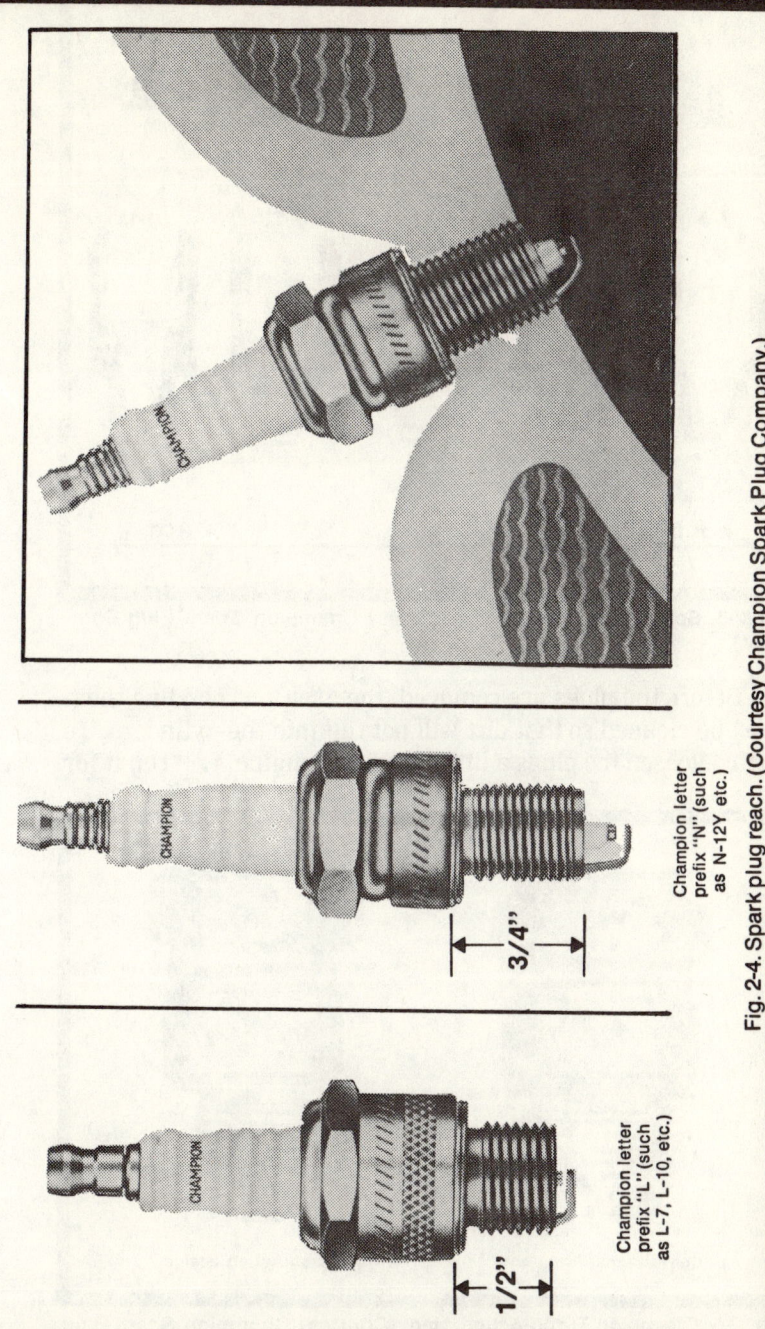

Fig. 2-4. Spark plug reach. (Courtesy Champion Spark Plug Company.)

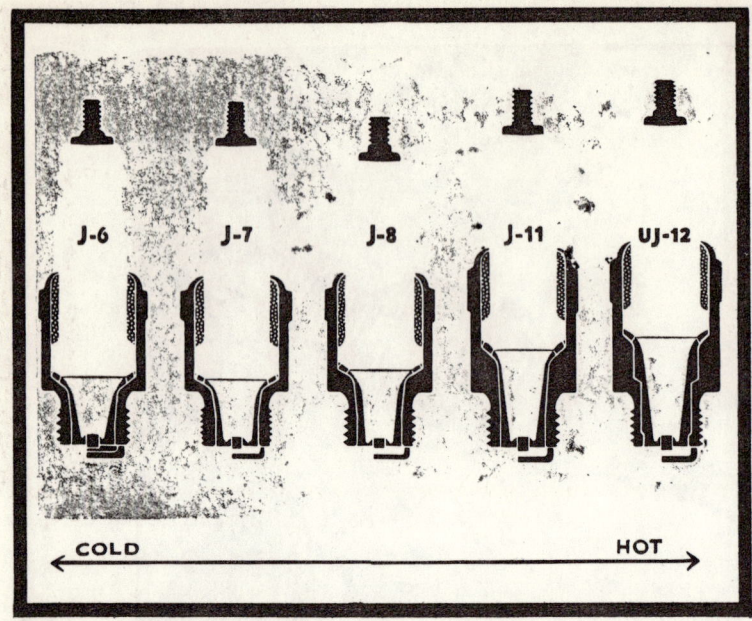

Fig. 2-5. Spark plug heat range. (Courtesy Champion Spark Plug Company.)

Before the plugs are removed, the area surrounding them must be cleaned so that dirt will not fall into the cylinders. To do this, loosen the plugs a little, start the engine, and run it for

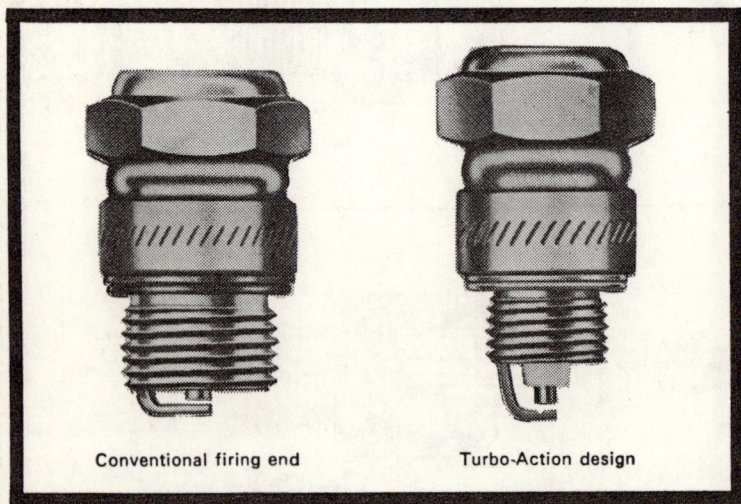

Fig. 2-6. Champion Turbo-Action plug. (Courtesy Champion Spark Plug Company.)

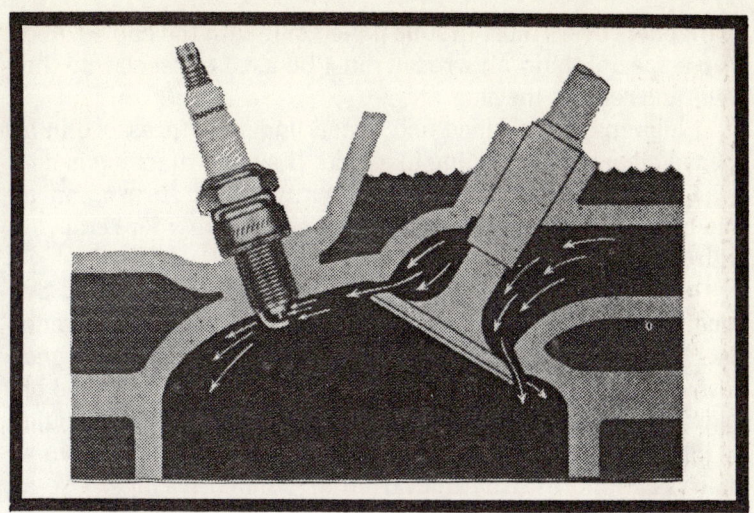

Fig. 2-7. Charge cooling of Turbo-Action plug. (Courtesy Champion Spark Plug Company.)

1–3 minutes. The leakage of compression around the loosened plugs will blow the dirt and loosened carbon away. Ford recommends loosening the plugs two turns and then using compressed air to blow the dirt from around the plugs.

Some engines, such as the Chrysler *Hemi* engine, have the spark plug mounted in wells as shown in Fig. 2-8. On these,

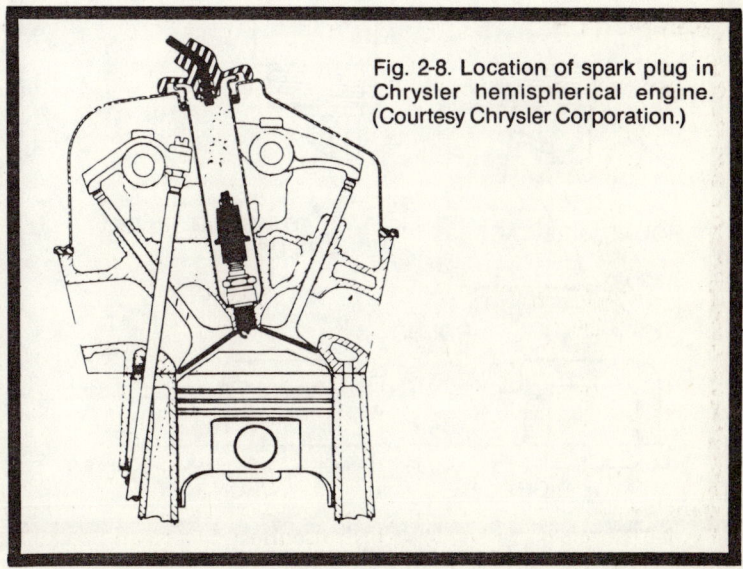

Fig. 2-8. Location of spark plug in Chrysler hemispherical engine. (Courtesy Chrysler Corporation.)

spark plug covers must first be pulled out, with the cables, and then a special thin-wall wrench must be used to reach into the wells and remove the plug.

Plugs may be cleaned and tested under air pressure in a special cleaning and testing machine. If such a machine is not available, they may be cleaned with a wire brush, or a thin-bladed knife if the carbon deposit is too heavy for removal with the brush.

When the plug is cleaned, the gap should be reset by bending the outer electrode after filing the center electrode flat. *Never bend the center electrode, as this will crack and destroy the porcelain.* Figure 2-9 shows the correct method of gaging and setting the plug gap. The center electrode should be filed flat because the high-voltage sparks will leave from a sharp edge more easily than from a rounded surface. Use a round—not a flat—gage to check the gap as shown in Fig. 2-9. Be sure to consult a manufacturer's chart for correct gap settings. While th majority of cars on the road today have a spark plug gap recommendation of 0.030 to 0.035 in., some General Motors car models use a 0.040 gap. More recent engines equipped with electronic ignition systems have gap specifications ranging from 0.044 in. in some Ford engines to 0.080 in. in some General Motors engines.

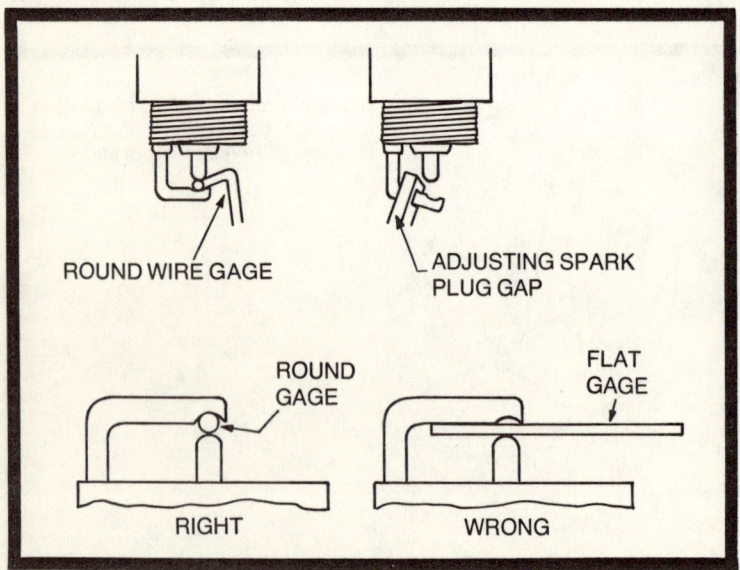

Fig. 2-9. Gaging and setting of spark plug gap.

The factory gap setting of a new plug is determined by the most popular application of that number of plug. Before installing any new spark plug, compare the gap to that recommended on the manufacturer's specification chart.

"Reading" Plugs

The ability of a mechanic to "read" spark plugs that have been in service for some time and determine if problems exist in the plugs, the ignition system, or in some other part of the engine is a great boon in his profession. A chart of a few conditions observed in used spark plugs appears in Fig. 2-10. This chart also lists recommendations for the elimination of problems causing damage to the plugs and resulting in poor engine performance.

The best (and certainly the quickest) method of pinpointing ignition troubles is by the use of an oscilloscope. For some of the late-model transistor ignition systems, a scope is absolutely essential not only for troubleshooting but for making accurate adjustments in the system.

ENGINE TROUBLESHOOTING

A chart for troubleshooting the ignition—showing conditions, possible causes, and corrections—rounds out this chapter. The checks for possible causes can all be made on conventional ignition systems without the use of a scope. Some of the conditions listed may be caused by fuel problems or other engine problems not necessarily connected with the ignition system. Some examples of such conditions and problems might be:

Engine will not crank: discharged battery or shorted cell; loose, corroded, or broken battery cable; burned-out starter; inoperative starter drive; starter drive locked into flywheel; wornout starter solenoid; water in cylinder; starter switch inoperative.

Engine cranks but will not start: no fuel, engine flooded with fuel, no spark. Available spark may be checked by removing the coil wire from the distributor cap and holding within ¼ in. from the engine block. Crank the engine with ignition switch on. If the spark will jump this gap, ignition is not the problem.

NORMAL

Brown to grayish tan color and slight electrode wear. Correct heat range for engine and operating conditions.

RECOMMENDATION. Properly service and reinstall. Replace if over 10,000 miles of service.

SPLASHED DEPOSITS

Spotted deposits. Occurs shortly after long delayed tune-up. After a long period of misfiring, deposits may be loosened when normal combustion temperatures are restored by tune-up. During a high-speed run, these materials shed off the piston and head and are thrown against the hot insulator.

RECOMMENDATION. Clean and service the plugs properly and reinstall.

HIGH SPEED GLAZING

Insulator has yellowish, varnish-like color. Indicates combustion chamber temperatures have risen during hard, fast acceleration. Normal deposits do not get a chance to blow off, instead they melt to form a conductive coating.

RECOMMENDATION. If condition recurs, use plug type one step colder.

CARBON DEPOSITS

Dry soot.

RECOMMENDATION. Dry deposits indicate rich mixture or weak ignition. Check for clogged air cleaner, high float level, sticky choke or worn breaker contacts. Hotter plugs will temporarily provide additional fouling protection.

OIL DEPOSITS

Oily coating.

RECOMMENDATION. Caused by poor oil control. Oil is leaking past worn valve guides or piston rings into the combustion chamber. Hotter spark plug may temporarily relieve problem, but positive cure is to correct the condition with necessary repairs.

ASH DEPOSITS

Light brown to white colored deposits encrusted on the side or center electrodes or both. Derived from oil and/or fuel additives. While non-conductive, excessive amounts may mask the spark, causing misfire.

RECOMMENDATION. If excessive deposits accumulate in short mileage, corrective measures may include installation of valve guide seals to prevent seepage of oil into combustion chamber.

TOO HOT

Blistered, white insulator, eroded electrodes and absence of deposits.

RECOMMENDATION. Check for correct plug heat range, overadvanced ignition timing, cooling system level and/or stoppages, lean fuel/air mixtures, leaking intake manifold, sticking valves, and if car is driven at high speeds most of the time.

MECHANICAL DAMAGE

Mechanical Damage to the plug's firing end is caused by some foreign object in the combustion chamber. It may also be due to the piston striking the firing tip of improper reach plugs. When working on an engine, be sure to keep the carburetor throat and any open plug holes covered. Consult the catalog for proper reach plugs.

Fig. 2-10. Analyzing used spark plugs. (Courtesy Champion Spark Plug Company.)

IGNITION SYSTEM TROUBLESHOOTING CHART

Condition	Possible Cause	Check/Correction
Engine cranks okay but will not start.	Open primary circuit	Check primary circuit connections.
	Coil primary grounded.	Replace coil.
	Points not opening.	Adjust points.
	Points burned.	Replace points and eliminate cause of burning.
	Out of time.	Retime. and repair problem causing timing change.
	Defective capacitor.	Replace capacitor.
	Coil secondary open or grounded.	Replace coil.
	High voltage leakage.	Check plugs. plug cables. and cap for dampness. Check for broken rotor.
	Spark plugs fouled or broken.	Clean and adjust. or replace. Repair cause of fouling.
Engine starts but will not continue to run.	Open ballast resistor.	Replace ballast resistor.
	Ignition switch problem.	Check for loose connection or poor contact at IGN contact of switch.
Engine is hard to start.	Timing off.	Check and adjust.
	Improper point opening.	Adjust point clearance and dwell.
	Faulty capacitor.	Replace.
	Loose connection.	Check all connections in primary circuit.
	Grounded primary wiring or capacitor pigtail.	Check for bare spots and repair or replace as necessary.
	Wornout or fouled spark plugs.	Check and adjust or replace as necessary.
Under capacity coil.	Faulty distributor cap or rotor.	Replace coil. Check for loose rotor or excessive rotor gap. Always replace cap and rotor as a set.

IGNITION SYSTEM TROUBLESHOOTING CHART

Condition	Possible Cause	Check/Correction
Engine runs but misses on one cylinder.	Defective spark. Defective distributor cap or plug lead.	Clean and adjust. or replace. Check cap for crack and lead for internal break. Replace as necessary.
	Engine defect such as stuck valve or broken ring.	This defect can often be detected by listening at exhaust pipe for "wheeze."
Engine runs but misses on different cylinders.	Ignition timing off.	Retime ignition.
	Worn spark plugs or wrong plugs.	Clean and adjust. or replace with correct plugs.
	Leaky capacitor.	Replace.
	Cracked cap.	Replace.
	Defective advance mechanisms.	Repair or replace.
	Defective high-voltage cables.	Replace cables as a set.
	High-voltage leakage.	Check coil head. distributor cap, rotor, and leads.
	Cylinder crossfiring.	Check plug leads for placement causing inductive pickup.
	Weak coil.	Replace.
	Incorrect point setting or dwell.	Clean and adjust to specifications.
	Changing dwell or timing.	Check for worn distributor shaft or bushings. Check point spring tension. Repair and adjust. or replace.
Engine lacks power	Timing off.	Retime ignition.
	Mechanical advance not working.	Repair or replace mechanism.
	Vacuum advance not working.	Check for vacuum leaks in line and diaphragm.
Engine overheats.	Late ignition timing.	Retime ignition.
Engine backfires.	Ignition timing off. Ignition crossfiring.	Retime ignition. Check plug wiring. cap, and rotor for leakage paths.
	Wrong spark plugs.	Install correct heat range plugs.

IGNITION SYSTEM TROUBLESHOOTING CHART

Condition	Possible Cause	Check/Correction
Engine knocks or pings.	Timing off.	Retime ignition.
	Faulty advance mechanisms.	Rebuild or replace distributor.
	Point clearance off.	Adjust point clearance and dwell.
	Distributor shaft bent or worn.	Rebuild or replace distributor.
Pitted contact points at low mileage.	Wrong value of capacitor.	Replace with correct capacitor.
	Capacitor or point leads improperly arranged.	Renew points and capacitor and rearrange leads.
Burned contact points.	Excessive resistance in points or capacitor circuit.	Eliminate high resistance in circuit before replacing points and capacitor.
	High voltage on primary circuit.	Check alternator output and regulation.
	Points not aligned properly.	Clean, align, and adjust or replace.
	Weak point spring tension.	Adjust tension to specifications.
	Oil on points.	Check for over-lubrication of cam or for oil entering distributor.
Spark plugs appear defective.	Cracked insulator.	Careless installation. Install new plug.
	Sooty plug.	Install hotter plug; correct condition in engine causing excessive fuel or oil in cylinder.
	Plug white or gray with blistered insulator.	Install colder plug. Check for air leak in intake manifold causing an over-lean mixture.

Chapter 3

Semiconductor Devices for Automobiles

Semiconductor devices, or solid-state devices as they are often called, are used in many automotive applications. While it is not necessary for the mechanic to know and understand much of the theory of solid-state electronics, it is essential that he recognizes the devices in common automotive use and knows what each device does and how it works.

It has been a common practice of mechanics to lump all solid-state devices under the catchall term *transistor*, and if the device is suspect, change it or the entire unit which contains it. This has occurred because many automotive units are difficult or impossible to repair. However, a working knowledge that will enable a mechanic to pinpoint the faulty device will also enable him to replace only it. This can result in a considerable saving in time and money, especially when an automobile employs more than one electronic unit in its operation, each at a price approaching $100.

The semiconductor devices most often used in automotive applications, particularly in transistor ignitions, are the diode, zener diode, (or just zener) light-emitting diode (LED), silicon controlled rectifier (SCR), NPN transistor, PNP transistor, phototransistor, and Darlington power transistor.

RECTIFYING DEVICES

A diode is made of specially treated crystals of silicon or germanium, called P-material and N-material. They are fused together in a *junction*. The P-material has a shortage of electrons, and the N-material has an excess of electrons. Although the diode in this sense appears to have a positive and negative polarity, it will not in itself cause a current flow as will a battery. The diode can conduct current, however, if a sufficient voltage is applied to it in the proper way.

Electric current flows from negative to positive, so when a voltage of proper polarity is applied to the diode—negative to N-material and positive to P-material—a current will flow through the diode. This is known as *forward-biasing* the diode. The value of current increases with the applied voltage. The current that can be safely passed without damage to the diode is the current rating of that particular type of diode.

When a reverse-polarity voltage is applied to a diode—negative to P and positive to N—no current will flow (this is reverse bias). If the applied reverse voltage on the diode is increased to a high enough value, the barrier between the crystals opposing current will be destroyed; current will flow in the reverse direction, and the diode will be rendered useless. The maximum value of reverse voltage that can be

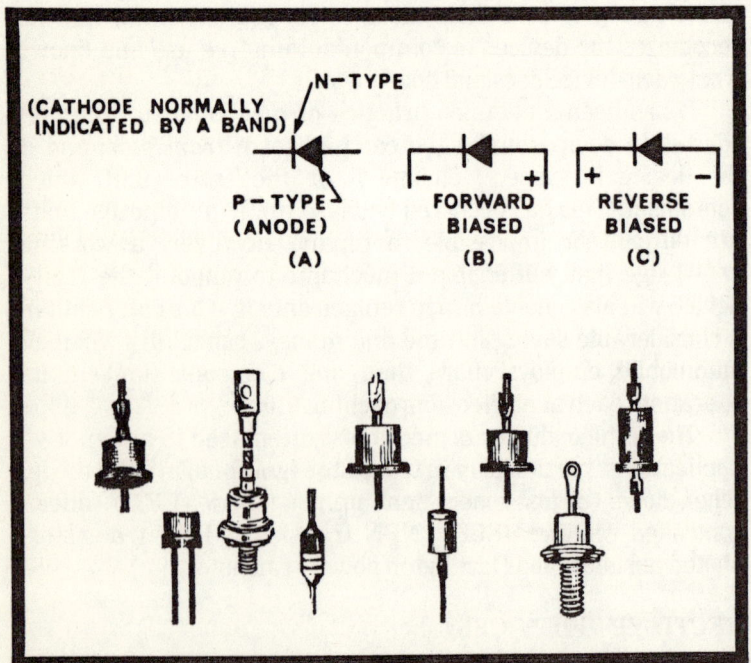

Fig. 3-1. The diode and its biasing.

applied to a diode without damaging it is the peak-inverse-voltage (PIV) rating of that particular type of diode.

The diode is also called a *rectifier* because of its action of passing current in only one direction. This is the type of action that takes place in alternator diodes.

Diodes used with alternators and some diodes used in transistor ignition systems are classified as either positive or negative diodes. This designation pertains to stud-mounting and press-in-mounting diodes and denotes whether the anode (positive) or cathode (negative) connection of the diode is common to the mounting end. This type of diode is always mounted in some type of heat dissipating device, called a *heatsink*. A heatsink is necessary for high-current diodes and power transistors, as the current they pass generates considerable heat, which must be dissipated.

Diodes are always marked with connection-identifying symbols. Where space permits, the standard diode symbol (Fig. 3-1) is used. The bar represents the cathode, or *negative*, connection, and the wide mouth of the funnel the anode, or *positive*, connection. On very small diodes a colored band denotes the cathode connection.

Testing Diodes

Diodes may be tested by an ohmmeter, a 12V test lamp with a voltage supply, or a regular diode tester. When the negative lead of the ohmmeter is connected to the cathode, and the positive lead to the anode, the meter should show low resistance. This forward resistance should be about 10 ohms for high-current diodes of silicon or germanium around and around 100 ohms for low-current germanium diodes. When the lead connections are reversed, high-current diodes should show resistance of 1000 ohms or more and low-current germanium diodes from several megohms to infinity. More important than the absolute values of the readings is their ratio, which should be 100 or more.

The above readings should be taken with the ohmmeter in the $R \times 100$ range. If the ohmmeter readings show very high resistance in both directions, the diode is said to be *open* and must be replaced. If the resistance is low in both directions, the diode is said to be *shorted*, and again it must be replaced.

A diode tester usually indicates GOOD or BAD when the diode is connected and tested in accordance with the directions accompanying the meter.

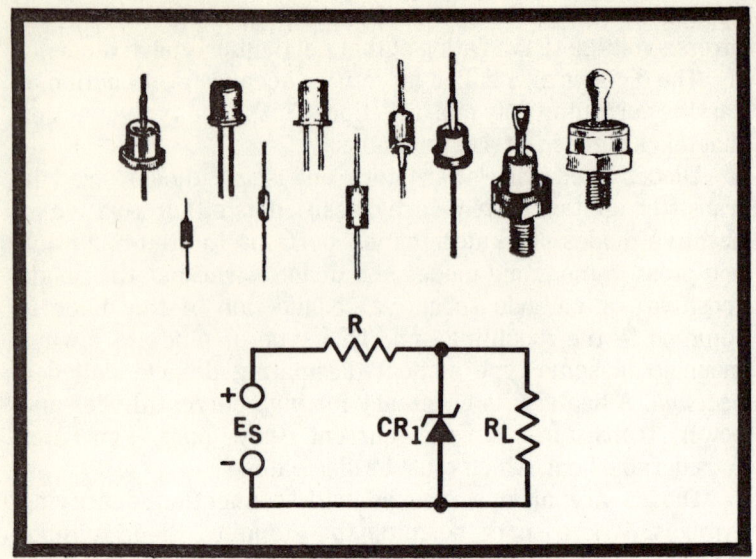

Fig. 3-2. Zener diode and typical circuit.

Zeners

The *zener*, or *breakdown*, diode has its PN junction modified in the manufacturing process to withstand a certain reverse breakdown voltage without damage to the diode. Once the breakdown voltage is reached, the zener will conduct current freely and will maintain a constant voltage drop. This makes it useful for establishing voltage references.

Each zener has a specific breakdown voltage (zener voltage) and operates over a small voltage range determined by its design characteristics. Zener voltages may vary from less than 2V to over 20V, and hence a zener must be selected individually for the desired operating voltage.

Many charging circuits of motorcycles and small cars, as well as automotive pollution control devices and ignition systems, are regulated by zeners. They are also used for surge protection, as arc reducers across contact points, as reverse-polarity gates in control circuits, and as biasing elements.

Zeners are rated as to (1) zener voltage and (2) allowable reverse current or allowable dissipation in watts. High-current zeners must be mounted in a heatsink.

Figure 3-2 shows a zener used in a basic DC voltage-regulating circuit. A diode is selected that has a breakdown voltage equal to the desired regulated output voltage. A limiting resistor R is then chosen that will drop the voltage difference between the inut voltage and the desired output voltage while maintaining the diode current at the correct operating value. When the input voltage rises or the load current (through the device being supplied with power R_L) decreases, current through the diode increases, and the voltage drop across R increases so that the output voltage (across R_L) remains constant. Conversely, when the input voltage decreases or the load current increases, the diode current and the voltage drop across R decrease to maintain a constant output voltage.

Note: Zeners cannot be checked by using the same methods used to check rectifier diodes. Such testing would not harm a zener, but neither would it give a meaningful indication.

Light-Emitting Diode

Light-emitting diodes, or LEDs, are semiconductor diodes, generally made from gallium arsenide, that can serve as a source of light when a voltage is applied. When the voltage is applied continuously, the light is emitted continuously. The LED serves as an indicator lamp of very low current consumption and low applied voltage. When the applied voltage is pulsed, the light is pulsed accordingly. The PN junction of the LED can be made very small and enclosed in an evacuated glass envelope shaped to control the direction of light so as to require very little space. The LED, whose schematic symbol and physical appearance are shown in Fig. 3-3, is used in automotive applications as an indicator and, more recently, as the light source in light-triggered transistor ignition systems.

Silicon Controlled Rectifier

The *silicon controlled rectifier*, or SCR, is a PNPN 4-layer semiconductor device that normally acts as an open circuit but switches rapidly to a conducting state when an appropriate signal voltage is applied to the *gate* terminal. The SCR is used as a current switch in transistor ignitions.

The SCR is illustrated by Fig. 3-4. Another type of SCR, the *light-actuated* SCR (LASCR), is beginning to make its appearance in automotive applications. Its action is similar to that of

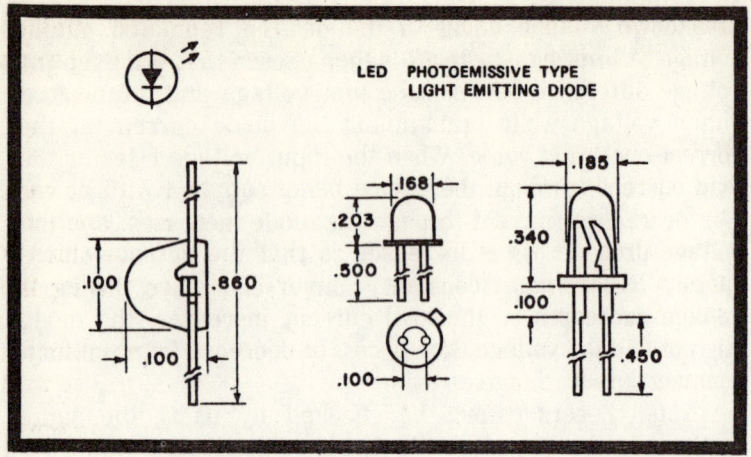

Fig. 3-3. LED symbol and shapes. (Courtesy RCA Solid State.)

the SCR, but it is triggered by light rather than by the application of a triggering voltage.

Photodiode

Another type of diode used in automotive applications is the *photodiode*. The photodiode is a specially constructed junction diode so arranged that it is possible to use variations in the light striking the diode to produce variations in its current.

The small physical size, high efficiency, low power consumption, and circuit simplicity it promotes make its use

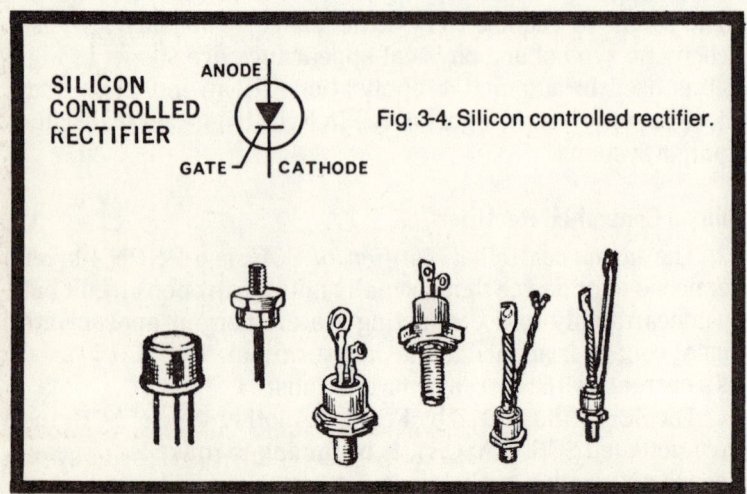

Fig. 3-4. Silicon controlled rectifier.

particularly advantageous. However, it is adversely affected by temperature changes and humidity, and this limits to some extent its use in automotive applications.

TRANSISTORS

The *transistor* consists of two semiconductor diodes back to back, with the center element common to both junctions. Transistors are either NPN or PNP, depending upon which is the common element. This is illustrated along with the schematic symbols for each type in Fig. 3-5.

Transistors of either type have three connections—emitter, base, and collector. The base is the control

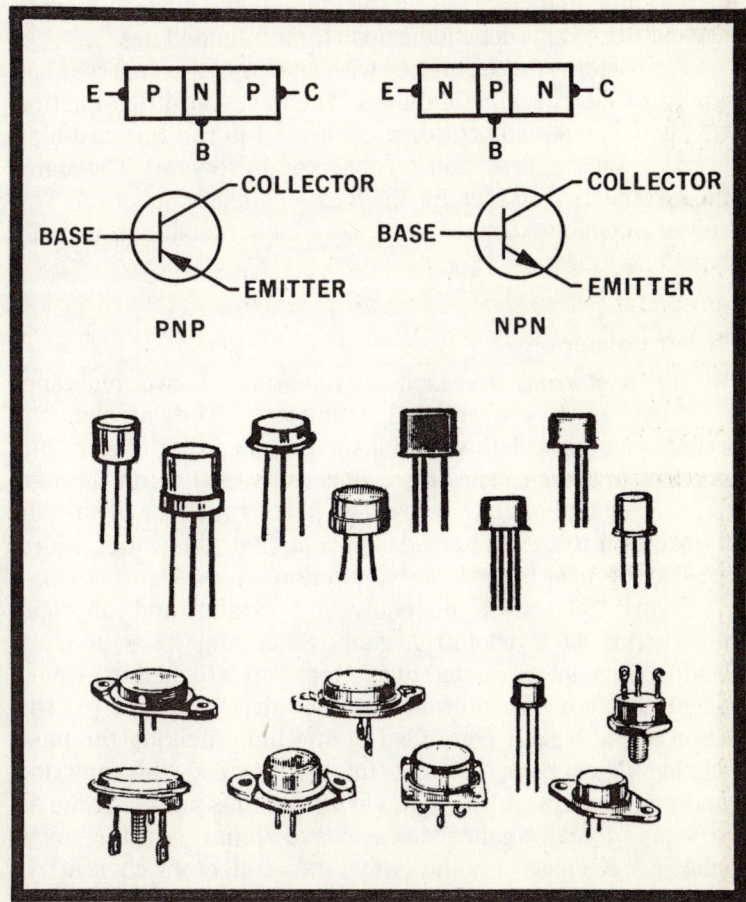

Fig. 3-5. Transistor symbols, construction, and shapes. (Courtesy RCA Solid State.)

connection, allowing current flow through the transistor when it is forward-biased (with respect to the emitter) and shutting off current flow when it is negative biased. The value of current is dependent upon the value of bias voltage applied.

Figure 3-5 illustrates a few of the many different shapes and sizes of transistors used in automotive applications. It will be necessary when replacing a transistor to consult a transistor manual for the correct replacement number. This is mandatory for several reasons. An NPN transistor cannot be distinguished from a PNP except by its number or by an ohmmeter test (and perhaps not then if the transistor is open or shorted). Also, the placement of the leads on transistors is not the same in all cases. And the voltage and current ratings of transistors vary, depending upon their intended use.

Transistors can be checked with an ohmmeter in a manner similar to the checking of diodes. The base—emitter junction will show low resistance when connected in the forward-bias direction and high resistance connected in reverse. The same measurements hold true for the base—collector junction. The emitter—collector connections show high resistance in both directions.

Phototransistor

The *phototransistor* is a combination of two junctions arranged as a conventional transistor. The mechanical arrangement is such that light is focused on either one or both junctions in order to vary the conductivity of the unit through its collector and emitter leads. The phototransistor is similar in operation to the photodiode, except that it is much more sensitive because of the transistor action.

Figure 3-6 shows the equivalent circuit and physical construction of a phototransistor. Since the base is truly floating (it is not connected to any input or returned to ground except through the internal base—emitter resistance), the action at the base is controlled by the light striking the base junction. Variations in light intensity cause the junction conductivity to vary. The light variations thus act the same as an input signal applied to a conventional emitter—base junction. Because of the way the collector current is controlled, the phototransistor can be used as a light-sensitive switch.

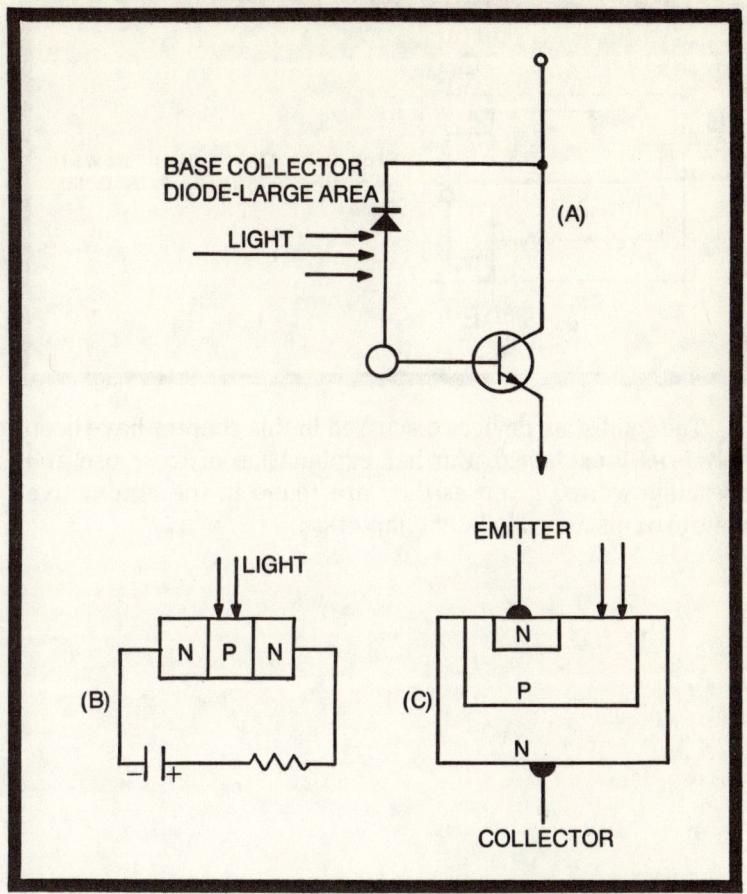

Fig. 3-6. The phototransistor—its equivalent circuit (A), its physical construction (B) and (C).

Darlington

A *Darlington power transistor* is a current amplifier consisting essentially of two separate transistors mounted in a single transistor housing and having the same external terminations or connections as a single transistor. This arrangement of two transistors in one can provide current gains in excess of 1000.

The arrangement of transistors for a Darlington amplifier is shown by its schematic symbol in Fig. 3-7. The Darlington has the same physical appearance of other power transistors, and as it has a high current-carrying ability, it usually is mounted in a heatsink.

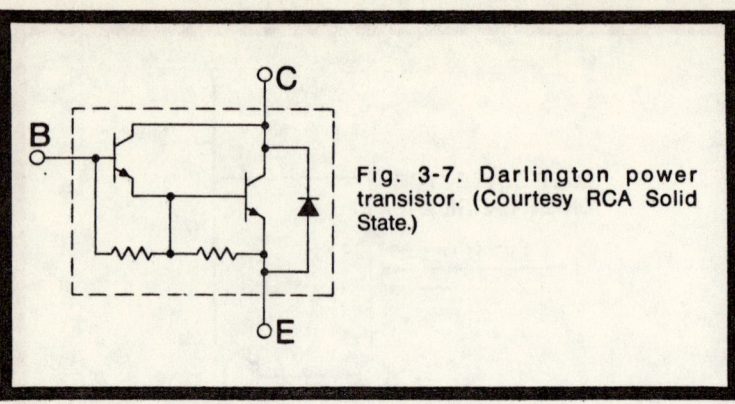

Fig. 3-7. Darlington power transistor. (Courtesy RCA Solid State.)

The solid-state devices discussed in this chapter have been only briefly explained. Further explanation of their use and operation will be given as they are found in the automotive units to be discussed in later chapters.

Chapter 4

Transistor Circuits

The transistor circuits used in ignition systems are: amplifier circuits, control circuits, regulator circuits, timing circuits, and sensing circuits. All transistor ignition systems are made up of various combinations of these circuits and, of course, a mechanical method of timing to an engine.

A brief description of each circuit and how it operates will be given in this chapter to enable the mechanic to (1) recognize the particular circuit by inspection of the components and how they are connected, or by comparison with the schematic diagram of the system and (2) to troubleshoot the system, locate the malfunctioning components, and make the necessary repair or replacement.

AMPLIFIER CONFIGURATIONS

A transistor (either NPN or PNP) may be connected in three different amplifier circuit configurations—common base, common emitter, and common collector. Each configuration demonstrates different characteristics and so is selected to accomplish a particular purpose.

Common Base

In the common-base configuration (Fig. 4-1), the input signal, or control signal, is applied between the emitter and base, and the output signal is taken between the collector and base. The base is common to both the input and output circuits,

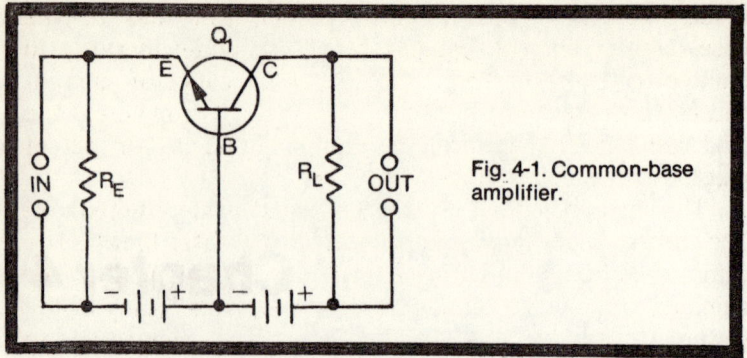

Fig. 4-1. Common-base amplifier.

hence the term *common-base* amplifier.

Note: For purposes of explanation, the circuits shown in this chapter show battery symbols for power supply. In a working system, the circuit power would be supplied by voltages available within the system.

In the common-base configuration, the emitter−base junction is forward-biased and the base−collector junction is reverse-biased. Any change in emitter−base current will cause a change in emitter−collector current. The collector current I_C is equal to the emitter current I_E minus the small base current I_B. Therefore, the collector current is slightly less than the emitter current. Varying the emitter current causes the collector current to vary in the same direction—to increase or decrease.

The input impedance of this configuration is low and the output impedance is high. This low-to-high impedance change can provide a high voltage gain, though the current gain is less than 1. It also makes the circuit a valuable impedance-matching device.

Common Emitter

The common-emitter configuration is the most often used transistor amplifier circuit. In the common-emitter configuration, the input signal is applied between the base and emitter, and the output signal is taken between the collector and emitter. The emitter is common to both the input and output circuits. The common-emitter amplifier circuit of an NPN transistor is shown in Fig. 4-2.

In the common-emitter circuit, the emitter−base junction is forward-biased, and the emitter−collector junction is reverse-biased. A positive-going signal will add to the base—emitter current, causing a corresponding increase in emitter—collector current. The increased collector current causes a corresponding increase in the voltage drop across the load resistance. Therefore, the output signal is 180° out of phase with the input voltage across R_B.

The input and output impedances are considered medium. The current and voltage gains are always greater than 1. The common-emitter configuration provides the highest power gain due to the large voltage and current gains. Many of the power transistors used in ignitions are connected in common-emitter circuits.

Common Collector

In the common-collector amplifier, the input signal is applied between the base and collector; the output signal is taken between the emitter and collector. The collector is common to both the input and output circuits. This circuit is also referred to as an *emitter follower*. The common-collector configuration of an NPN transistor is illustrated in Fig. 4-3. Both schematics are electrically identical, but B is the more common way of drawing the circuit.

In this circuit, the emitter—collector junction is forward-biased, and the collector—base junction is reverse-biased. The input signal either aids or opposes the forward bias and causes an increase or decrease in the emitter current. The collector is connected in the circuit to allow emitter current flow. The emitter circuit is the output circuit.

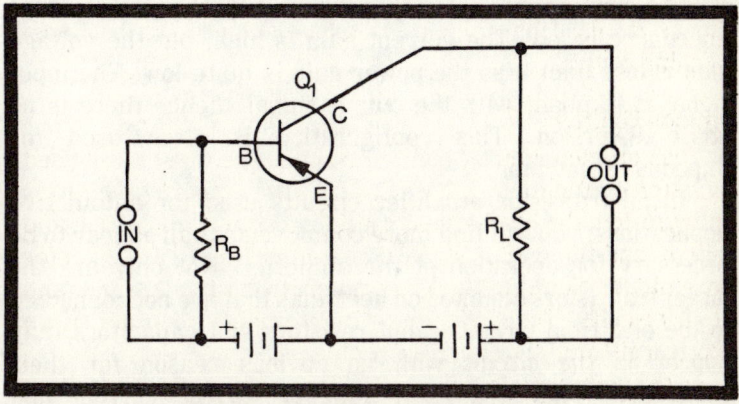

Fig. 4-2. Common-emitter amplifier.

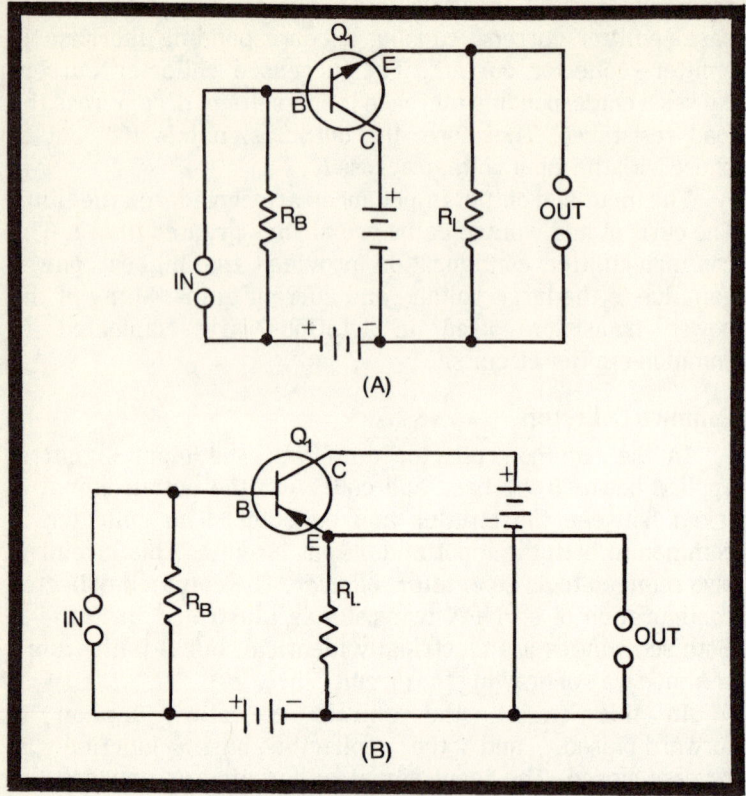

Fig. 4-3. Common-collector amplifiers.

The varying emitter current causes a corresponding varying output voltage across the emitter load resistance R_L.

The input impedance of this circuit is high, and the output impedance is low. The current gain is high, but the voltage gain is less than 1, so the power gain is quite low. The input signal is in phase with the output signal; hence there is no phase inversion. This configuration is often used for impedance matching.

In all transistor amplifier circuits used for automotive applications, you will find more components than appear to be necessary for operation of the amplifier. Not only are the larger transistors mounted on heatsinks that are not connected in the electrical circuitry, but resistors and capacitors may appear in the circuit with no obvious reason for their connection. They *are* vital, however, to the correct and continuous operation of the circuit.

BIAS STABILIZATION

The heatsink is used when a transistor must dissipate considerable power. The transistor is very sensitive to heat. A transistor subject to a change in its surrounding (ambient) temperature may suffer adverse effects in its operation. A transistor operated beyond its ability to disipate the resultant heat may be destroyed. Bias stabilization circuits have been devised to counteract the current increase due to a rise in temperature. One of the more frequently used bias stabilization circuits employs fixed bias combined with emitter bias, and it is illustrated in Fig. 4-4.

Resistor R_L is the collector load resistor, and capacitors C_1 and C_2 are coupling capacitors. Resistors R_1 and R_2 form a voltage divider and set the fixed-bias level. Their values are selected to provide the required bias current. Resistor R_E and capacitor C_E form the emitter bias circuit. The emitter current is equal to the sum of the base and collector currents. Current through R_E will develop a voltage drop that will oppose the base bias. Thus any increase in the voltage drop across R_E due to temperature changes will oppose the input bias and reduce the collector current. Capacitor C_E bypasses

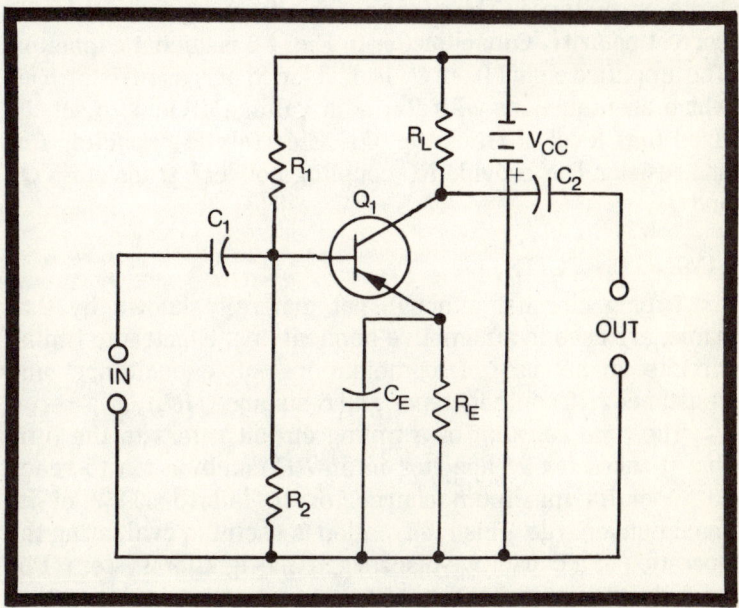

Fig. 4-4. Amplifier bias stabilization.

the AC signal; otherwise the AC gain of the stage would be reduced by the effect of R_E.

COUPLING

In automotive circuits, as well as most other electronic circuits, several transistors may be connected in cascade to provide sufficient gain to accomplish the intended purpose. This presents a problem of matching the output impedance of a transistor, which is relatively high, to the low input impedance of the following stage. In spite of its poor impedance matching, *RC* (resistor−capacitor) coupling is often used since it is inexpensive, requires few components, and handles the frequencies of automotive circuits very well. Figure 4-5 shows an *RC*-coupled 2-transistor amplifier stage.

The coupling capacitor (C_{C2}) serves the function of isolating the DC voltage at the collector of Q_1 from the base of the next transistor, Q_2. The coupling capacitor must also have a low reactance to signal voltages and, therefore, be relatively large in value. Typical values are from 1 to 30 μF. Another reason for using large coupling capacitors is the low input impedance of the next stage.

Electrolytic capacitors are small in physical size but of large capacitance. These capacitors must be installed with correct polarity. Capacitor C_{C2} in Fig. 4-5 is such a capacitor. The amplified signal from Q_1 is developed across resistor R_{B2}, which also functions with R_{F2} as a voltage divider to set the fixed bias level of transistor Q_2. Electrolytic capacitor C_{C2} and resistor R_{B2} provide *RC* coupling between transistors Q_1 and Q_2.

TIMING CIRCUITS

Timing circuits, although not generally known by that name, are used in automotive applications. Electronic timing circuits make use of combinations of capacitance and resistance (*RC*) or inductance and resistance (*RL*).

The *time constant* of a timing circuit refers to the time that it takes for a capacitor in an *RC* combination to reach 63.2% of its maximum charge, or to fall to 36.8% of its maximum charge. This information is useful in evaluating the operation of a capacitive-discharge (CD) ignition system. For an inductance−resistance (*RL*) circuit, the time constant refers to the time that it takes for the current to reach 63.2% of

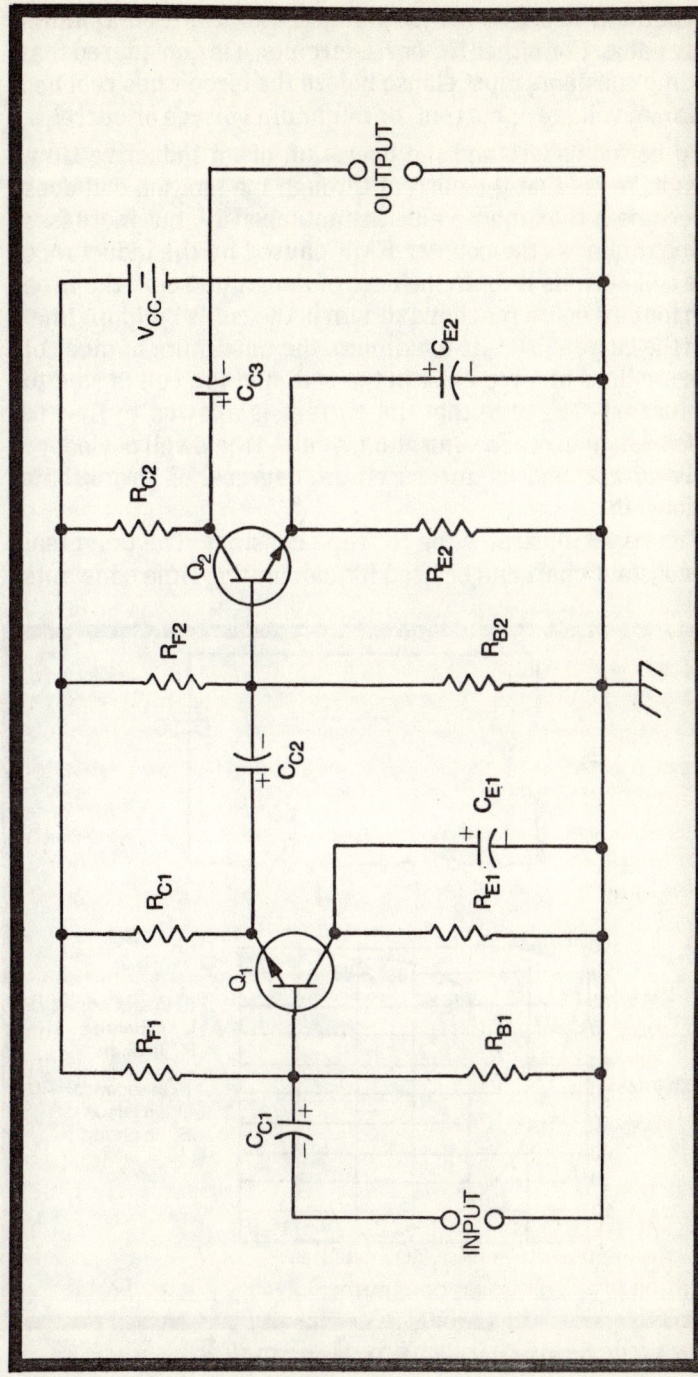

Fig. 4-5. An RC-coupled 2-transistor amplifier.

its maximum steady value, or to fall to 36.8% of its maximum steady value. For either *RC* or *RL* circuits, it is considered that five time constants must elapse before the circuit has reached maximum voltage or current, or minimum voltage or current.

To better understand the operation of an inductive time constant, recall that the current through the ignition coil does not become a maximum value instantaneously, but increases to a maximum as the counter EMF caused by the inductance of the coil permits it to. In the case of an ignition coil, the time taken for current to reach maximum is the coil's buildup time. When the current is at its maximum, the maximum number of magnetic lines of force exist in the coil, and the coil is said to be saturated. The time that the current is allowed to flow to enable the coil to reach saturation is called the dwell period, or simply *dwell*, and is measured in degrees of crankshaft rotation.

Figure 4-6 illustrates the *RC* time constant. The universal time constant chart can be used for calculating time constants

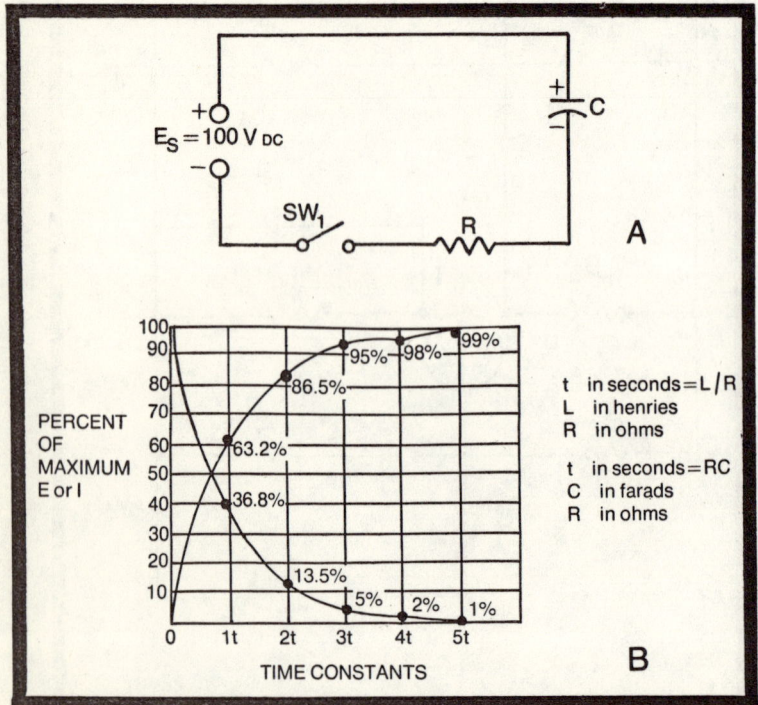

Fig. 4-6. RC time constant—(A) RC network. (B) Time constant chart.

74

of both *RC* and *RL* circuits, as well as for both charge and discharge times. On this chart, t is time, L is inductance, R is resistance, and C is capacitance.

Refer to the *RC* circuit of Fig. 4-6 and consider capacitor C as discharged, and switch SW_1 open. When switch SW_1 is closed, the only instantaneous opposition to current flow in the circuit is the resistance of R, and current is maximum. Capacitor C begins to build up or store a countervoltage (CEMF) which opposes the source voltage. This causes current to decrease as C charges, resulting in a decrease of the voltage drop across R (since $E = IR$). When capacitor C is fully charged, the voltage across the capacitor is equal to the source voltage, and current flow through R is reduced to zero. A definite time elapses during the charging of capacitor C; and if the values of R and C are known, the time may be found from the rising curve in Fig. 4-6B. For example, if R equals 1M (one megohm or 1,000,000 ohms) and C equals 1 μF (one microfarad or 0.000001 farad), then

$$t = RC = 1,000,000 \times 0.000001 = 1 \text{ sec}$$

With an input voltage of 100V, the voltage across the capacitor at the end of one time constant would be 63.2V.

With the charging voltage replaced by a short and the capacitor discharging through R, the rate of discharge would be as noted by the other curve on the chart. Note that if a capacitor were only charged for one time constant, a one-time-constant discharge would reduce the charge value to 36.8% of the value to which it actually became charged in one time constant, or to 36.8% of 63.2V instead of 36.8% of 100V. Maximum can only be reached in five time constants.

SENSING AND CONTROL CIRCUITS

There are many types of control circuits used in conjunction with emission control apparatus and transistor ignitions. One type is the photocell circuit shown in Fig. 4-7.

The operation of the circuit in Fig. 4-7 depends upon bias changes in transistor Q_1. The photocell and potentiometer R_3 form a voltage divider for Q_1, which is used in a common-collector configuration. Since the output impedance of the common-collector stage is low, it can be directly coupled to the base of Q_2. Assume that the photocell is in darkness and, therefore, its resistance is high. The base—emitter voltage, or

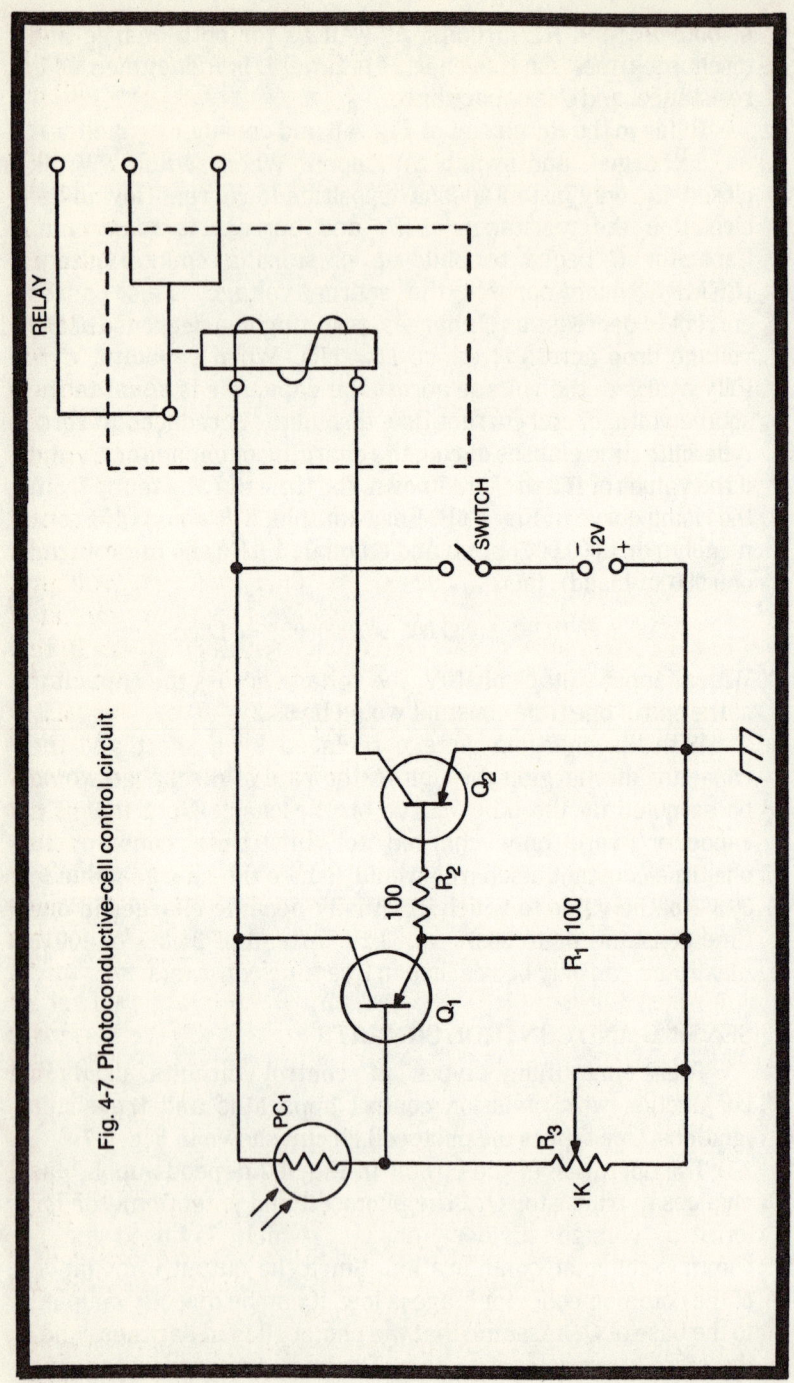

Fig. 4-7. Photoconductive-cell control circuit.

forward bias, of Q_1 will be relatively low, because the base will be relatively close electrically to the positive supply terminal. Therefore Q_1 will not conduct, and the relay will not be activated.

When light strikes the photocell, its resistance falls rapidly, making the base more negative with respect to the emitter of transistor Q_1. There is then forward bias and transistor Q_1 turns on, causing transistor Q_2 to be biased on, which activates the relay.

Resistor R_2 limits the forward bias of Q_2 to a safe level. Potentiometer R_3 is used to compensate for stray light, which might activate the relay. As the value of R_3 is decreased, it makes the base of Q_1 positive going with respect to the emitter, and it can be adjusted to cut Q_1 off. Resitor R_3 might be termed a sensitivity control.

There are several types of sensors and sensor circuits used in conjunction with transistor ignitions and emission control equipment—sensors of heat, temperature, pressure, vacuum, etc. For purposes of explanation, the humidity sensor circuit of Fig. 4-8 will be used. Note that this circuit, like others in this book, shows the circuit output driving relay. The output can be designed to drive amplifiers, electric valves, transistor switches, and other devices.

The circuit of Fig. 4-8 is a common-emitter amplifier used to control a relay. The bias on the transistor Q_1 is controlled by the resistance of the sensor H and the compensation potentiometer R_2. Humidity sensors have a high resistance in very dry surrounding air and change to a very low resistance when the surrounding air becomes very moist. Because of this response to a change in humidity, the potentiometer can be adjusted to operate the relay when the humidity is over or under a certain value. Similar circuits with different sensors can be used to advance or retard timing, control air/fuel mixtures, and so forth.

VOLTAGE REGULATION CIRCUIT

For a transistor ignition to operate at its optimum, it should have a well regulated input voltage. While the zener makes a fairly good DC voltage regulator when used in a simple circuit, the more sophisticated regulator circuits use transistors and zeners in combination.

The circuit shown in Fig. 4-9 is a transistorized version of a series regulator. Note that transistor Q_1 is effectively in series

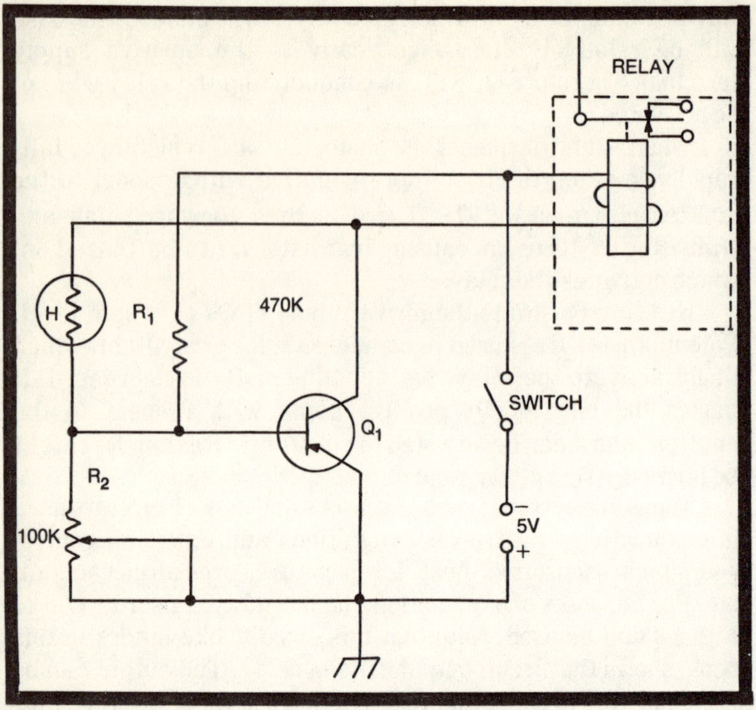

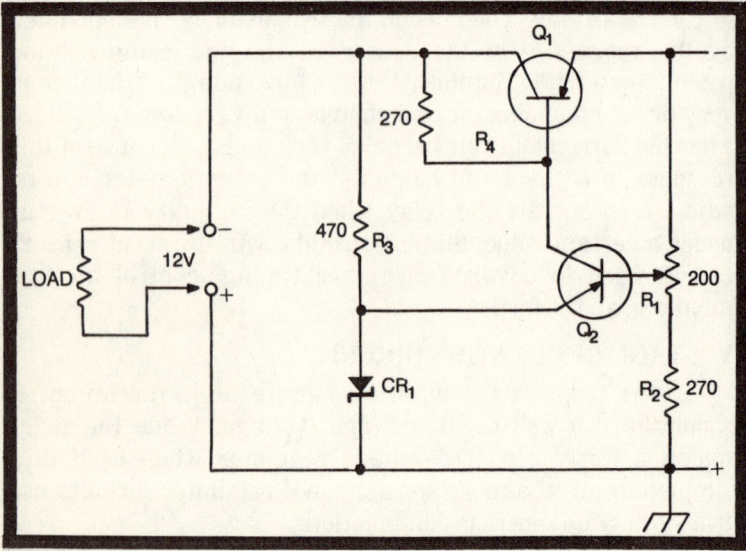

Fig. 4-8. Humidity-sensor control circuit.

Fig. 4-9. Series voltage regulator.

with the negative lead from the unregulated DC supply; the positive lead runs straight through to the positive terminal of the regulated output. This series transistor is commonly called a *pass* transistor. Its resistance depends upon the level of its forward bias. When its base becomes more negative with respect to the emitter, the resistance decreases.

Transistor Q_2 is the control transistor. It determines how positive or negative the base of Q_1 will be and, hence, the series resistance of Q_1. The voltage input to the regulator is always higher than the required DC output (load) voltage.

Note that the potentiometer and resistor R_2 are placed in parallel with the DC output terminals (through) Q_1. This is the voltage-sensing network. When the DC load current becomes less, the DC output voltage tends to rise. As it starts to rise, the sensing network changes the base bias of Q_2, and this in turn makes the base of Q_1 more positive. As a result, the resistance of Q_1 increases to counter the tendency of the output voltage to rise. When a large current is drawn by the load, the voltage on the sensing network tends to fall. This changes the bias on Q_2 in such a way as to cause the base of Q_1 to become more negative. This in turn lowers the resistance of Q_1. Its voltage drop is less, and the tendency of the DC load voltage to fall is countered.

The zener serves two purposes. First, it compensates for changes in the DC input voltage. Its second, and very important, function is to maintain a constant reference voltage at the emitter of Q_2. The voltage sensed by the sensing network is compared to this, and the voltage difference is used to bias Q_2, which in turn controls the resistance of Q_1 and hence the output voltage. The output voltage is thus pegged to a very stable zener reference voltage and held steady.

This type of regulator has the advantage of being able to regulate higher DC output voltages and currents than the zener alone. The regulated voltage can also be made variable.

Chapter 5

Transistor Ignition

The transistor ignition system has been developed primarily because the increased power outputs and higher sustained speeds of the modern high-compression engine have taxed the conventional ignition system to its capacity and beyond.

The need for more frequent and expensive tuneups on the high-power, high-compression engines to avoid poor gasoline mileage as well as poor performance was a large factor in this development. Many of these engines required a tuneup costing in excess of $100 at intervals of approximately 5000 miles to maintain desired performance and gasoline mileage. The requirement for maintenance of emission control was another factor in the development of a better ignition.

PROBLEMS OF CONVENTIONAL IGNITIONS

The weak point of the conventional ignition system has always been the mechanically operated breaker points. Normal point wear affects the operation of other components of the ignition system, even leading to the need for early replacement of some components, such as spark plugs.

In normal operation, the points pit and burn and metal transfer occurs. This metal transfer due to arcing takes place even with a proper value of capacitor in the circuit because the current through the points varies with speed and the capacitor must be selected for an average current. At low speeds current flows for a longer period of time, longer than is necessary for coil saturation. This causes both the points and the coil to heat, and leads to poor performance and emission control. At high speeds, the dwell time is too short; not enough current flows to saturate the coil, resulting in poor high-voltage output, incomplete combustion, and fuel waste.

This changing current flow, which may be anywhere in the range of 2A to 6A, causes the points to pit, increasing point resistance and creating a snowball effect. As point resistance increases, less current is available for coil saturation, and again, available high voltage is decreased.

ADVANTAGES OF TRANSISTOR IGNITIONS

The problem of point resistance and insufficient dwell time at high speeds is nearly eliminated by the transistor ignition system. Figure 5-1 illustrates a conventional ignition system and a basic transistor ignition for comparison.

Circuit A (Fig. 5-1) is that of a conventional ignition system. The breaker points are in series with the ignition coil primary winding. The current-carrying capacity of the points

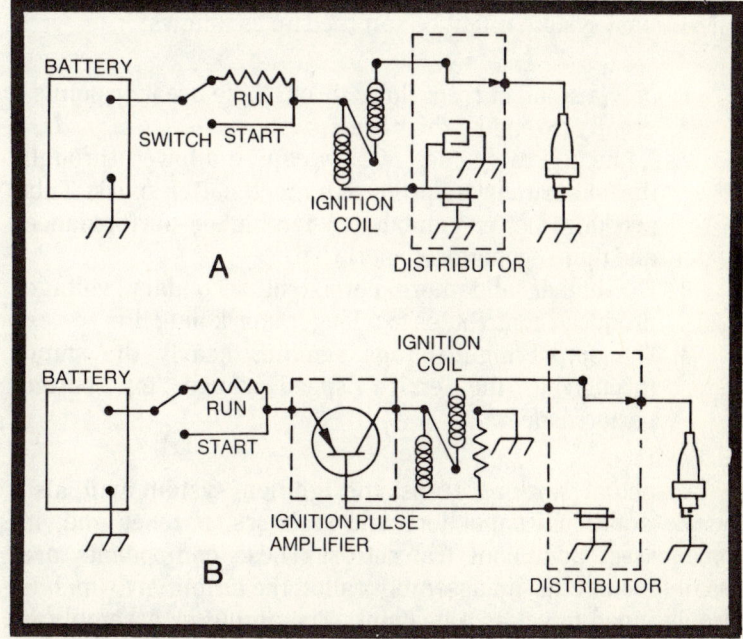

Fig. 5-1. Comparison of conventional (A) and transistor (B) ignition systems.

is the factor that determines how much current can pass through the coil. With a limited strength in the primary circuit, there is a proportionately limited secondary circuit output.

Figure 5-1B is a schematic of a basic transistor ignition system that employs breaker points to mechanically trigger the transistor into conduction. The breaker points are now connected only in the base circuit of the transistor and must pass only enough current to turn the transistor on and off. (A transistor is an excellent fast-acting electronic switch.)

Since the base circuit permits only a very small current flow, the breaker points now handle only 0.5A or less. Arcing across the points is practically nonexistent with this light current, so the capacitor has been eliminated. A current of around 6A can be used in the coil primary circuit. Coil magnetic saturation is now virtually instantaneous, with a corresponding increase in secondary circuit output. The coil should be designed to accommodate the greater primary current. Coil saturation will definitely be faster than in the conventional system, and be virtually unaffected by high-speed operation.

The advantages of a transistor ignition system over the conventional system might be summed up as follows:

1. Only a small current flows through the breaker points, greatly extending their life.
2. A much greater current flow can be allowed through the coil primary to produce a much hotter spark. This produces better combustion for higher performance and more economy of operation.
3. The higher and more persistent secondary voltage produced contributes to a longer spark plug life.
4. The output high voltage remains nearly the same throughout the entire speed range for better performance.

An actual working transistor ignition system will also include additional capacitors and resistors, a zener and, in some cases, additional transistors. These components are usually mounted in an assembly called the amplifier, which is also designed to act as a heatsink. The amplifier assembly is usually mounted near the distributor and on body metal rather than on the engine for purposes of heat dissipation.

FORD CONTACT-CONTROLLED IGNITION

Figure 5-2 is a complete wiring diagram of the Ford contact-controlled transistor ignition system, which uses a single transistor. The term *contact controlled* means that the conventional breaker points are used, but only to trigger the base circuit of the transistor, thus allowing conduction through the emitter—collector circuit.

Point Circuit

The *point circuit* current, as shown by the double-headed arrows, flows from the battery through the ground; the ignition points (when closed); the 7.1—7.9-ohm resistor; the base and emitter of the transistor; the 0.33-ohm resistor, which is common to the entire primary circuit; and returns to the positive battery post via the ignition switch. This point current is approximately 0.5A.

The transistor used is a PNP, so the direction of point current—negative to positive, base to emitter—presents forward bias, and the transistor will conduct. The collector—emitter circuit is the switch in the coil primary circuit and, when biased on, it allows current to flow in the primary.

Primary Circuit

The coil primary current flows from the battery negative terminal through ground, the coil primary, the 0.43-ohm resistor, and the collector—emitter circuit of the transistor, joining with the point current through the common 0.33-ohm resistor and returning to the battery positive post via the ignition switch. The coil current is from 5A to 6A.

When the points open, the point circuit is broken and current flow stops in the base—emitter circuit and through the 10-ohm resistor that provided forward bias for the transistor. With forward bias removed, the transistor stops conducting, or turns off. This action opens the coil primary circuit, allowing the magnetic field to collapse and induce the high voltage necessary to fire the spark plugs.

Circuit Protection

The zener connected between the collector and emitter of the transistor is a protection diode. When the field of the coil collapses, it induces a voltage in the primary that can approach 100V. If this voltage were allowed to "flash" the

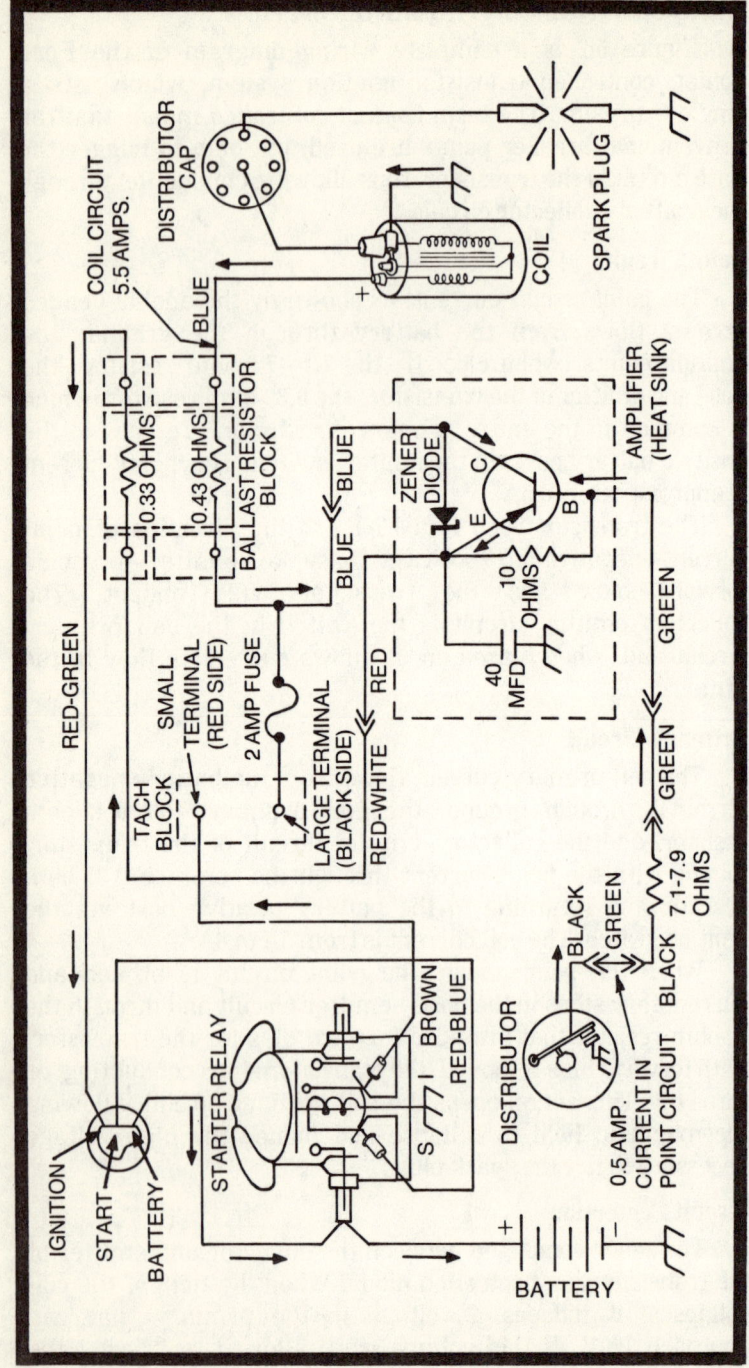

Fig. 5-2. Contact-controlled transistor ignition. (Courtesy Ford Motor Company.)

transistor, the transistor would be ruined. Before the induced voltage reaches a level that would damage the transistor, the zener "fires" and conducts current around the transistor and back to the battery. When the voltage falls below the danger level, the zener stops reverse conduction and coil current is again passed through the transistor. Thus, the zener acts as a voltage limiter for the transistor.

The 7.1–7.9-ohm resistor connected between the distributor and the base of the transistor is to protect the transistor from excess base current flow. The forward-bias voltage for the transistor base is built up across the 10-ohm resistor. This resistor also prevents the coil current from being bypassed through the base–emitter circuit when the points are closed.

The 0.43-ohm collector resistor and 0.33-ohm emitter resistor serve as current-limiting resistors. Due to the action of these two resistors and the two resistors noted in the preceding paragraph, the point current is limited to 0.5A and the coil current allowed to approach 6A.

The 40 μF capacitor is connected between the emitter and ground to protect the transistor from being damaged by voltage spikes, or pulses, from the alternator. Such voltage spikes can be caused by loose or corroded battery terminals, loose circuit connections, a faulty alternator voltage limiter, or by the battery becoming disconnected (broken cable) during operation.

The transistor in this system is well protected from damage by overvoltage in the circuit, but it and the zener are very heat sensitive. To prevent damage from overheating, the transistor, zener, base resistor, and capacitor are mounted in a finned aluminum heatsink. The heatsink dissipates heat readily, and when mounted in a relatively cool place, protects the entire assembly (amplifier) from heat damage.

The disadvantages, or problems, encountered in the point-triggered ignition system are strictly point problems. The quality of solid-state devices available today has virtually eliminated the problems in the electronics. The use of a small current through the points considerably lengthens point life, but points are still susceptible to rubbing-block wear (which changes dwell and timing), sticking or slow action, and point bounce at high speeds.

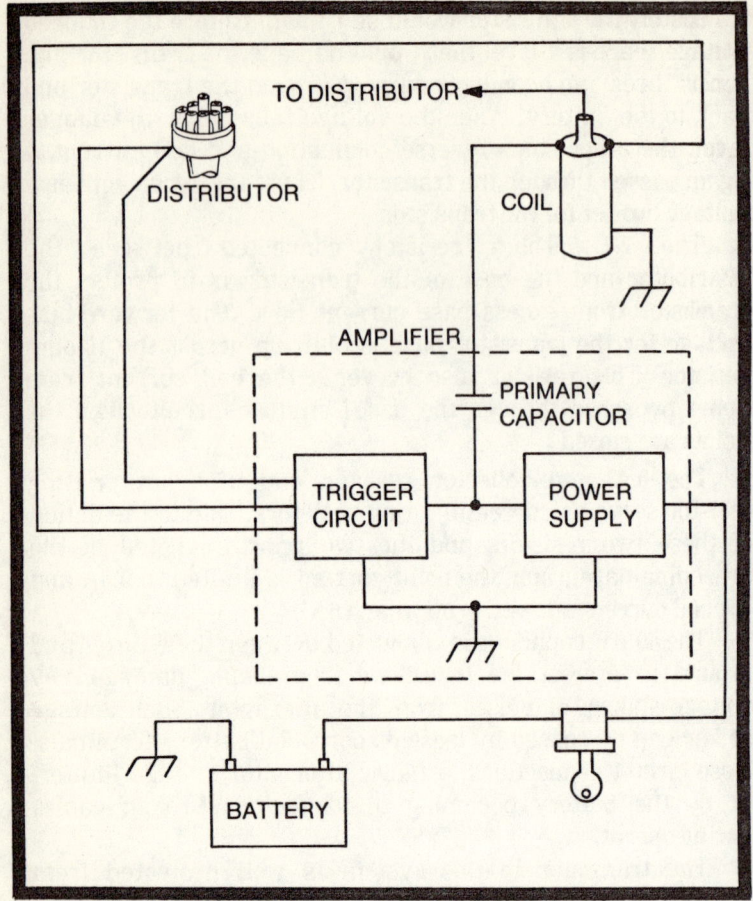

Fig. 5-3. Simplified diagram of capacitive-discharge ignition.

CAPACITIVE-DISCHARGE IGNITION

Another type of point-triggered transistor ignition system, said to have certain advantages over the "plain" transistor ignition, is the capacitive-discharge, or CD, ignition. A simplified diagram of a CD ignition is shown in Fig. 5-3.

In this system, point closing causes the transistor amplifier (trigger circuit) to operate the power supply and charge the capacitor to a value of 300V to 400V. When the points open, the trigger circuit is off, and the capacitor discharges through the coil primary, inducing the high voltage to fire the spark plugs. (This circuit will be explained in detail later.)

The advantage claimed for CD ignition stems from the extremely rapid rise time of the high voltage. The rise time is around 2 microseconds, as compared to a conventional ignition rise time of 100—150 microseconds. This gives the CD system an unusual ability to fire fouled spark plugs. Also, CD systems can produce a hot spark from a low battery or in subzero weather, and this is an aid in hard-starting problems. This system can operate successfully at very high RPM (8000 RPM), limited only by the point bounce problem.

Many CD ignition systems operate with stock points and a stock coil. However, more satisfactory results may be obtained by the use of a coil designed with a high-voltage (300—400V) primary. A comparison of the conventional coil and a coil designed for capacitive-discharge systems is shown in Fig. 5-4. Note that the secondary of the CD coil has its return directly to ground, rather than through the primary as is the case in the conventional coil. Also, the turns ratio of the coil will be different from that of the conventional coil.

POINTLESS IGNITIONS

Transistor and CD ignitions greatly extend point life, plug life, and plug-wiring life (the wires do not have to be handled as often), but some problems still remain with a mechanical triggering system.

A means of eliminating the breaker points in transistor ignition systems is to trigger the amplifier with a magnetic

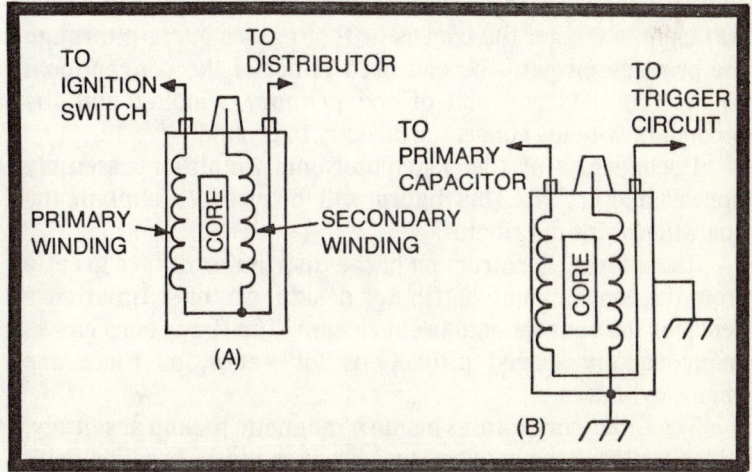

Fig. 5-4. Coil comparison—conventional (A) and CD type (B).

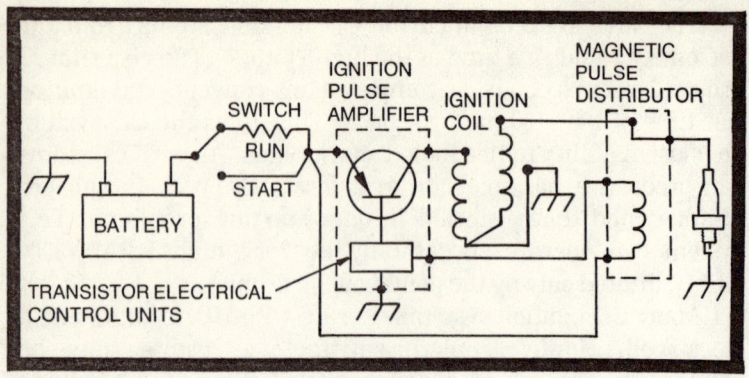

Fig. 5-5. Simplified version of magnetically triggered ignition. (Courtesy Delco Remy.)

pulse. The amplifier used is a 2- or 3-transistor type requiring a very low value of voltage to turn it on. This low value of triggering voltage is received from an engine-timed pulse generator located in the distributor in the space formerly occupied by the breaker plate, points, and capacitor.

Magnetic Triggering

Figure 5-5 is a simplified schematic of a magnetic-pulse-type transistor ignition. The triggering device, replacing the points, is shown as a coil winding located in the magnetic-pulse distributor. The control unit shown in the ignition pulse amplifier is a 2-transistor amplifier. It builds up the voltage pulse received from the distributor to a value sufficient to trigger the transistor that passes current through the primary circuit. The coil used is not of the conventional design, but has one end of the primary winding and the secondary winding connected directly to ground.

Photographs of the distributor and amplifier assembly appear in Fig. 5-6. This figure will be used to explain the operation of the distributor.

The internal construction of the distributor differs greatly from the conventional distributor design. An inner timer core replaces the conventional breaker cam. The timer core has as many equally spaced projections, or vanes, as there are engine cylinders.

The timer core rotates inside a magnetic pickup assembly, which replaces the conventional breaker plate, breaker point set, and capacitor. The magnetic pickup assembly consists of

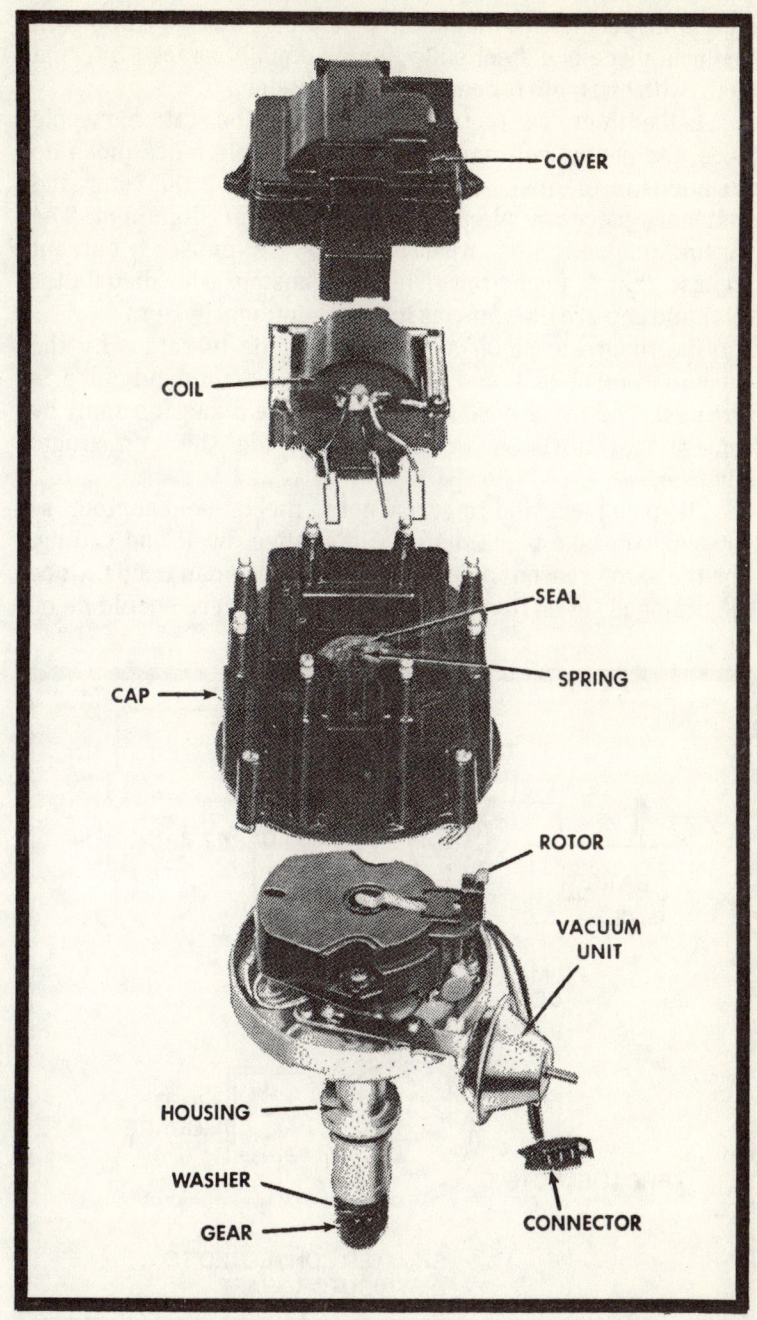

Fig. 5-6. Magnetic-pulse distributor and amplifier assembly. (Courtesy Delco Remy.)

a ceramic permanent magnet, a pole piece, and a pickup coil. The pole piece is a steel plate having equally spaced internal teeth, with one tooth for each engine cylinder.

As the timer core (rotor) rotates inside the stationary pole piece, the pickup coil mounted under the pole piece picks up variations in the magnetic flux as the teeth on the rotor and stationary piece are alternately in and out of alignment. The varying magnetic flux, weak as it may be, causes a current impulse that triggers the driver transistor. The distributor rotor and cap are the same as in a conventional system.

The magnetic picup assembly is made to rotate by the vacuum control unit and, in that way, vacuum advance is provided. The timer core is made to rotate about the shaft by conventional advance weights to provide the centrifugal advance.

The pole piece and rotor are not in mechanical contact, so no wear can take place that would change dwell and timing. For the same reason, no point lag or bounce can occur. Once the timing is set on this type of distributor, there should be no

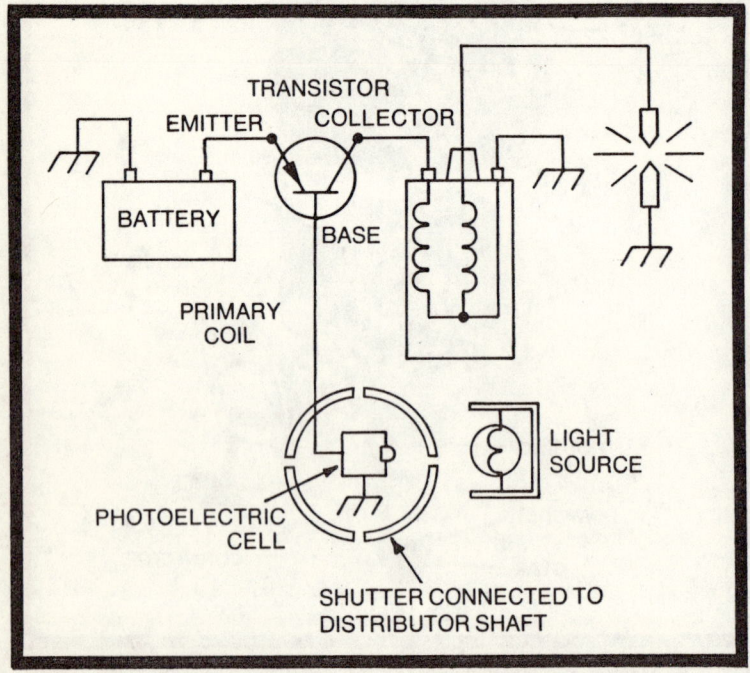

Fig. 5-7. Simplified version of light-triggered transistor ignition.

reason for the system to require further adjustment until the distributor has been removed and replaced.

Light Triggering

Another method of triggering a transistor ignition system is by light. A complete system of this type will be explained later. The simplified diagram of Fig. 6-7 shows the system to have the amplifier and coil used in many transistor ignition systems. The triggering mechanism consists of a light source, a photoelectric cell, and a rotating interrupter, or shutter. The source of light is most often an LED for low current drain and long life. The shutter is the timing device. It has as many equally spacd slots as there are cylinders in the engine.

Chapter 6

Auto Manufacturers' Transistor Ignitions

Chrysler Corporation may have been the first with transistor ignition as standard equipment. In 1971 transistor ignition was available as optional equipment on some Chrysler models, and it became standard on all models in 1973.

CHRYSLER MAGNETICALLY TRIGGERED IGNITION

This system, whose connection diagram is shown in Fig. 6-1, is similar in appearance to the Delco and Ford systems, but it does have important differences.

Note in the illustration of the distributor and its major parts (Fig. 6-2), that the distributor plate appears much the same as the breaker plate of a conventional ignition. The breaker points have been replaced by a pole piece and pickup coil mounted on the plate much the same as the breaker points were. The vacuum advance operates the pickup plate as it did the breaker plate. The distributor cam becomes a *reluctor*, with teeth replacing the lobes. The reluctor mounts on the centrifugal advance mechanism and operates the same as in the conventional distributor for centrifugal advance.

The weak magnetic field created in the pickup coil by the permanent-magnet pole piece is stationary when the reluctor is not turning, so no voltage is induced in the coil. When the reluctor is turning, at some points (Fig. 6-3) the field is quite weak, though moving, and little voltage is induced in the

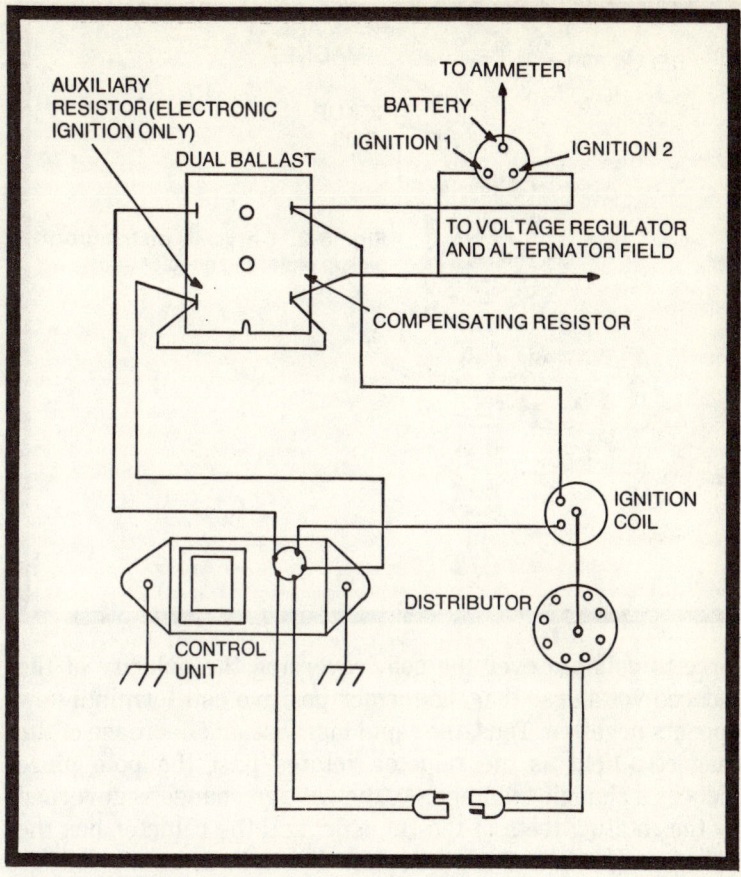

Fig. 6-1. Wiring diagram and major components of Chrysler magnetically triggered ignition.

pickup coil. As the rotating reluctor approaches the pickup, the air gap is decreased, increasing the magnetic field in the pickup. As the field strength increases, the lines of force move out over the pickup coil's windings, inducing a small voltage in the coil.

This small voltage will have a positive polarity at one of the coil terminals because of the direction of buildout of the magnetic lines of force. This positive voltage will continue to build until the reluctor tooth is directly opposite the pole piece as shown in Fig. 6-4.

As the reluctor tooth starts to leave the pole piece, the air gap begins to increase, which decreases the field strength. This decreasing field strength causes the magnetic lines of

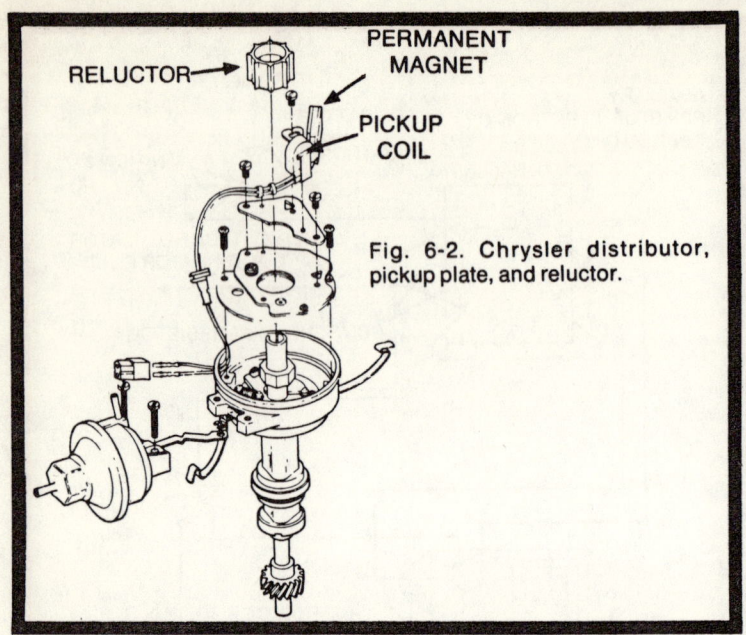

Fig. 6-2. Chrysler distributor, pickup plate, and reluctor.

force to collapse over the coil, reversing the polarity of the induced voltage so that the former positive coil terminal now appears negative. Thus, the rapid increase and decrease of the magnetic field as the reluctor rotates past the pole piece induces a changing voltage. As the voltage change is governed by the rotating teeth of the reluctor, and the reluctor has the same number of teeth as the engine has cylinders, one voltage pulse will occur for each cylinder with each complete revolution of the reluctor. The pulse induced in the coil by the rotating reluctor is a precisely timed signal to trigger the control circuit and cut the primary current off.

Figure 6-5 is the schematic diagram of the Chrylser electronic ignition, which incorporates as one circuit the reluctor and pickup in the distributor, the control amplifier, and the ignition coil. The following paragraphs, with the use of this diagram, explain the operation of this system.

In the beginning state, transistor Q_1 is biased into conduction, holding the anode of programmable unijunction transistor (PUT) Q_2 at essentially ground potential. Transistor Q_3 is reverse-biased and thus applies a forward bias to emitter follower Q_4, which in turn biases the power transistor Q_5 into conduction. Current flows through the

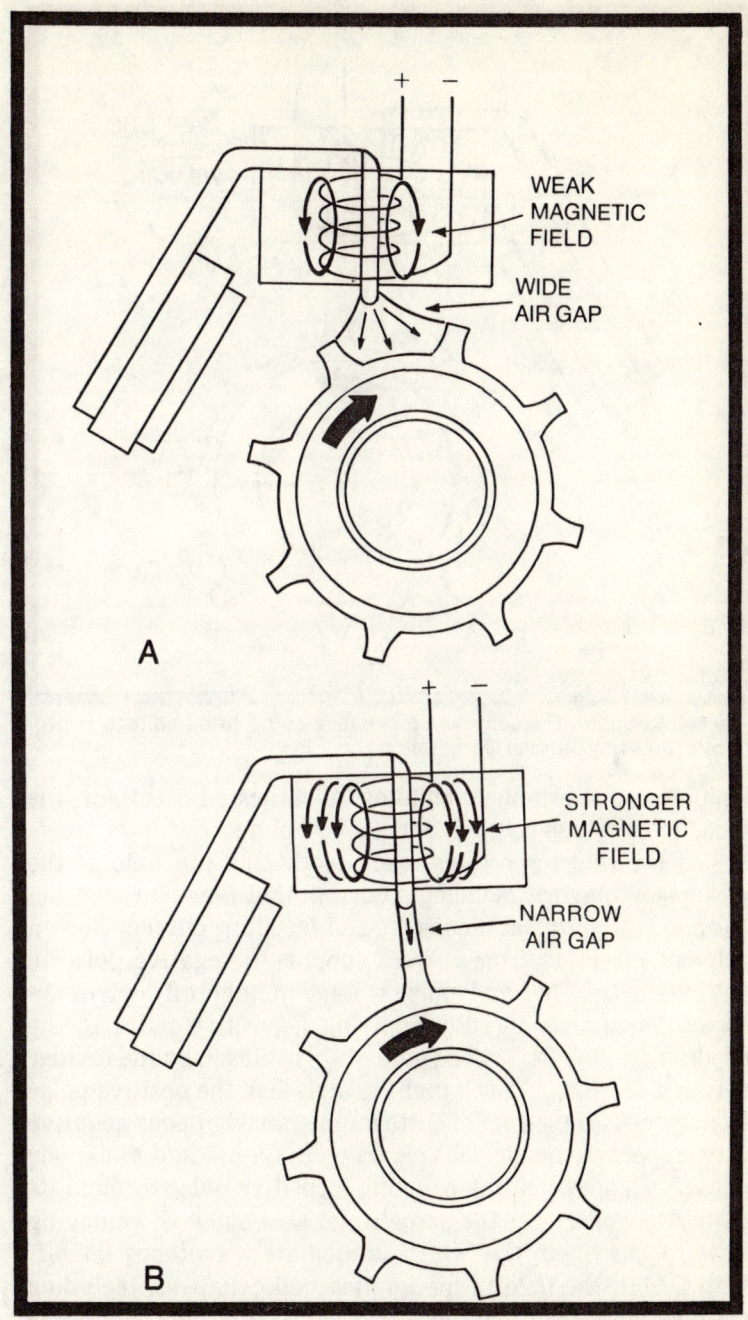

Fig. 6-3. Action of reluctor on magnetic lines of force. (Courtesy Chrysler Corporation.)

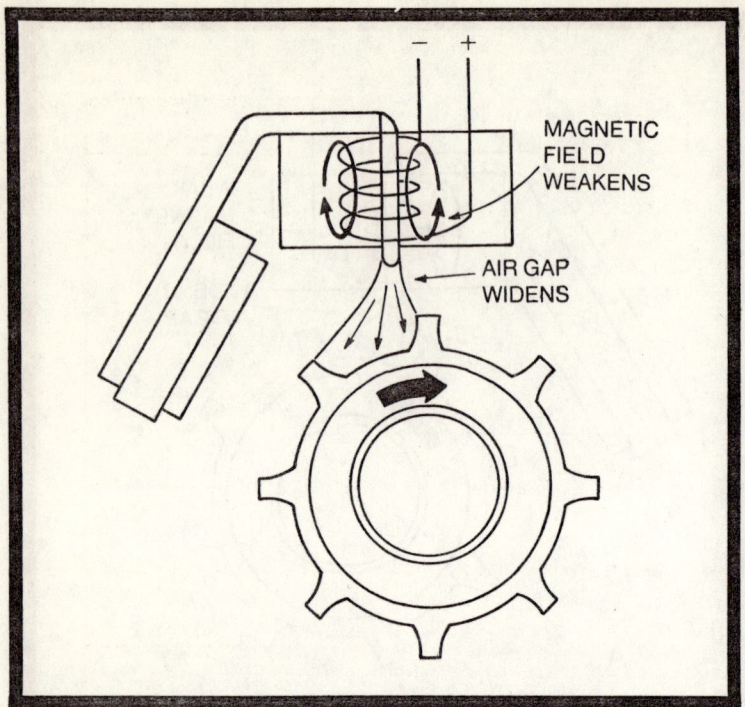

Fig. 6-4. Position of reluctor when negative-going firing voltage is produced. (Courtesy Chrysler Corporation.)

ignition coil's primary, building a saturated field for the induction of a high voltage for the spark plugs.

As the reluctor rotates, each tooth cuts the field of the pickup-coil magnet, inducing a current that flows through L_1, D_1, and D_2. Note that diodes D_1 and D_2 allow current flow in only one direction. This current supplies a negative pulse to the base of Q_1. The small pulse voltage momentaily drives Q_1 out of conduction, thereby applying a positive pulse to the anode of Q_2 (the PUT). The gate of Q_2 is biased by the divider network, R_4 and R_5, such that the arrival of the positive pulse from Q_1 causes the gate of Q_2 to momentarily appear negative with respect to the anode. This triggers Q_2 on, and the anode pulls the gate potential, coupling a positive pulse through C_3 to the base of Q_3. At the same time, Q_3 conducts, removing forward bias from Q_4, which immediately switches Q_5 off. With Q_5 off, the field in the ignition coil collapses, including the high voltage to fire the spark plugs. The high voltage is delivered to the plugs in the conventional manner.

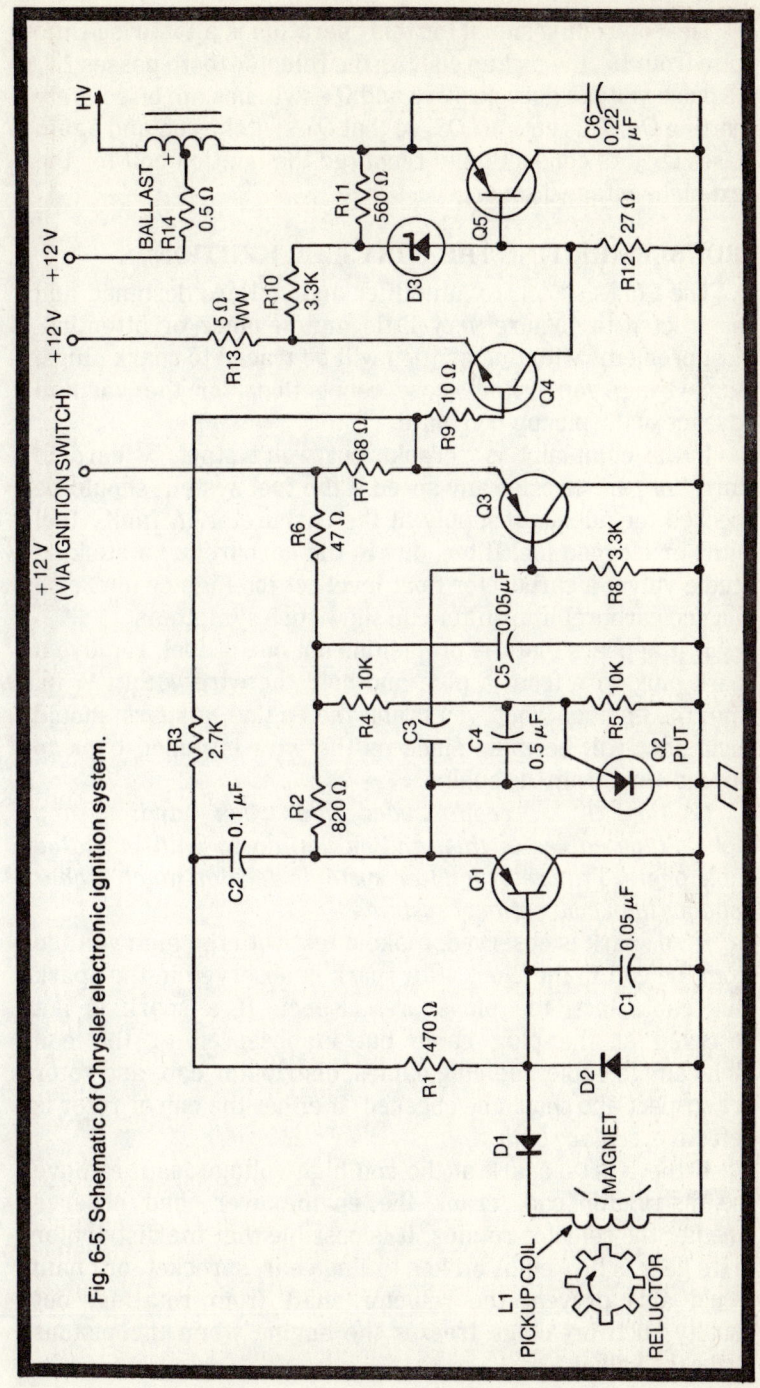

Fig. 6-5. Schematic of Chrysler electronic ignition system.

The controlling signal for this operation is a fast-rise-time pulse from L_1, the pickup coil. As the reluctor tooth passes L_1, the pulse voltage goes positive and Q_1 switches on, effectively shorting Q_2. This cuts off Q_3, so that Q_4 switches on and again biases Q_5 into conduction to recharge the ignition coil for the next high-voltage discharge.

TROUBLESHOOTING THE CHRYSLER IGNITION

The Chrysler control amplifier and coil are designed and constructed to require very little maintenance or attention. Most problems with this ignition will be traced to spark plugs, plug wiring, cap, rotor, loose connections, or the vacuum advance of the pickup-coil plate.

If the complaint is "cranks but won't start," "hard to start," or "misfires at any speed," the fuel system should be checked for adequate supply at the carburetor. A faulty fuel pump or clogged fuel filter, dirt in the carburetor, a sticking needle valve, a carburetor float level set too high or low, or a plugged carburetor air filter can show such symptoms.

If it appears that the problem is not one of fuel, remove a spark plug wire from a plug and hold the wire within ¼ in. from the engine. When you crank the engine, a spark should occur that will be maintained as the wire is pulled back to around ⅜ in. from the engine.

Caution: It is recommended that when handling any high-voltage cables of this ignition you do so with insulated cable pliers. Transistor ignition systems develop much higher voltages than conventional systems.

If no spark is observed, make a test with the high voltage from the coil to the block. If a spark is observed in the spark plug cable test, the plugs are suspect. If a spark is not observed at the plug cable but is observed at the coil high-voltage cable, the plug cables, distributor cap, and rotor are suspect and should be checked. If either the cap or rotor is defective, *replace both*.

If there is no spark at the coil high-voltage lead, remove the distributor cap, crank the engine over, and observe whether the reluctor rotates. It is possible that the distributor drive gear is broken. A broken timing gear, sprocket, or chain would also prevent the reluctor shaft from rotating, but usually such breakage freezes the engine when the pistons strike the valves.

If none of the foregoing tests reveals the problem and the complaint was "cranks but won't start" (no spark), it may be necessary to check out the ignition coil, pickup coil, and control amplifier.

Before proceeding with further checks, it is advantageous to be aware of certain precautions to observe when working on a transistor ignition system. This will prevent damage to the system that can occur during a check for defective components.

Precautions in Working on Transistor Ignitions

1. Disconnect the battery before doing work of any kind on a transistor ignition system.
2. Be extremely careful about using jumper wires to ground any part of the system. Unlike parts in the conventional system, transistors may easily be damaged by this practice.
3. When connecting a tachometer, always follow the instrument instructions. Damage to both the system and meter can result from wrong connections.
4. Be sure all lead connections in the system are clean and tight. High-resistance connections give poor system operation and erroneous test readings.
5. On point-controlled systems, proper lubrication of the distributor cam is extremely important.
6. Be sure the ground cables are not frayed or broken and that they make clean, tight connections.
7. Be careful not to ground any disconnected leads if the battery is still connected.
8. When it becomes necessary to crank the engine over without starting it, as for a compression test or static timing, remove the coil high-voltage cable from the distributor cap and ground it to the engine. *Never allow the coil to operate open circuited* (that is, with the high-voltage cable completely out of the coil tower). One firing in this condition can destroy the coil.
9. Always doublecheck the polarity of the coil's primary terminals. These leads are easily reversed.
10. Never install capacitor-type radio suppressors on the coil's primary terminals.

Testing the Pickup and Ignition Coils

The pickup coil can be tested with an ohmmeter. Disconnect the pickup coil connector and insert the ohmmeter leads into the connector. The resistance reading should be between 300 and 400 ohms. If the reading is infinite, the coil is open. If the meter reads below 300 ohms, the coil is shorted in the windings. Leave one lead of the ohmmeter in the connector and touch the other firmly to any metal part of the distributor. If any reading other than infinity is obtained, the coil is shorted to the pole piece. Check to be sure that the coil is not loose and floating on the pole piece.

The ignition coil can be checked for continuity and grounds by disconnecting its leads and using the ohmmeter. However, the transistor ignition coil is wound differently than the conventional coil, so if the ohmmeter check does not show a defect, the coil must be checked on a tester approved for transistor coils.

If all the above tests do not locate the trouble, the problem is in the amplifier or its grounding. If the grounding is not at fault, the amplifer should be replaced. It is possible to check the amplifier for defective components, but this procedure is not recommended.

Misfiring

If the complaint is one of misfiring, make fuel checks and then the following checks in sequence.

1. Check ignition timing for recommended setting. (The distributor may have slipped.)
2. Remove spark plugs and inspect. Clean, file, and gap, or replace as necessary.
    Note: If any are worn, replace the plugs in sets.
3. Check *all* ignition system wiring, both primary and secondary. Look for brittle or cracked insulation, loose connections, or corroded terminals. Check placement of spark plug cables (they must not be too close together). Be sure that high-voltage cables are all the way into the cap and on the plugs. Be sure cable and plug boots are all the way on and are not cracked from heat.
4. Check inside and outside surfaces of the distributor cap for cracks and carbon tracks. Check the rotor for looseness or cracks. If either the cap or rotor is defective, replace both.

5. Check pickup coil with ohmmeter as explained earlier.
6. Check metal part of control amplifier box for good no-resistance ground.
7. Check ignition coil on tester approved for transistor ignition coils.
8. If the preceding tests do not locate the cause of trouble, the amplifier is faulty and should be replaced.

Surging

If the complaint is one of surging, check the fuel system thoroughly, and if no problem is found, proceed with the following checks and tests.

1. Engine power surges can be caused by reversed leads in the pickup coil connections. Check the lead color coding and compare with the manufacturer's schematic for proper identification and connection.
2. Check the pickup coil for shorted windings or an intermittent open or ground, using an ohmmeter.
3. Since the pickup coil is moved by the vacuum advance and the reluctor is moved by the centrifugal advance, trouble in either of these units may cause an intermittent surge. To check the action of these units, connect a timing light to No. 1 plug and start the engine. With the vacuum line removed from the advance unit, rev the engine up to observe timing advance. Advance should be smooth, not jerky. An approximation of the total advance can be read from the timing marks on the balancer for comparison with the manufacturer's specifications. Install the vacuum line on the advance unit and again observe the advance pattern when engine vacuum is affecting the advance curve. Any malfunction of the centrifugal advance mechanism will require replacement or rebuilding of the distributor. A malfunction of the vacuum advance may require replacement of either the vacuum unit, the pickup plate, or both. Any disturbance of the pickup coil and its plate mechanism, or the replacement of these, will require resetting the pole-shoe-to-reluctor gap and retiming the engine.

Failure to Start

If the complaint is "won't start" and the problem has been traced to the absence of a spark, there are two checks for primary-circuit continuity that can be made to speed up location of the defective part. In the Chrysler transistor ignition, current will always flow in the primary circuit with the ignition turned on and the engine not running, provided the primary circuit is not broken. Check circuit continuity as follows:

1. Connect voltmeter from the ignition coil's positive primary terminal to ground. Turn ignition switch on and observe voltmeter reading. Reading should be 8V to 9V. If reading is battery voltage, there is an open in the primary winding, resistor, or wiring from the coil to ground. If the reading is zero, there is an open in the circuit between the battery and the voltmeter connection. This part of the circuit includes the ignition switch, resistor, distributor, amplifier, and related wiring.

2. Connect voltmeter from distributor side of resistor to ground. Turn ignition switch on and observe meter reading. If reading is zero, there is an open in the resistor, ignition switch, or wiring. If the reading is battery voltage, there is an open in the amplifier or wiring. If the wiring is not defective, replace the amplifier.

GENERAL MOTORS DELCOTRONIC IGNITION

The most popular type of magnetically triggered transistor ignition on General Motors engines is the *Delcotronic* system. This system is manufactured by the Delco Remy Division of General Motors for use as original equipment on GM engines and as a replacement ignition system for GM and other engines.

The *Delcotronic* system features a specially designed magnetic-pulse distributor, pulse amplifier, and a special coil. The other units in the system—the resistors or resistance wire, switch, and battery—are of standard design.

The external appearance of the distributor resembles that of a standard distributor. The internal construction and the operation are very similar to those of the Chrysler system.

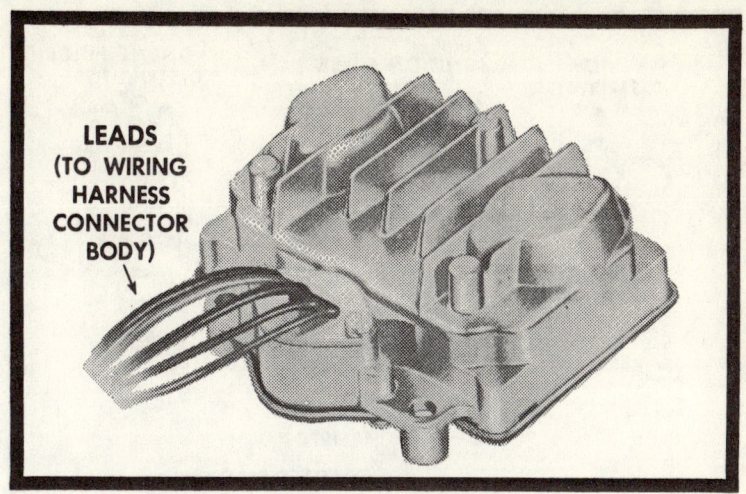

Fig. 6-6. Ignition pulse amplifier. (Courtesy Delco Remy.)

The ignition pulse amplifier, shown in Fig. 6-6, consists primarily of transistors, resistors, diodes, and capacitors mounted on a printed-circuit board. Since there are no moving or adjustable parts, and since the distributor shaft and bushings have permanent lubrication, no periodic maintenance is required. The distributor's lower bushing is lubricated by engine oil through a splash hole in the distributor housing, and a housing cavity next to the upper bushing contains a supply of lubricant which will last between engine overhauls. At engine overhaul, the upper bushing may be lubricated by removing the plastic seal and adding SAE 20 oil to the packing in the cavity. A new plastic seal will be required since the old one will be damaged during removal.

A diagram showing the wiring of the *Delcotronic* ignition is presented in Fig. 6-7. Note that there are two separate resistors used in this circuit. The resistor connected directly to the switch is bypassed during cranking, while the other resistor is always in the circuit. The use of two resistors permits the required value of resistance to be bypassed during cranking.

To fire the spark plugs, it is necessary to induce a high voltage in the ignition coil's secondary winding by opening the circuit of the primary winding. This is accomplished as explained next. For the purposes of this discussion, I am assuming *conventional* current flow, that is, from positive to

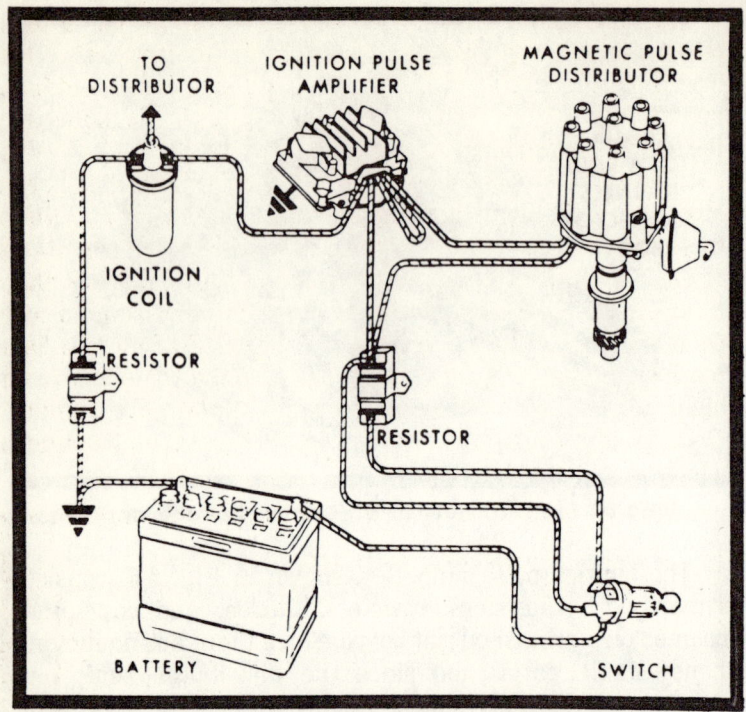

Fig. 6-7. Wiring diagram of typical ignition system. (Courtesy Delco Remy.)

negative. The important thing here, however, is not the current's direction but its path.

When the switch is closed, with the engine not running, a current flows through a part of the circuit as shown in Fig. 6-8. The current can be traced from the battery through the switch and resistor R_6 to the amplifier. Current then flows through transistors Q_1 and Q_2, resistors R_1, R_2, and R_3, the coil primary winding, and resistor R_7 to ground, thus completing the circuit back to the battery. It is important to note that under this condition current flows through the coil primary winding, and that capacitor C_1 is charged with the positive voltage towards transistor Q_2.

When the engine is running, the vanes on the rotating iron core in the distributor line up with the internal teeth on the pole piece. This establishes a magnetic path through the center of the pickup coil, causing a voltage to be induced in the pickup coil. This voltage causes transistor Q_3 to conduct, resulting in current flow in the circuit as shown in Fig. 6-9.

The charge on capacitor C_1 causes transistor Q_2 to turn off, which in turn causes transistor Q_1 to turn off. This interrupts the circuit to the ignition coil's primary winding, and the high voltage needed to fire the spark plug is induced in the secondary winding.

The current paths shown in Fig. 6-9 exist until the charge on capacitor C_1 has been dissipated through resistor R_3. When this happens, the system reverts back to the current conditions of Fig. 6-8. The system is then ready to fire the next spark plug.

Resistor R_5 is a *feedback* resistor; its purpose is to turn Q_3 off when Q_2 returns to the *on* condition. Resistor R_1 is a biasing resistor for Q_1. Zener D_1 protects transistor Q_1 from high voltages which may be induced in the coil primary. Capacitors C_2 and C_3 protect transistor Q_3 from high voltages which appear in the system.

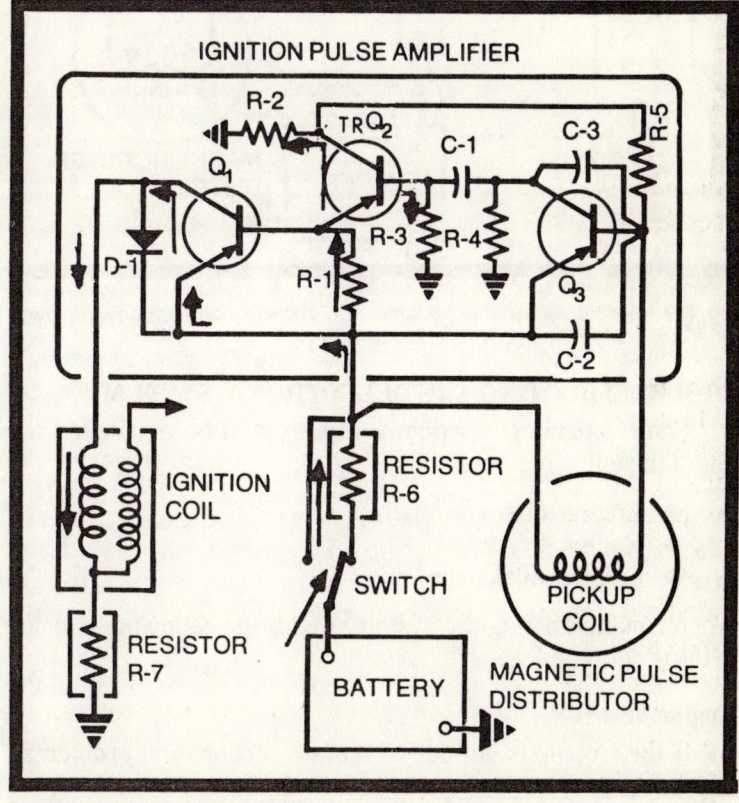

Fig. 6-8. Internal wiring of ignition pulse amplifier, showing current flow (arrows) with switch on and engine not running. (Courtesy Delco Remy.)

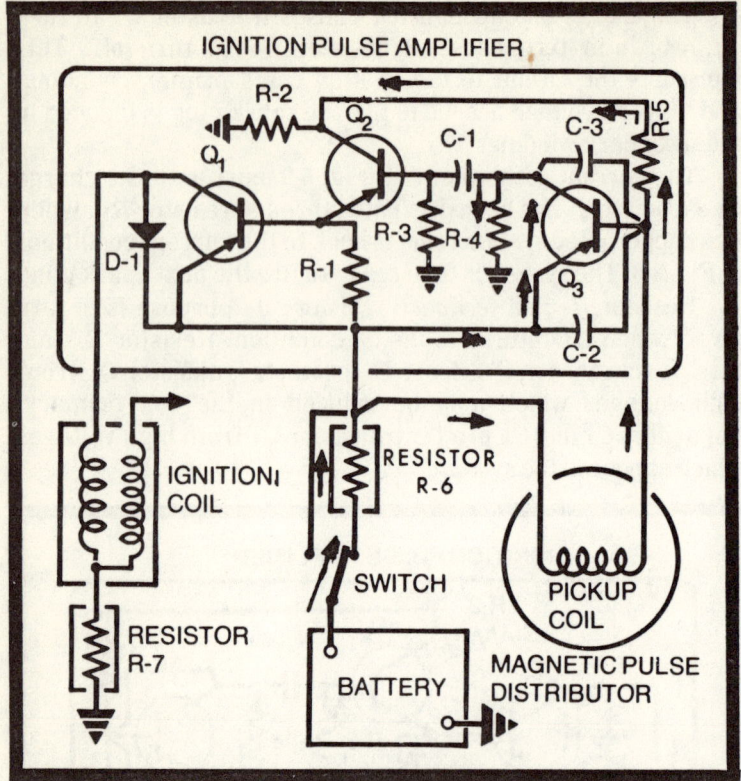

Fig. 6-9. Internal wiring of pulse amplifier, showing current flow (arrows) when spark plug fires. (Courtesy Delco Remy.)

TROUBLESHOOTING THE DELCOTRONIC SYSTEM

Faulty engine performance usually will be evidenced by one of the following conditions:

- Engine misses or misfires
- Engine surges
- Engine will not run

When troubleshooting the system, make the following checks in the order listed.

Engine Misses

If the trouble is not due to fuel or carburetion problems, check the ignition system as follows.

Timing. The timing should be checked in accordance with the vehicle or engine manufacturer's recommendations.

Spark Plugs. Removal of the spark plugs followed by a visual inspection will often reveal conditions which may adversely affect ignition performance. Spark plug servicing is covered in an earlier chapter of this book.

Wiring. All the wiring should be visually inspected for brittle or cracked insulation, broken strands, and loose or corroded connections. The high-voltage cables in the coil and distributor cap should be checked to make sure they are pressed all the way down in their inserts. If rubber boots are used, they too should be tightly in place over the connections. Also, the outside of the distributor cap and the coil cover should be inspected for carbon paths, which would allow high-voltage leakage to ground. Remove the distributor cap so the rotor and inside of the cap can be checked for cracks and carbon paths.

Distributor. The pickup coil in the distributor may be checked by separating the harness connector and connecting an ohmmeter across the coil. The resistance of the coil should be 300 to 400 ohms. If the reading is infinite, the coil is open; and if the reading is low, the coil is shorted. Remember that the resistance of the coil will increase slightly as the coil temperature rises. The pickup coil may be checked for grounds by connecting the ohmmeter from either coil lead to the distributor housing. The reading should be infinite. If it is not, the coil is grounded.

The centrifugal advance and vacuum advance may be tested in a distributor-testing machine. However, this involves the removal of the distributor from the engine and may be unnecessary. An indication of how well the advance mechanisms are operating may be had by running the engine and using a timing light to observe the advance and retard of the timing mark on the vibration dampener.

Ignition Coil. The ignition coil primary can be checked for an open condition by connecting an ohmmeter across the two primary terminals. An infinite reading indicates the primary to be open. If the engine runs but misses at times, the primary open must be intermittent. The coil secondary can be checked for an open by connecting an ohmmeter from the high-voltage tower to either primary terminal. If the reading is infinite, the secondary winding is open.

There are a number of coil testers available. Before using such a tester make sure the tester can test this special coil. Then check it exactly as the tester manufacturer directs.

Pulse Amplifier. If all previous checks fail to reveal the problem, and if the amplifier is properly grounded, the engine miss is probably caused by a defective ignition pulse amplifier. Replacement of the amplifier is the best solution, as it is extremely difficult and time consuming to bench-repair the amplifier.

Engine Surges

An engine surge of a nature much more severe than that caused by a lean carburetor may occur because the two distributor leads are reversed in the connector body, or it may be due to an intermittent open in the distributor pickup coil. The distributor white and green leads should be located in the connector body as shown in Fig. 6-10. If the leads are reversed, severe surging will result. A surge condition may also result from the action of the vacuum unit causing an intermittent break in the distributor pickup coil's wiring. To check this, disconnect the vacuum line and observe engine behavior at idle speed.

To complete the checks on the pickup coil, connect an ohmmeter to the two distributor pickup-coil leads in the connector body. The resistance should be 300 – 400 ohms. If the resistance is infinite, the coil is open; and if the resistance is low, the coil is shorted. Also connect the ohmmeter from either terminal to the distributor housing. The reading should be infinite. If it's not, the winding is grounded.

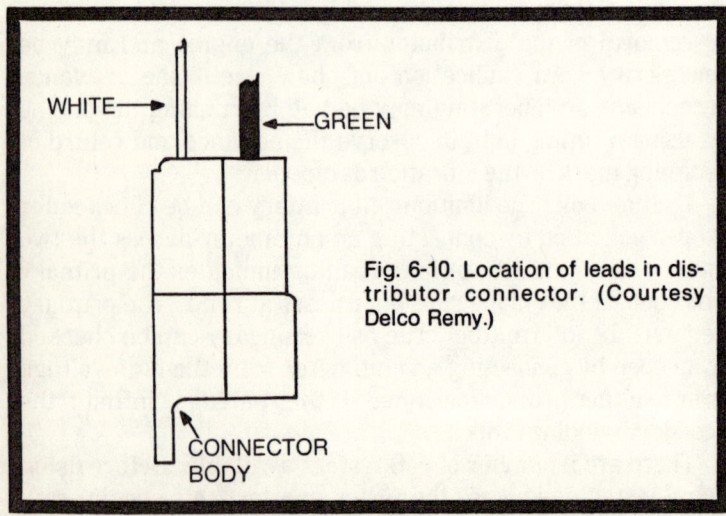

Fig. 6-10. Location of leads in distributor connector. (Courtesy Delco Remy.)

Engine Will Not Run

If the engine will not run, remove the lead from one of the spark plugs and hold about ¼ in. from the engine block while cranking the engine. If a spark occurs, the trouble most likely is not ignition. If a spark does not occur, check the ignition system as follows.

Wiring. All the wiring should be visually inspected for brittle or cracked insulation, broken strands, and loose or corroded connections. The high-voltage cables in the coil and distributor cap should be checked to make sure they are pressed all the way down in their inserts. If rubber boots are used, they too should be tightly in place over the connections. Also, the outside of the distributor cap and the coil cover should be inspected for carbon paths which allow high-voltage leakage to ground. Remove the distributor cap so the rotor and inside of the cap can be checked for cracks and carbon paths.

Ignition Coil. The ignition coil primary can be checked for an open by connecting an ohmmeter across the two primary terminals. An infinite reading indicates an open primary.

The coil secondary can be checked for an open by connecting an ohmmeter from the high-voltage center tower to either primary terminal. (Use the RX 1000 scale.) If the reading is infinite, the coil secondary winding is open. This coil can be tested on a coil tester if the tester manufacturer advises that the instrument will test this special coil. Follow the exact procedure recommended by the tester manufacturer.

Continuity. Further checks for continuity can be made by connecting a voltmeter from the ignition coil's positive terminal to ground (step 1 in Fig. 6-11). Turn on the ignition switch and observe the reading.

- If the reading is approximately 8V to 9V, proceed to the next section (*Distributor*).
- If the reading is the battery voltage, there is an open in the circuit between this point and ground. This circuit consists of the coil primary winding, resistor, and wiring.
- If the reading is zero, there is an open circuit between this point and the battery. Proceed to the next paragraph.

Connect the voltmeter from the other resistor to ground (step 2 in Fig. 6-11). Observe the reading with the switch on.

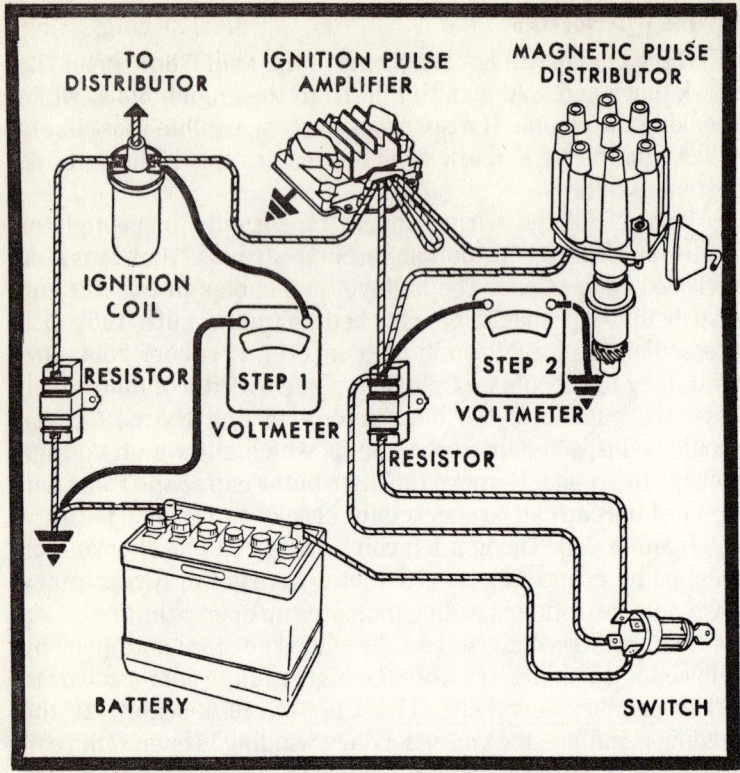

Fig. 6-11. Voltmeter connections for current checks. (Courtesy Delco Remy.)

- If the reading is zero, there is an open between this point and the battery. This circuit consists of the resistor, ignition switch, and wiring.
- If the reading is the battery voltage, there is an open in the circuit between this resistor and the ignition coil. This circuit consists of the ignition pulse amplifier and the wiring.

If the wiring checks satisfactorily, replace the amplifier.

Distributor. The pickup coil in the distributor may be checked by separating the harness connector and connecting an ohmmeter across the coil. The resistance of the coil should be 300–400 ohms. If the reading is infinite, the coil is open; and if the reading is low, the coil is shorted. Remember that the resistance of the coil will increase slightly as the coil temperature rises.

The pickup coil may be checked for grounds by connecting the ohmmeter from either coil lead to the distributor housing. The reading should show infinity. If it does not, the coil is grounded. If the distributor checks out okay, replace the pulse amplifier.

DELCO REMY HIGH-ENERGY IGNITION

The Delco Remy *High-Energy Ignition* (HEI) system is a magnetic-pulse-controlled system with all units contained in the distributor and cap, and designed to provide up to 35,000V for spark plug firing. The HEI system is easily recognized by the larger-than-average distributor and the lack of additional system units such as coil, amplifier, and connecting wiring.

The HEI system has a built-in ignition coil, an electronic module, and a magnetic pickup assembly. The module and pickup assembly take the place of the conventional contact points and capacitor. This system is designed to provide high-output secondary voltages and is said to be a completely maintenance-free unit. The system is energized by one wire from the ignition switch, and the six or eight spark plug leads complete the entire external circuit (Fig. 6-12). With the separately mounted coil and amplifier eliminated, the wiring is greatly simplified. A terminal is provided to which a tachometer can be connected (see Fig. 6-13). A connector plugs into the cap to connect the pickup assembly and module to the ignition coil.

The pickup assembly is mounted over the main bearing on the distributor housing, and it is made to rotate by the vacuum control unit (Fig. 6-14), thus providing vacuum advance. The

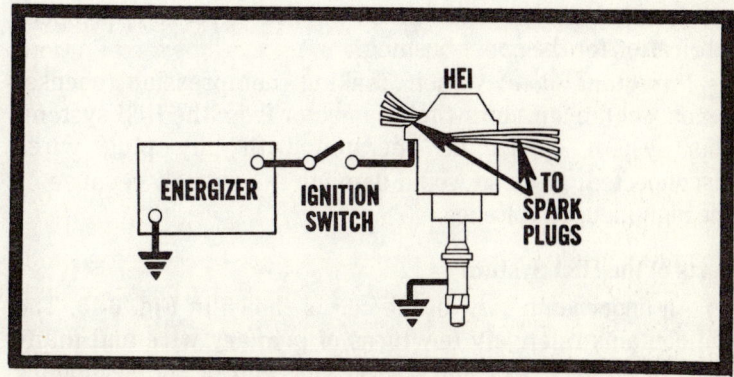

Fig. 6-12. Connection of the HEI distributor in an ignition system.

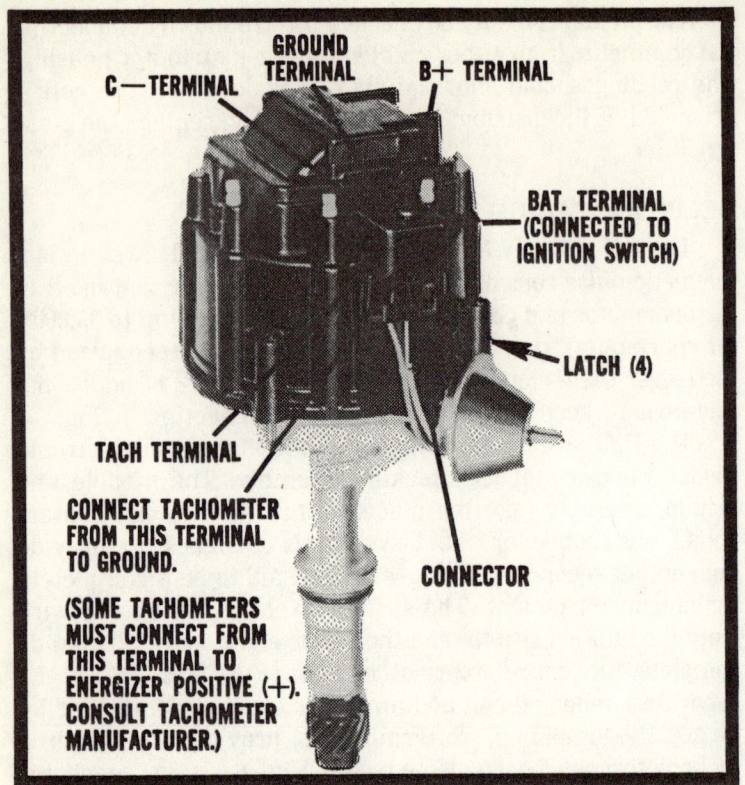

Fig. 6-13. Typical HEI distributor (Courtesy Delco Remy.)

timer core is made to rotate about the shaft by conventional advance weights, thus providing centrifugal advance.

No periodic lubrication is required. Engine oil lubricates the lower bushing, and an oil-filtered reservoir provides lubrication for the upper bushing.

Important note: When making compression checks, disconnect the ignition switch connector from the HEI system. This system cannot be operated with any plug wires disconnected; to do so would damage the system because of the high-induced voltages.

Parts of the HEI System

An underneath view of the coil is shown in Fig. 6-15. The coil contains relatively few turns of primary wire and many turns of smaller secondary wire. One end of the secondary winding is connected to the coil output terminal. This terminal

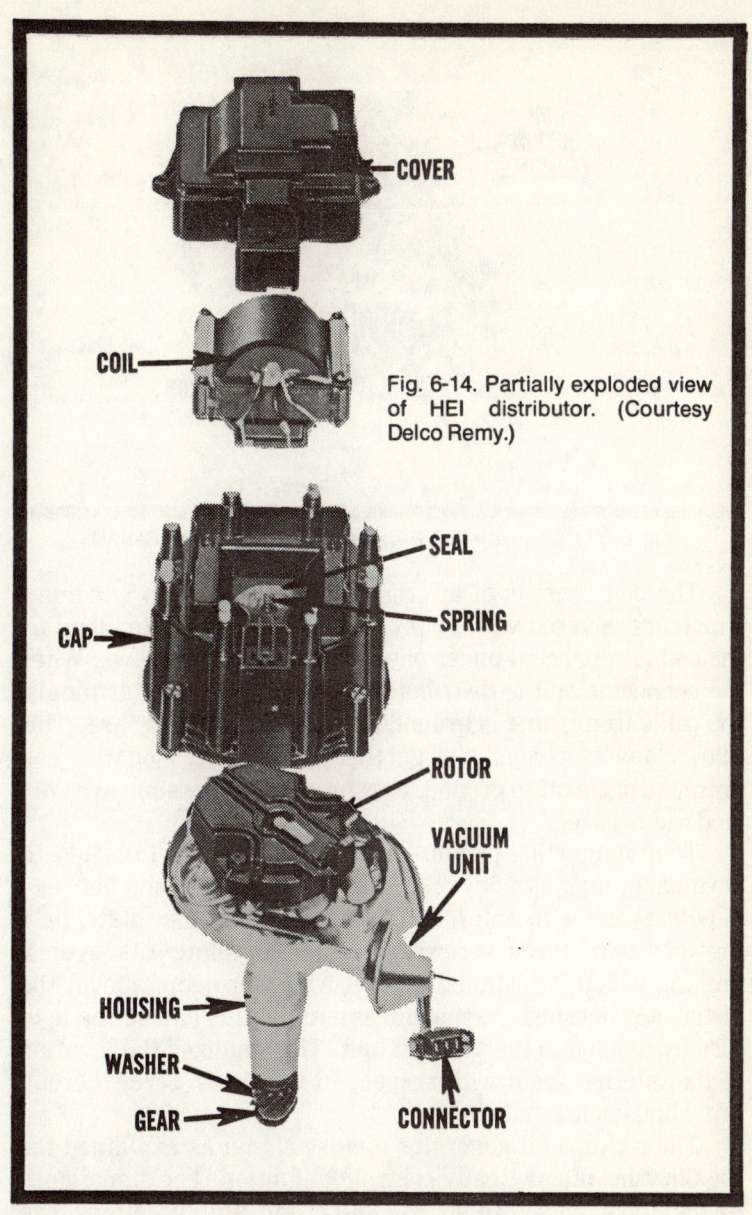

Fig. 6-14. Partially exploded view of HEI distributor. (Courtesy Delco Remy.)

touches the spring in the cap, when assembled, and directs the high secondary voltage into the rotor spring. The voltage is then directed from the rotor segment to one of the cap inserts, and then through the high-voltage secondary wire to the spark plug.

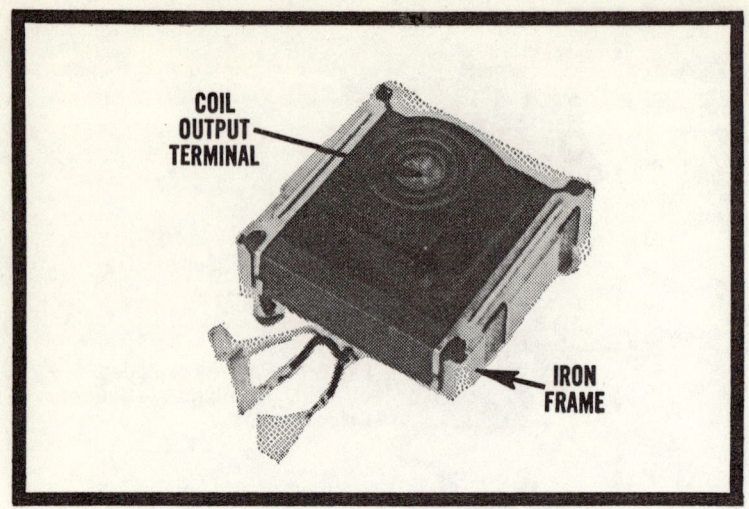

Fig. 6-15. Coil used with HEI system. (Courtesy Delco Remy.)

The coil consists of an iron frame and the two windings, which are covered with epoxy insulation. The center lead on the coil is connected under one of the mounting screws. When the connector on the distributor is attached to the terminals, the coil's iron frame is grounded to the distributor base. This allows any electrical charge that accumulates on the coil frame to drain off to ground, thus preventing possible arcover and radio noise.

The magnetic pickup assembly (Fig. 6-15) has a permanent magnet and pickup coil, both sandwiched between a pole piece with internal teeth and a bottom plate held together with three screws. The bottom plate fits over a bushing which is installed in, and which projects above, the distributor housing. The pickup assembly thus can be made to turn by linkage to the vacuum unit. This changes the location of the internal teeth with respect to the timer core, thereby providing vacuum advance.

The pickup coil generates a pulse signal as explained for the Chrysler magnetically controlled ignition. The signal goes to the module, shown in Fig. 6-17, for amplification. The module contains a microminiature electronic element (integrated circuit), which is not repairable. The module can be serviced by replacement only.

The amplifier receives a signal voltage from the pickup coil and then allows primary current to flow. When the timer

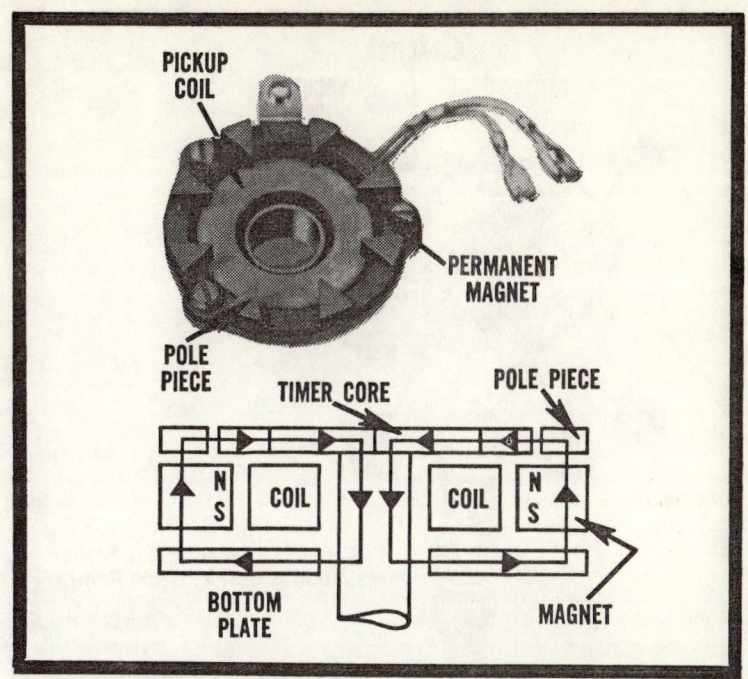

Fig. 6-16. Magnetic pickup assembly. (Courtesy Delco Remy.)

core teeth move away from the pole piece teeth, the signal disappears and the module turns the primary current off, thus inducing the high voltage in the secondary to fire the spark plugs. The module, therefore, switches the coil primary current.

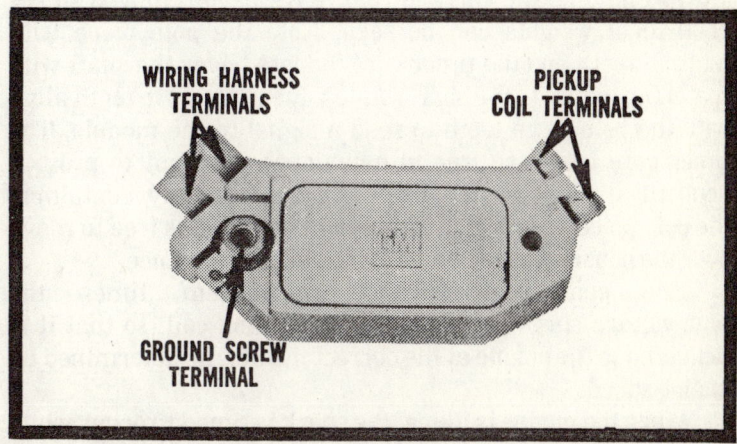

Fig. 6-17. Electronic module of HEI system. (Courtesy Delco Remy.)

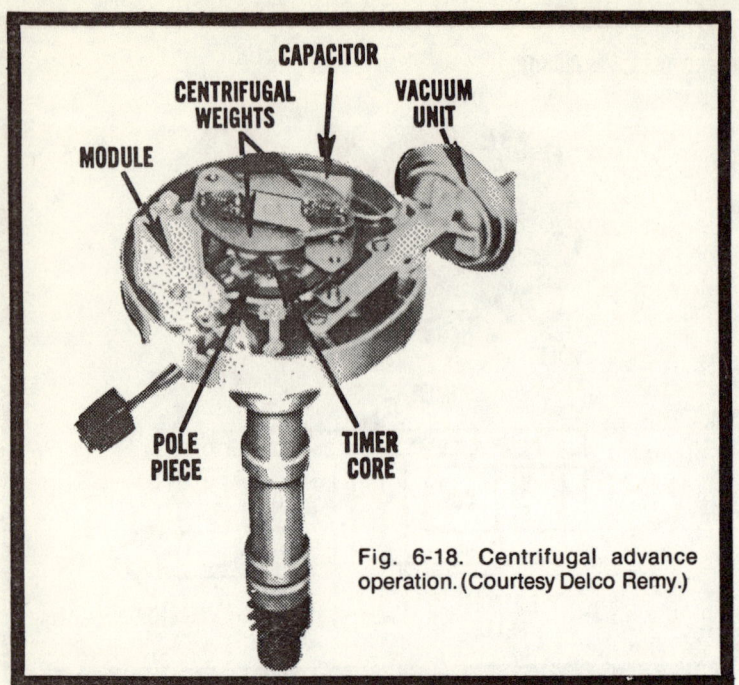

Fig. 6-18. Centrifugal advance operation. (Courtesy Delco Remy.)

Centrifugal Advance in HEI System

The centrifugal advance mechanism in an electronic ignition is like that of a conventional ignition. It will be useful to review some of the principles of centrifugal advance to see just how they are applied to an electronic ignition.

In Fig. 6-18, the cap and rotor have been removed so the centrifugal weights can be seen. Note the pole piece with internal teeth and the timer core mounted over the shaft with matching teeth. As the shaft rotates, the timer core teeth align with the pole piece teeth to send a signal to the module. The timer core teeth are free to move over the shaft to provide centrifugal advance; and the pickup coil assembly, containing the pole piece, is linked to the vacuum unit and is free to move over the housing bushing to provide vacuum advance.

The centrifugal advance mechanism times the high-voltage surge produced by the ignition coil, so that it is delivered to the engine at the correct instant, as determined by engine speed.

When the engine is idling, the spark is timed to occur while the piston is near top dead center. At higher engine speeds, however, there is a shorter time available for the air/fuel mixture to ignite, burn, and give up its power to the piston. Consequently, to obtain the maximum amount of power from the mixture, it is necessary at higher engine speeds for the ignition system to deliver the high-voltage surge to the cylinder earlier in the cycle.

As previously mentioned, the timing of the spark to engine speed is accomplished by the centrifugal advance mechanism, which is assembled on the distributor shaft. The mechanism consists primarily of two weights and a timer core assembly. The weights throw out against spring tension as engine speed increases. This motion of the weights turns the timer core assembly so that the timer core is rotated in the direction of shaft rotation to an advanced position with respect to the distributor drive shaft. The higher the engine speed, the more the weights throw out and the more the timer core is advanced.

The centrifugal advance required varies considerably among various engine models. To determine the advance for a given engine, the engine is operated on a dynamometer at various speeds with wide-open throttle. Spark advance is varied at each speed until the range of advance that gives maximum power is found. The cam assembly weights and springs are then selected to give this advance. Timing, consequently, varies from no advance at idle to full advance at high engine speed, where the weights reach the outer limits of their travel. Typical centrifugal advance curves for four engines are shown in Fig. 6-19.

Vacuum Advance in HEI System

Vacuum advance operation is illustrated in Fig. 6-20. Under part-throttle operation a high vacuum develops in the intake manifold, and a smaller amount of air and gasoline enters the cylinder. Under these conditions, additional spark advance (over and above advance provided by the centrifugal advance mechanism) will increase fuel economy. To realize maximum power, therefore, ignition must take place still earlier in the cycle.

To provide a spark advance based on intake manifold vacuum, many distributors are equipped with a vacuum advance mechanism. This mechanism has a spring-loaded diaphragm connected by linkage to the distributor. The

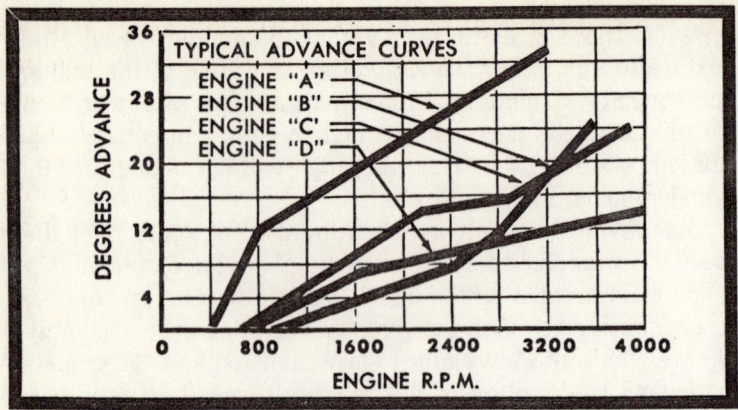

Fig. 6-19. Typical advance curves. (Courtesy Delco Remy.)

spring-loaded side of the diaphragm is airtight, and is connected in many cases by a vacuum passage to an opening in the carburetor. This opening is on the atmospheric side of the throttle when the throttle is in the idling position. In this position, there is no vacuum in the passage.

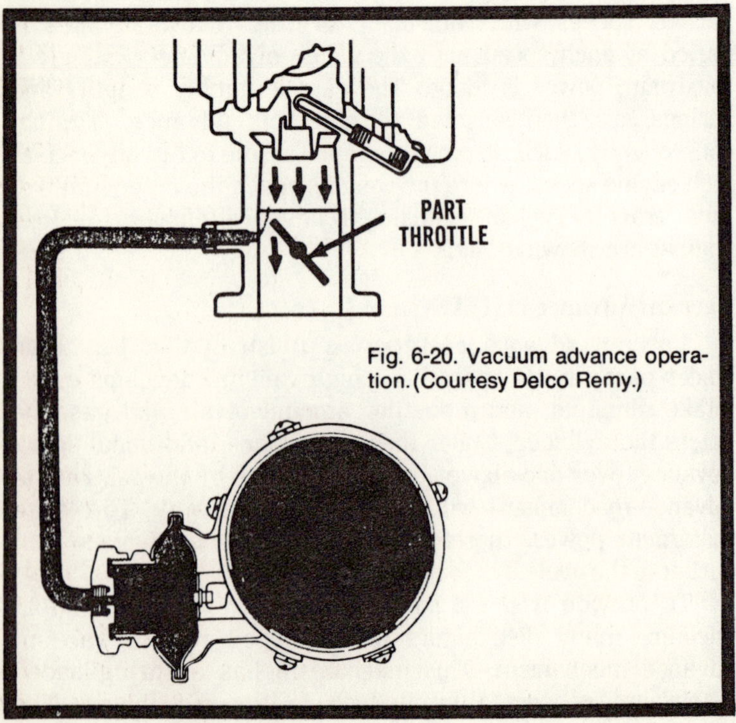

Fig. 6-20. Vacuum advance operation. (Courtesy Delco Remy.)

When the throttle is partly opened, it swings past the opening of the vacuum passage. Intake manifold vacuum then can draw air from the airtight chamber in the vacuum advance mechanism, and this causes the diaphragm to be moved against the spring. This motion is transmitted by linkage to the pole piece assembly, causing it to rotate. The amount of rotation is governed by the amount of vacuum in the intake manifold, up to the limit imposed by the design of the vacuum advance mechanism.

When the pole piece is rotated, its teeth are carried around to an advanced position so that they meet the timer core teeth earlier in the cycle. This provides a spark advance based on the amount of vacuum in the intake manifold. Thus, for varying compressions in the cylinder, the spark advance will vary, permitting greater economy of engine operation. It should be recognized that the additional advance provided by vacuum control is effective in providing additional economy only in part-throttle operation.

The wiring diagram of the HEI system is shown in Fig. 6-21. Only those components in the module necessary to explain basically how the module turns the ignition coil primary on and off are illustrated. Since the module is not repairable, it must be replaced as a unit if it becomes defective in any way.

In Fig. 6-21A, with the spark plug not firing, the circuits conducting current are shown in heavy lines. The iron frame of the ignition coil is grounded to bleed off any charge that may accumulate on the frame. The capacitor is connected across the circuit to prevent radio noise. The current is supplied by the battery (or alternator if the engine is running).

With current flowing through R_5, D_1, the pickup coil, and resistor R_9 to ground, the voltage between R_2 and R_3 is reduced to such a low value that Q_1 will not turn on. Hence there is no ignition coil primary current, since this circuit can be traced from the battery through the switch, the coil primary, Q_1, and R_1 to ground. This condition occurs when the timer core teeth are not aligned with the pole piece teeth.

As the teeth approach alignment, a voltage is induced in the pickup coil with positive polarity at terminal G. This stops current flow through the pickup coil and establishes the current conditions shown in heavy lines in Fig. 6-21B. Transistor Q_3 turns on, which lowers the voltage between R_4

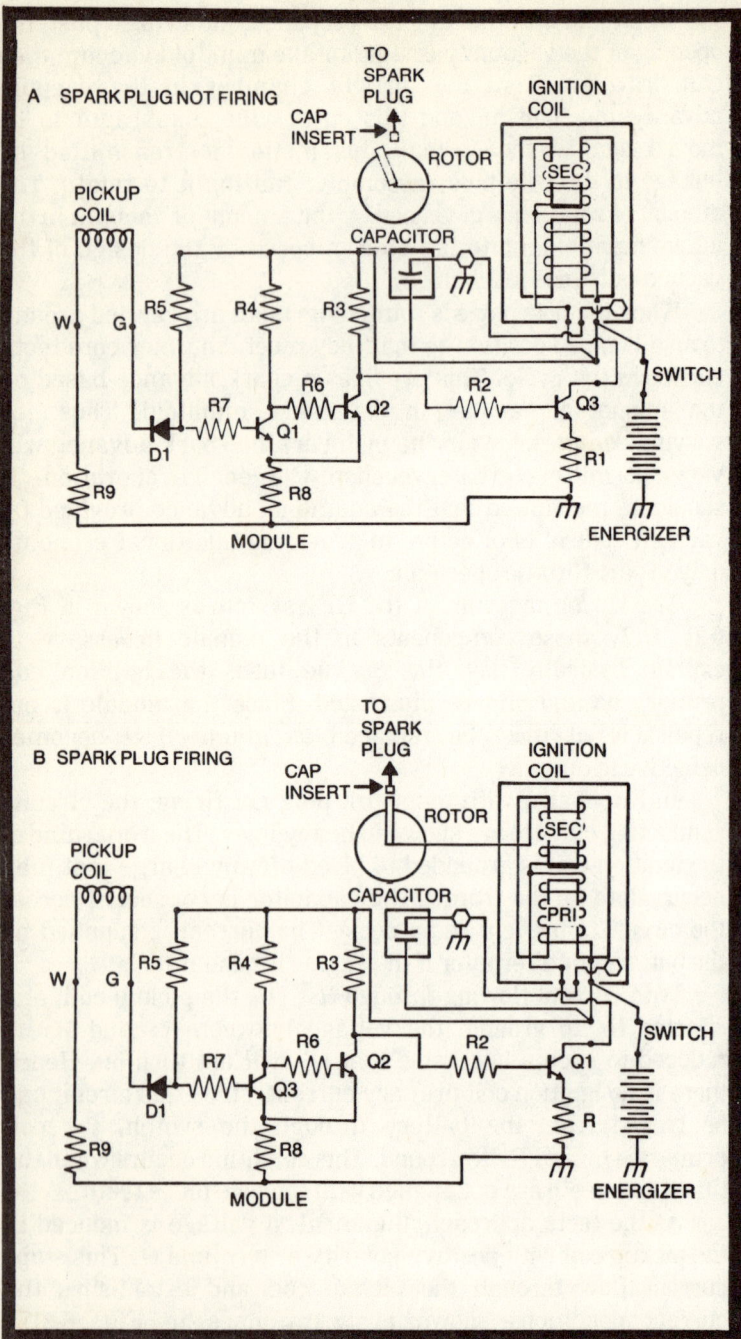

Fig. 6-21. Wiring diagrams of HEI system. (Courtesy Delco Remy.)

and R_6 such that Q_2 turns off. This allows Q_1 to turn on, and current then flows in the ignition coil's primary winding.

As the teeth start to separate again, the pickup coil's voltage polarity is reversed and the system reverts back to the current conditions shown by heavy lines in Fig. 6-21A. But for this condition to prevail, the primary current must decrease, which induces the voltage in the ignition coil's secondary to fire the spark plug.

Troubleshooting the High-Energy Ignition

The manufacturer's recommended procedures for troubleshooting the HEI ignition system as used on V-8 and V-6 engines are given in Fig. 6-22. Figure 6-23 illustrates the test connections.

The manufacturer's recommended procedures for troubleshooting the HEI ignition system as used on 4-cylinder and in-line 6-cylinder engines are slightly different than for the V-8 and V-6 engines and so are given in Fig. 6-24. The illustrations in Fig. 6-25 are to be used with the chart of Fig. 6-24.

FORD MAGNETICALLY TRIGGERED IGNITION

The Ford solid-state ignition system (see Fig. 6-26) is similar to the magnetically triggered systems already discussed. A small control box, or electronic module, is connected between the ignition coil's primary circuit and the battery, through the ignition switch. The electronic module allows battery current to flow into the coil's primary windings; it also acts to interrupt this current on a signal from the distributor. The stoppage of current in the primary winding causes its magnetic field to collapse. This induces a high voltage in the coil's secondary winding, which in turn is delivered to the spark plug. The action of the electronic module is quite similar in its effect on the system to what happens when the points open and close in a conventional ignition system.

Timing circuitry in the electronic module senses when the coil has fired and, then, redirects electric current to the primary circuit of the coil. The dwell varies with engine speed. This is normal and cannot be altered; thus any dwell measurement is meaningless.

The coil for this ignition system appears much like the standard Ford coil but is not interchangeable with it. The

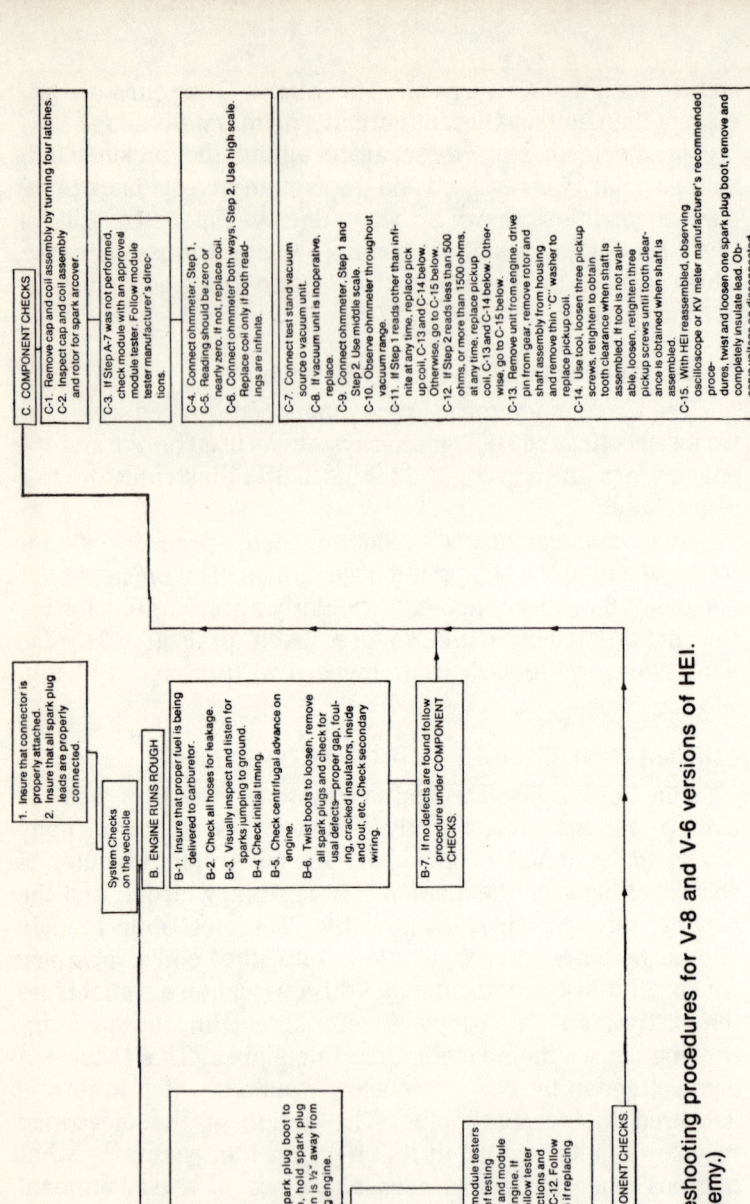

Fig. 6-22. Troubleshooting procedures for V-8 and V-6 versions of HEI. (Courtesy Delco Remy.)

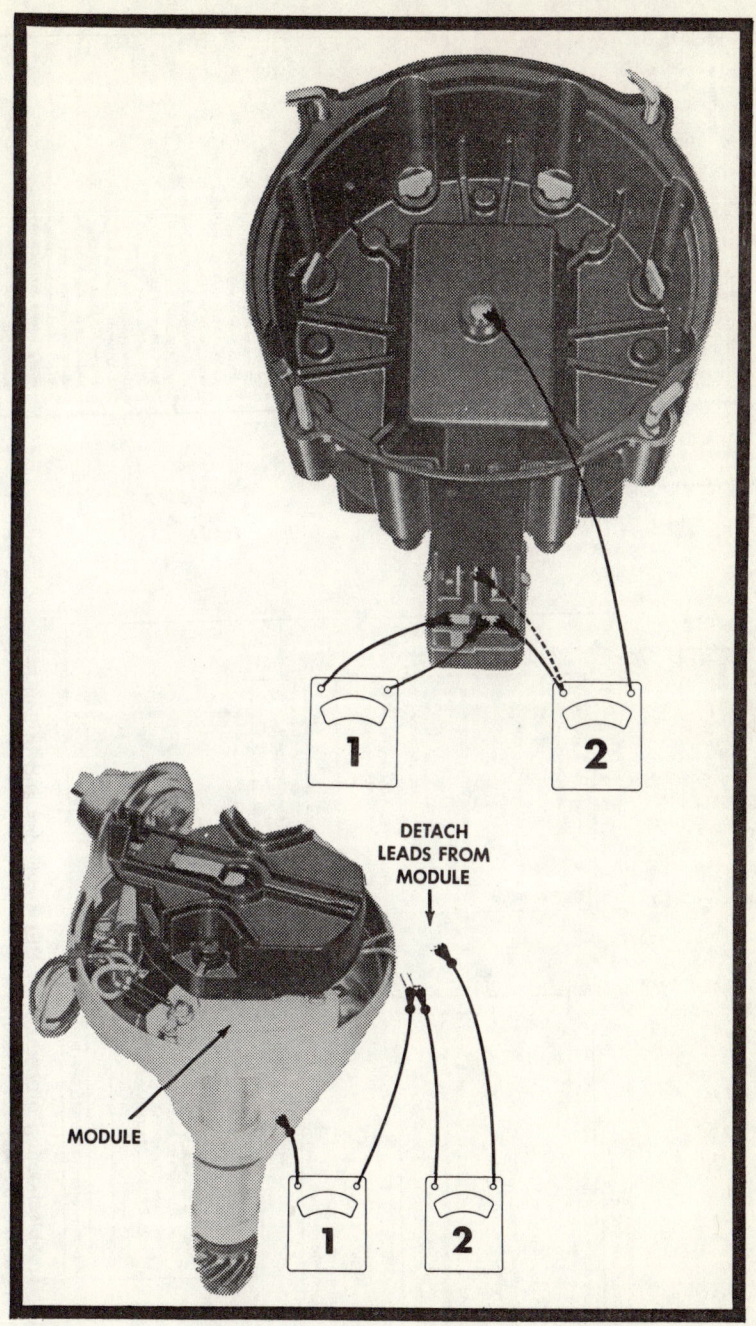

Fig. 6-23. Illustrations for use with troubleshooting chart of Fig. 6-22. (Courtesy Delco Remy.)

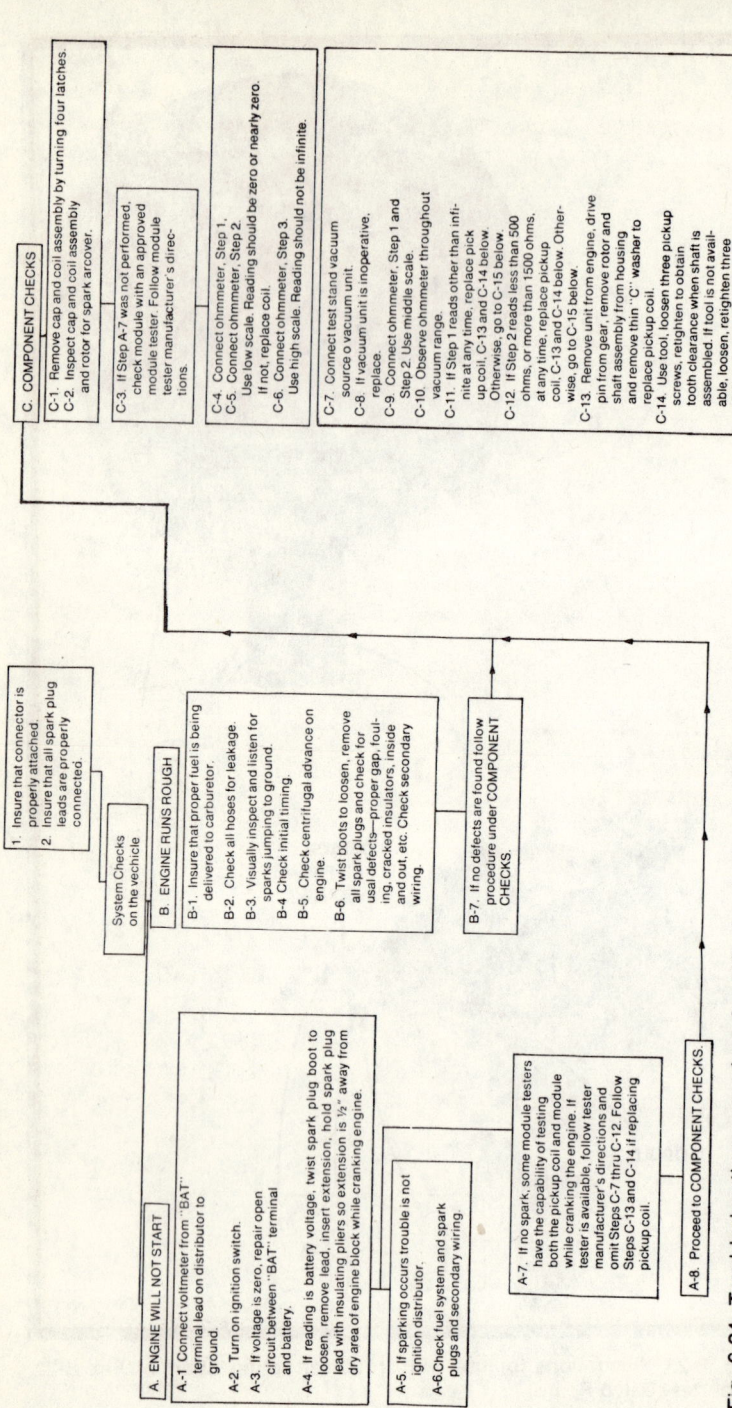

Fig. 6-24. Troubleshooting procedure for HEI 4-cylinder and in-line 6-cylinder engines. (Courtesy Delco Remy).

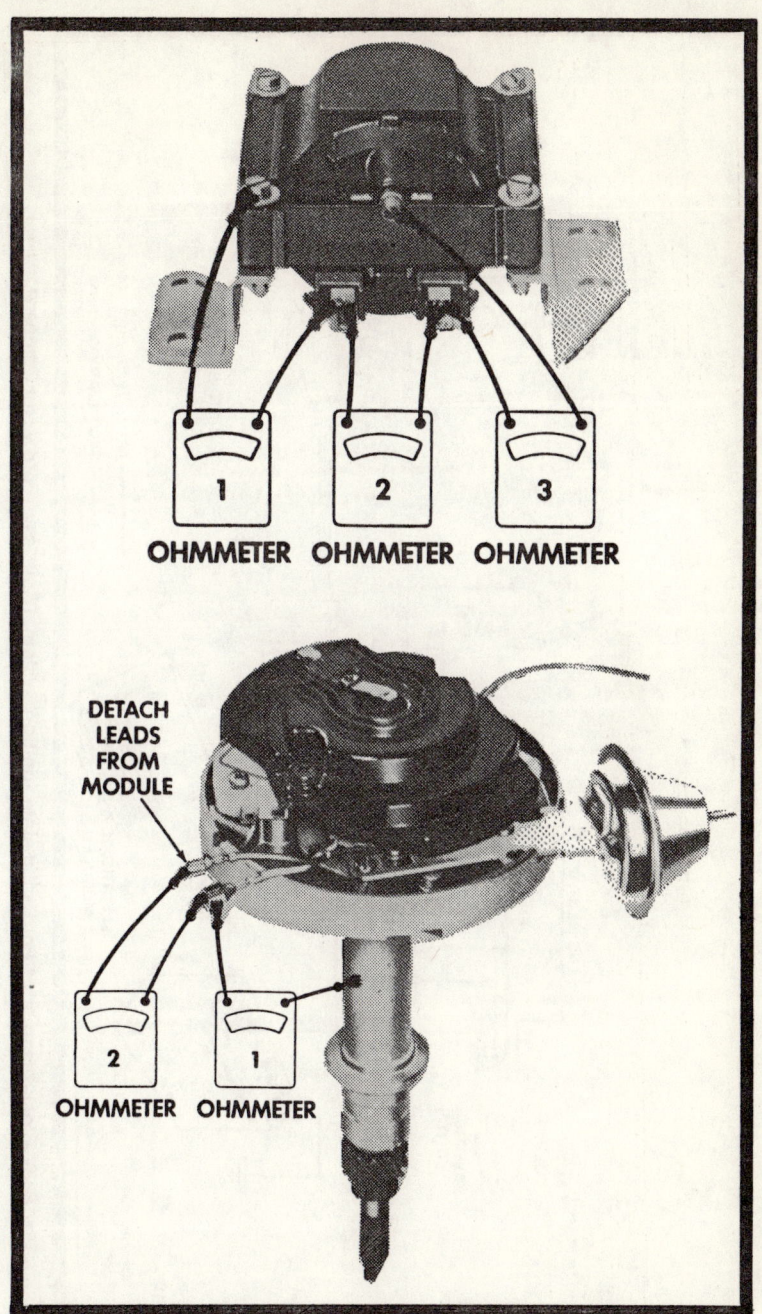

Fig. 6-25. Illustrations for use with troubleshooting chart of Fig. 6-24. (Courtesy Delco Remy.)

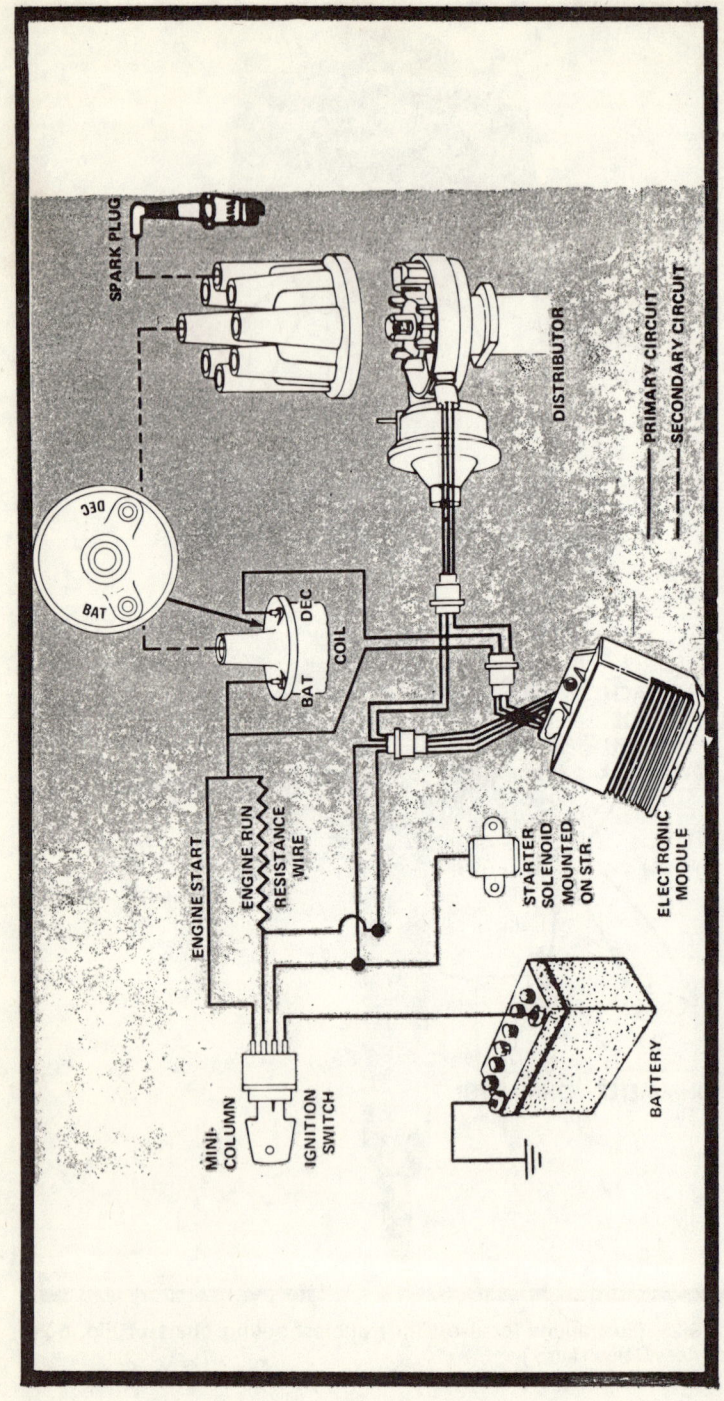

Fig. 6-26. Block diagram of Ford solid-state ignition system. (Courtesy Ford Motor Company.)

primary terminals on the solid-state ignition coil are labeled BAT. for battery (or switch) side, and DEC, for distributor electronic control. The use of any other ignition coil with the Ford solid-state ignition system will cause the system to malfunction and may damage the electronic module.

The Ford solid-state distributor and the Ford point-contact distributor are similar in appearance and construction. Both distributors are mounted and driven in the same way. The breaker plate has been replaced by a magnetic pickup (stator) assembly (Fig. 6-27), which provides the signal to the control module. This assembly contains the pickup coil and a permanent magnet. The armature is mounted on the sleeve-and-plate assembly. It has the same number of teeth as there are cylinders in the engine.

High voltage from the coil to the plugs is directed through the distributor in the same way as in the conventional system. Also, automatic advance or retard of the spark is controlled in the same way as in a conventional system. The advance mechanism moves the plate holding the pickup coil.

There has been no change in the shaft, gear, weights, springs, cap, and rotor. They are of the same design for both the solid-state and conventional Ford systems.

The Ford solid-state distributor works similarly to the Chrysler distributor already discussed. It develops electrical pulses that periodically turn off the electronic module, which interrupts the current in the ignition coil's primary. Interruptions of the primary current cause high-voltage pulses to be induced in the secondary for firing the spark plugs.

Preliminary Checks of the Ford Ignition

When the ignition system is suspected in complaints of failure to start, misfiring, loss of power, or erratic performance, first make sure there are no loose, corroded, or disconnected terminals at the ignition coil or distributor. Repair, clean, or tighten connections as necessary.

If the engine is still not running properly, then check for loose, damaged, or corroded connectors at the electronic control module. (The location of this module varies among the various Ford and Lincoln-Mercury car lines and with the engine used.) Make certain that all connectors are snug and tight, repairing or replacing connectors as necessary. Try the engine again.

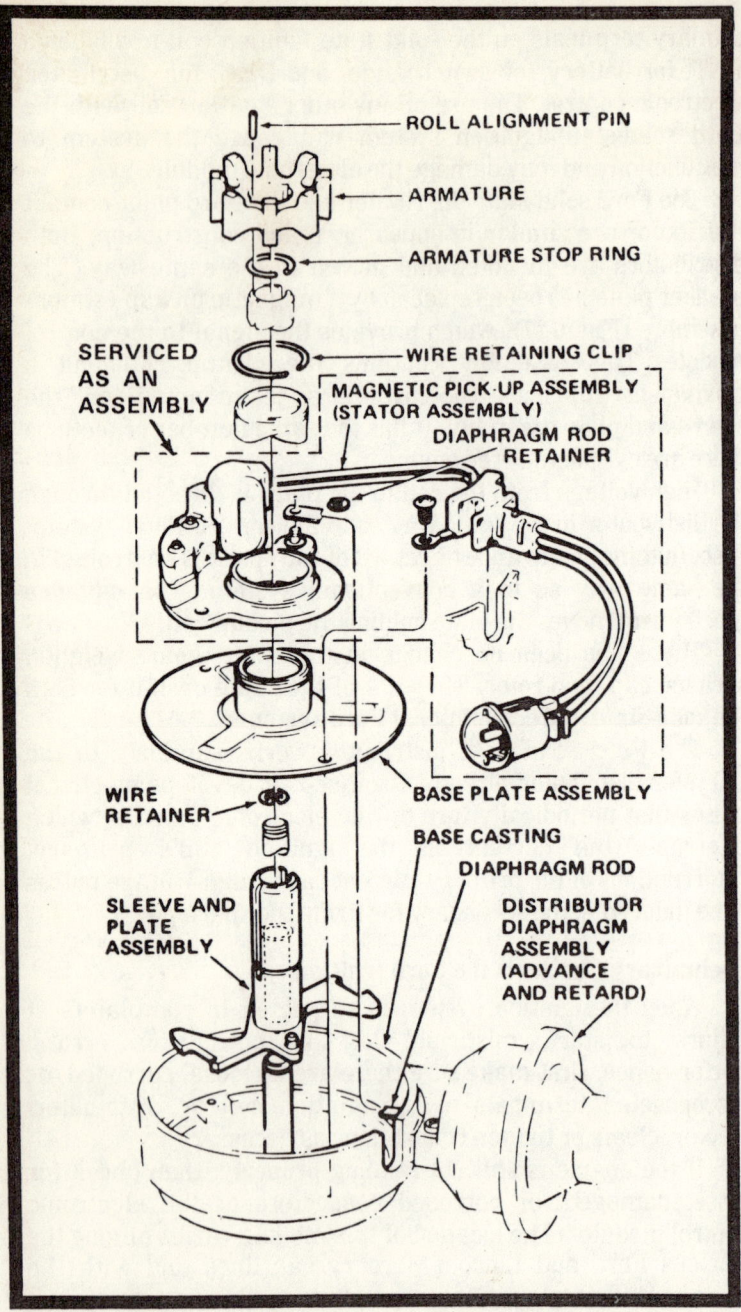

Fig. 6-27. Exploded view of solid-state ignition distributors. (Courtesy Ford Motor Company.)

If the engine still does not perform as it should, then make a simple spark intensity test at the coil. Disconnect the high-voltage wire from the center tower of the distributor. Hold it ¼ in. away from a good ground at the engine and crank the engine over. You should get a good fat spark jumping the gap regularly. If the observed spark appears okay but the engine still does not operate properly, then make the secondary tests listed below.

Check spark intensity at each spark plug except as follows: *Never pull the No. 1 or No. 5 spark plug wire on 6-cylinder engines or the No. 1 or No. 8 spark plug wire on 8-cylinder engines.* Doing so may cause internal arcing within the distributor.

Check resistance of spark plug wires where the weak spark is observed. If the spark is weak or intermittent, then check the ignition coil. Check the distributor cap for cracks, hairline fractures, moisture, or any signs of damage.

Note: The secondary circuit in a solid-state ignition system is exactly the same as that in a conventional ignition system. Thus, all secondary tests are performed exactly the same way. If the secondary circuit checks out properly, then the engine condition is not the fault of the ignition system.

If the engine still does not function properly and faulty ignition is indicated, then proceed with the ignition tests in the following section and in the order listed.

Caution: Make tests on the harness side of the 3- and 4-wire connectors coming from the module, which is the socket side. Do not test at the blade side of the module. Test the distributor on the distributor side of the 3-wire pigtail connector, which is the bladeside.

Troubleshooting Procedure for the Ford Ignition

1. Disconnect the 3- and 4-wire connectors at the module.
2. Using a voltmeter, test the voltage between socket No. 3 (Fig. 6-28) and a good ground at the engine. The ignition switch must be in the ON position. If the voltmeter reads battery voltage within plus or minus 0.1V, then socket No. 3 is receiving the correct voltage from the battery and through the ignition switch and connections. If you do not get this reading, then repair the wiring to the module. (Note Fig. 6-29 for tracing this circuit.)

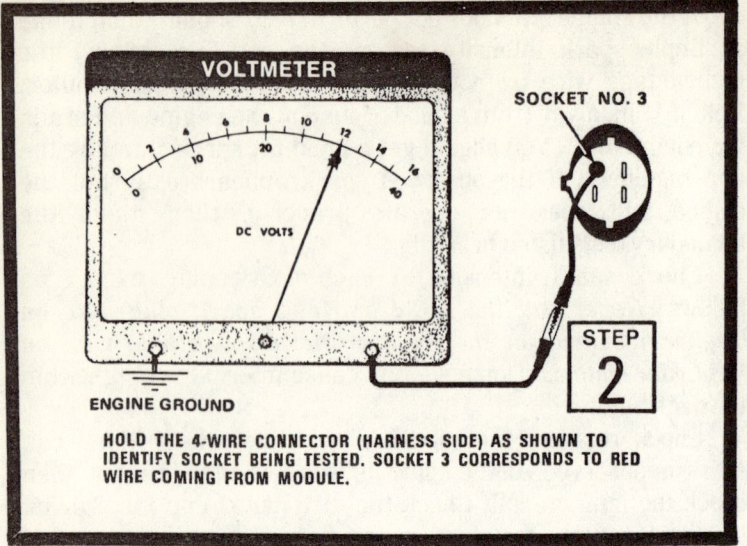

Fig. 6-28. Checking voltage between socket 3 and engine ground. (Courtesy Ford Motor Company.)

3. Using a voltmeter, test the voltage between socket No. 5 and a good ground at the engine (Fig. 6-30). The ignition switch must be in the ON position. If the voltmeter reads battery voltage within plus or minus 0.1V, then socket No. 5 is receiving the correct voltage from the battery, ignition switch, and connections. If you do not get this reading, then proceed to step 4. However, if you get the correct voltage reading, skip step 4 and proceed to step 5.

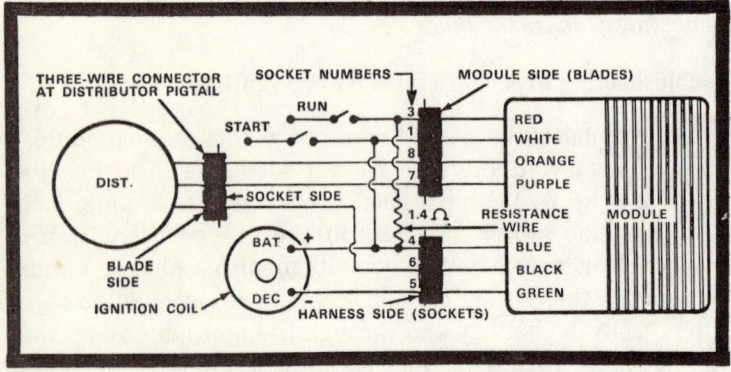

Fig. 6-29. Wiring diagram of the Ford ignition. (Courtesy Ford Motor Company.)

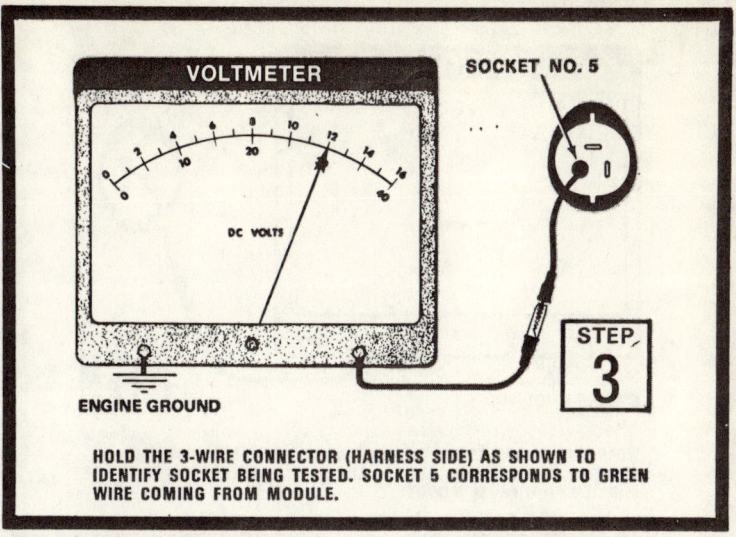

Fig. 6-30. Testing voltage between socket 5 and engine ground. (Courtesy Ford Motor Company.)

4. The voltmeter reading should be 4.9V to 7.9V in the connection of Fig. 6-31. To make this test, do not disconnect the coil. Connect the voltmeter leads to the BAT terminal at the coil and to a good ground. Connect a jumper wire from the DEC terminal at the coil to a good ground. Turn all lights and accessories off and turn the ignition on. *If the voltage is below 4.9V,* then check the primary wiring for worn insulation, broken strands, or loose or corroded

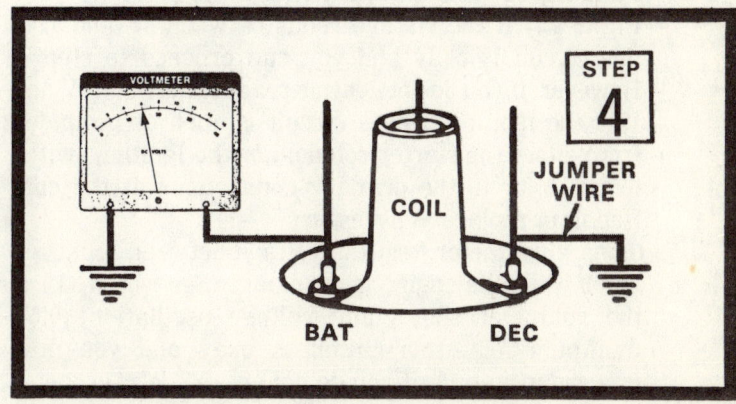

Fig. 6-31. Battery source test. (Courtesy Ford Motor Company.)

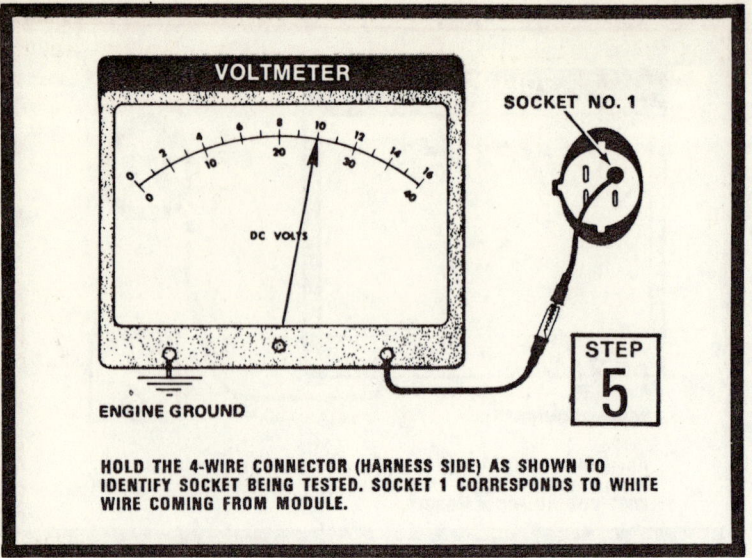

Fig. 6-32. Checking voltage between socket 1 and engine ground. (Courtesy Ford Motor Company.)

terminals. Repair or replace as necessary. *If the voltage is above 7.9V,* replace the resistance wiring.

5. Using a voltmeter, test the voltage between socket No. 1 and a good ground while the engine is cranking. (See Fig. 6-32.) If the voltage reads between 8V and 12V, this circuit is okay, so proceed to step 6. If you do not get this voltage, then repair or replace the wiring to the module. (Refer to Fig. 6-29 for wiring diagram.)
6. Using a voltmeter, test the voltage between socket No. 5 and a good ground while the engine is cranking. (See Fig. 6-30.) If the voltage reads between 8V and 12V, this circuit is okay and you can proceed to step 7. However, if you do not get this reading between 8V and 12V, the ignition bypass circuit is open or grounded from either the starter solenoid or the ignition switch to No. 5, or in the primary connections at the coil. Repair or replace as necessary.
7. Using a voltmeter, test the voltage between sockets 7 and 8 while the engine is cranking. (See Fig. 6-33.) If the voltmeter shows any voltage oscillation (0.5V minimum AC), this circuit is okay and you may proceed to step 10. If you do not get the correct meter reading, proceed to step 8.

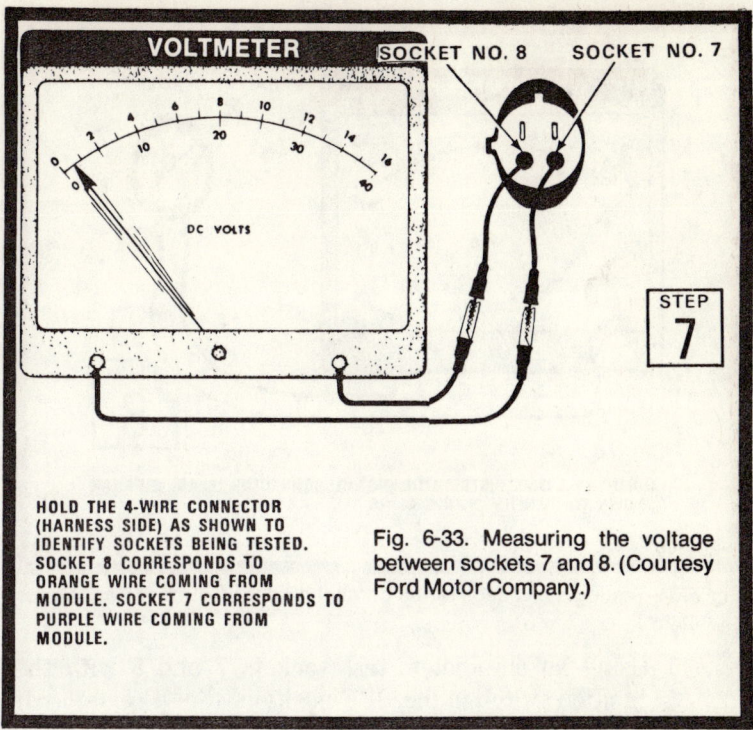

Fig. 6-33. Measuring the voltage between sockets 7 and 8. (Courtesy Ford Motor Company.)

8. Disconnect the 3-wire weatherproof connector at the distributor pigtail. Using a voltmeter, test the voltage of the parallel blades while the engine is cranking. (See Fig. 6-34.) With the voltmeter on the low scale and connected to the parallel blades as shown in Fig. 6-34, the meter needle should oscillate slightly or read 0.5V minimum AC. If it does not oscillate, repair or replace the harness leading to the 3-wire pigtail connector at the distributor. If there is still no oscillation, proceed to steps 9 and 10.

9. Remove the distributor cap and rotor. Check for visible damage. Check that the armature is tight on the sleeve and that it rotates when the engine cranks. If you find there is no problem with the cap, rotor, or armature, then replace the magnetic pickup assembly and the 3-wire pigtail connector at the distributor. If you find distributor cap or rotor damage, repair or replace as necessary and test the car. If engine operation is still not okay, proceed to step 10.

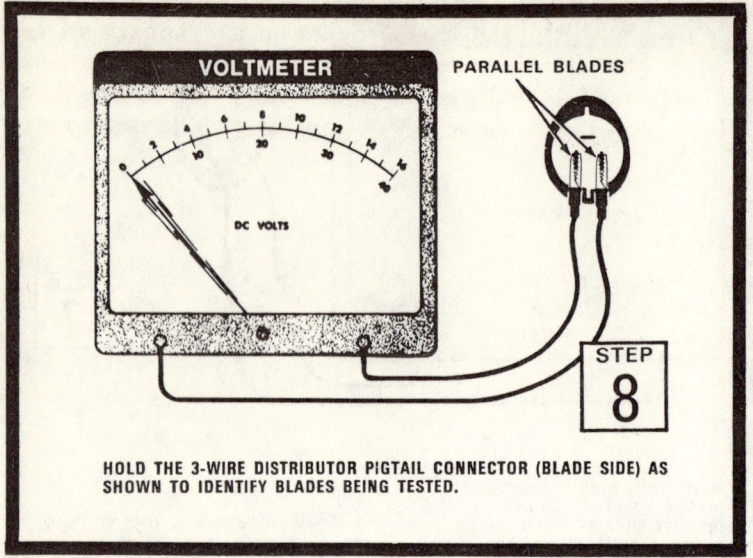

Fig. 6-34. Testing the voltage of the parallel blades. (Courtesy Ford Motor Company.)

10. Using an ohmmeter, test sockets 7 and 8 with the ignition switch in the OFF position. (See Fig. 6-35.) If you get a reading of anywhere between 400 and 800 ohms, skip step 11 and go to step 12. If you do not get the correct reading, proceed to step 11.

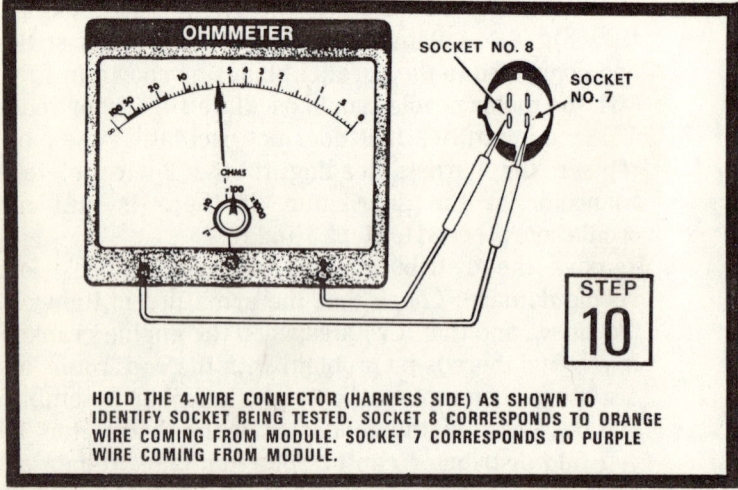

Fig. 6-35. Using an ohmmeter to test sockets 7 and 8. (Courtesy Ford Motor Company.)

11. Disconnect the 3-wire connector at the distributor pigtail. Using an ohmmeter, test the parallel blades with the ignition in the OFF position. If you now get a reading of anywhere between 400 and 800 ohms, replace the harness leading to the 3-wire pigtail connector at the distributor. If you do get the correct reading, then replace the magnetic pickup assembly (stator). Proceed to step 12 if the engine still does not run right. Reconnect the 3-wire pigtail connector at the distributor before performing step 12.
12. Using an ohmmeter, test between socket No. 6 and a good ground at the engine (Fig. 6-36). Be sure the ignition switch is in the OFF position. If you read zero ohms (dead short), it indicates this circuit is okay, so skip step 13 and proceed to step 14. If the reading shows any resistance, proceed to step 13.
13. Disconnect the 3-wire weatherproof connector at the distributor pigtail. Using an ohmmeter, test between the third blade and a good ground at the engine (Fig. 6-37). Be sure the ignition switch is in the OFF position. If you read zero ohms, then repair or replace the wiring harness leading to the distributor pigtail connector. If you get a reading of some resistane (not

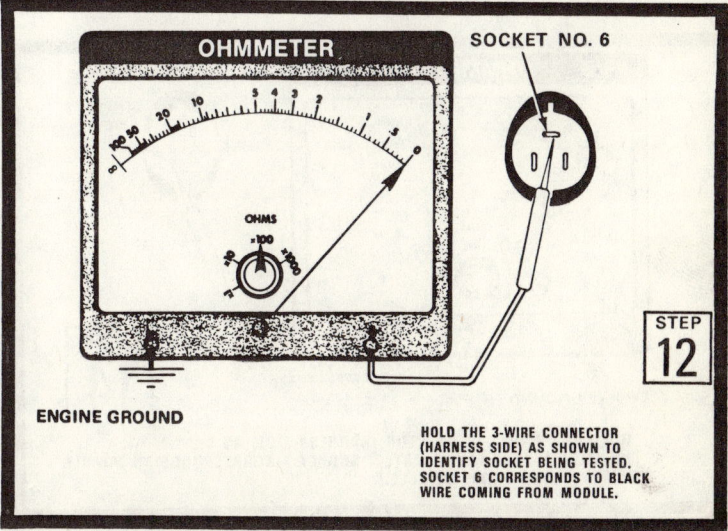

Fig. 6-36. Measuring resistance between socket 6 and engine ground. (Courtesy Ford Motor Company.)

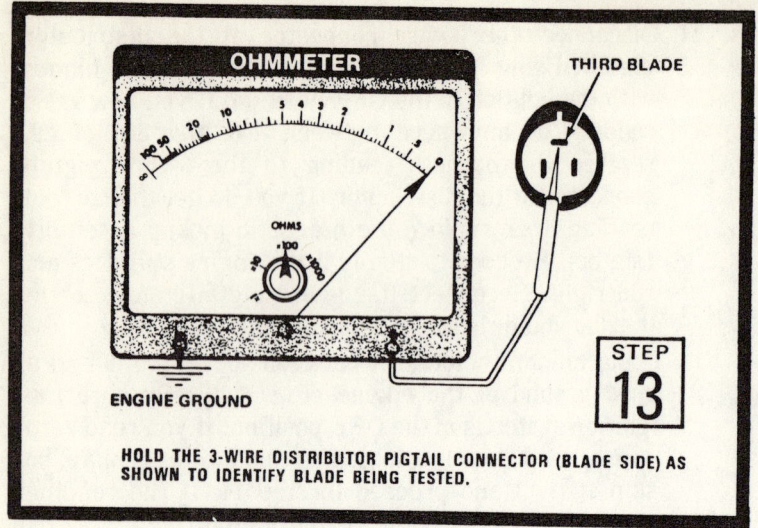

Fig. 6-37. Ohmmeter test between third blade of distributor pigtail connector and engine ground. (Courtesy Ford Motor Company.)

zero), replace the magnetic-pickup assembly (stator). If the car still does not perform properly, proceed to step 14.

14. Using an ohmmeter, test between socket No. 7 and a good ground at the engine (Fig. 6-38). Be sure ignition

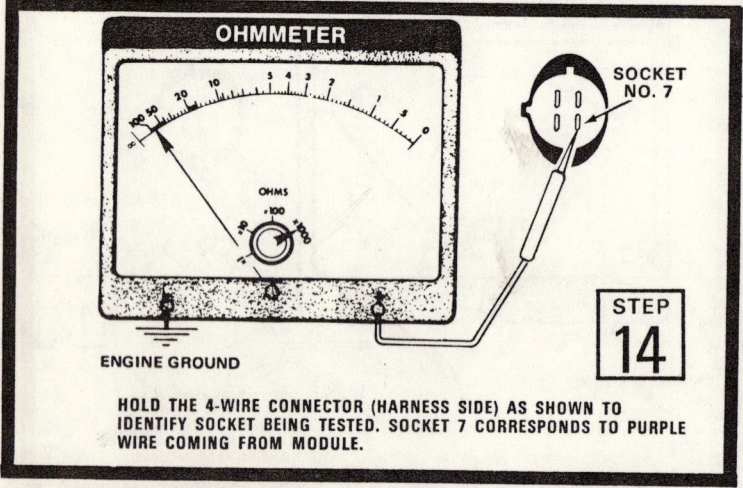

Fig. 6-38. Ohmmeter measurement between socket 7 and engine ground (Courtesy Ford Motor Company).

is in the OFF position. The ohmmeter reading should be more than 70,000 ohms. If it is okay, then proceed to step 15. If the reading is low, check to see if the harness is grounded. If the harness is okay, replace the pickup assembly (stator). If the engine still does not operate properly, go to step 15.

15. Using an ohmmeter, test between socket No. 8 and a good ground at the engine (Fig. 6-39). Be sure the ignition is off. The ohmmeter should read more than 70,000 ohms. If it reads okay, proceed to step 16. If the reading is low, check to see if the harness is grounded. If the harness is okay, replace the pickup assembly. If the engine still does not run properly, proceed with step 16.

16. Using an ohmmeter, test between socket No. 3 and the coil's high-voltage tower (Fig. 6-40). Be sure the ignition switch is in the OFF position. The resistance of the coil secondary should be between 7,000 and 13,000 ohms. If the reading is within this resistance range, proceed with step 17. If the resistance reading is not within the acceptable range, remove the coil from the engine and test it on a coil tester. *Be sure to follow the test equipment manufacturer's instructions.* If the coil tests bad, it must be replaced. If the coil

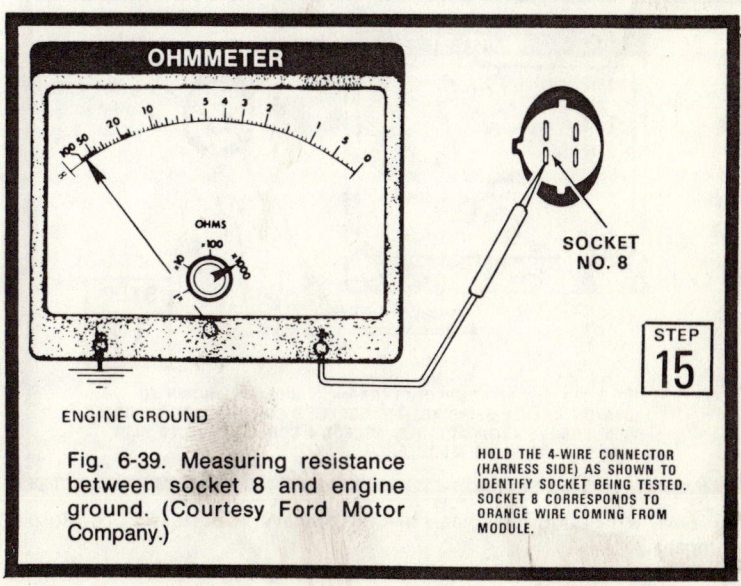

Fig. 6-39. Measuring resistance between socket 8 and engine ground. (Courtesy Ford Motor Company.)

HOLD THE 4-WIRE CONNECTOR (HARNESS SIDE) AS SHOWN TO IDENTIFY SOCKET BEING TESTED. SOCKET 8 CORRESPONDS TO ORANGE WIRE COMING FROM MODULE.

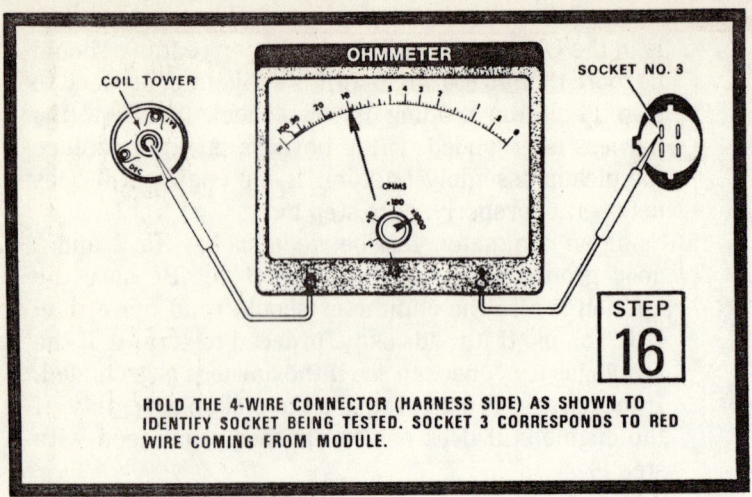

Fig. 6-40. Using an ohmmeter to check between socket 3 and coil tower. (Courtesy Ford Motor Company.)

    tests okay, replace the harness leading to the distributor pigtail. In either case, if the engine still does not operate properly, proceed to step 17.

17. Using an ohmeter, test between socket No. 5 and socket No. 4 with the ignition off (Fig. 6-41). The coil's primary resistance should be between 1.0 and 2.0

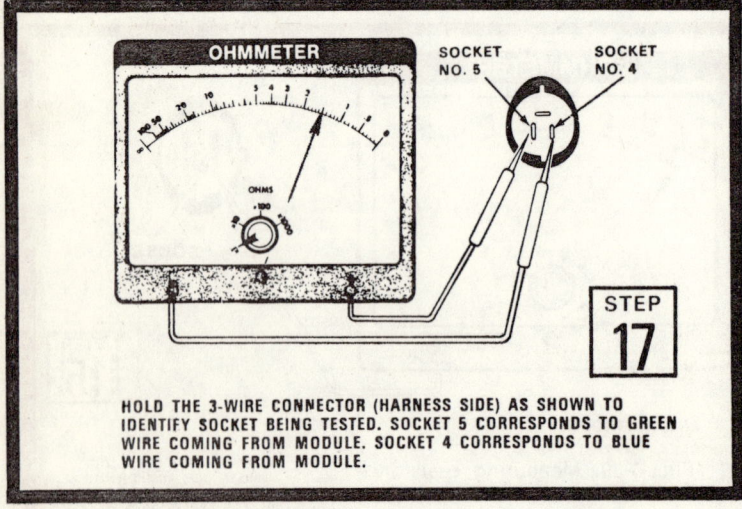

Fig. 6-41. Measuring resistance of coil primary. (Courtesy Ford Motor Company.)

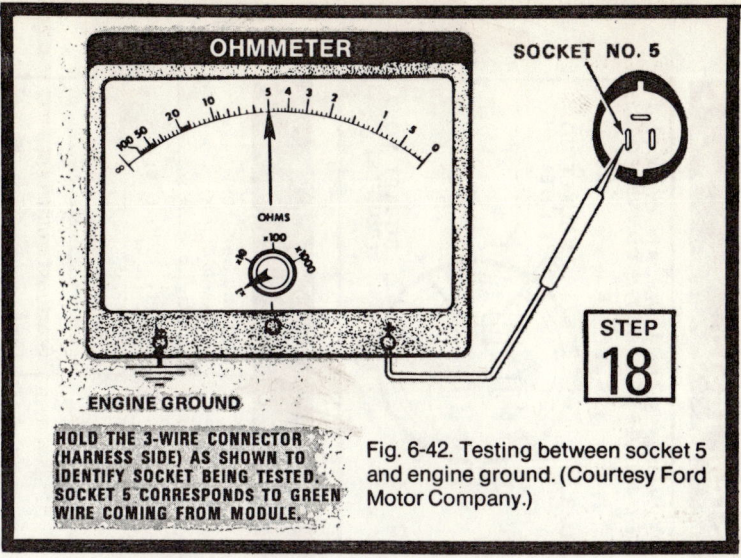

Fig. 6-42. Testing between socket 5 and engine ground. (Courtesy Ford Motor Company.)

ohms. If you do not get this reading, remove the coil and test it, following the equipment manufacturer's instructions. If the resistance reading is between 1 and 2 ohms, proceed to step 18.

18. Using an ohmmeter, test between socket No. 5 and a good ground at the engine. Be sure the ignition is off. (See Fig. 6-42.) The reading on the ohmmeter should

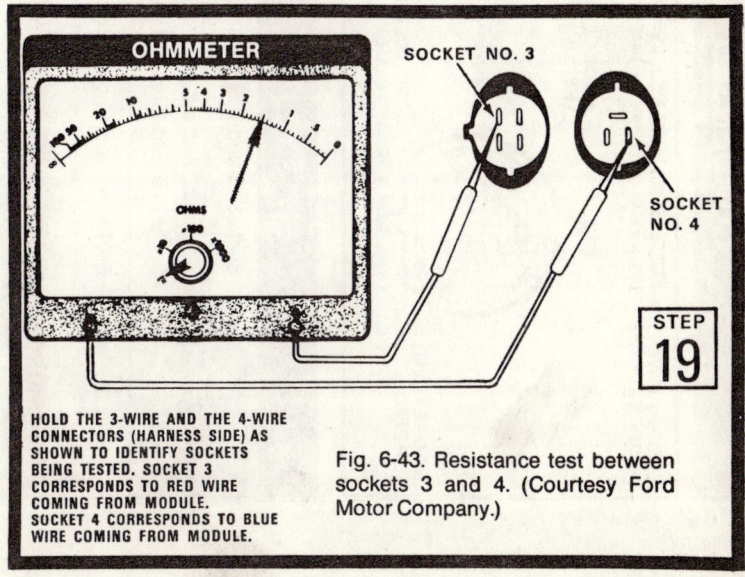

Fig. 6-43. Resistance test between sockets 3 and 4. (Courtesy Ford Motor Company.)

CONDENSED SUMMARY OF SYSTEM TESTS

SPECIAL NOTE • THE COLOR CODES NEXT TO EACH SOCKET NUMBER (HARNESS SIDE) INDICATE ONLY THE COLOR OF THE WIRES LEADING FROM THE MODULE TO THE BLADE SIDE (MODULE SIDE) OF THE CONNECTORS.

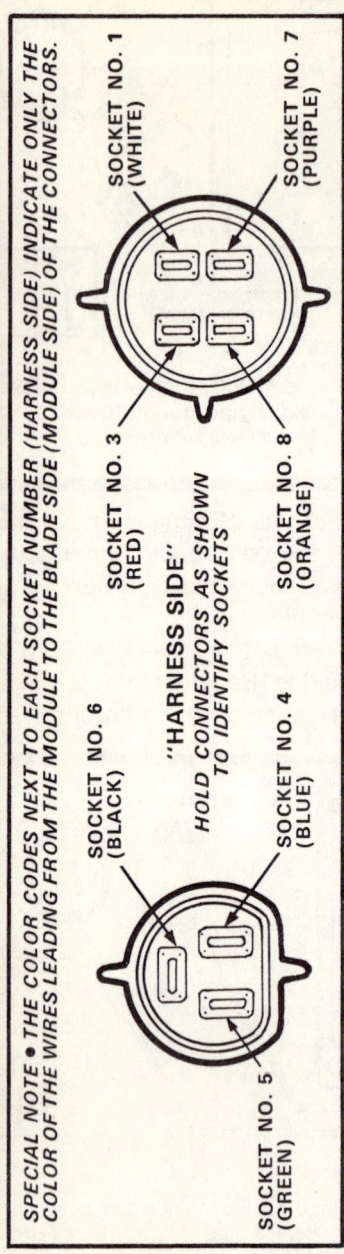

SOCKET NO. 6 (BLACK)
SOCKET NO. 5 (GREEN)
SOCKET NO. 4 (BLUE)
SOCKET NO. 1 (WHITE)
SOCKET NO. 3 (RED)
SOCKET NO. 7 (PURPLE)
SOCKET NO. 8 (ORANGE)

"HARNESS SIDE"
HOLD CONNECTORS AS SHOWN TO IDENTIFY SOCKETS

KEY ON	Socket #3 and Engine Ground	Battery Voltage ± 0.1V	Module Bias Test *(Power to Operate)*
	Socket #5 and Engine Ground	Battery Voltage ± 0.1V	Battery Source Test
	Socket #1 and Engine Ground	8 to 12 volts	Cranking Test
	Socket #5 and Engine Ground	8 to 12 volts	Starting Circuit Test
CRANKING	Socket #7 and Socket #8	Any D.C. volt wiggle or ½ volt A.C. min.	Distributor Hardware Test

KEY OFF	Socket #7 and Socket #8 Socket #6 and Engine Ground Socket #7 and Engine Ground Socket #8 and Engine Ground	400 to 800 ohms 0 ohms more than 70,000 ohms more than 70,000 ohms	Magnetic Pick-up (Stator) Test
	Socket #3 and Coil Tower Socket #5 and Socket #4	7000 to 13000 ohms 1.0 to 2.0 ohms	Coil Test
	Socket #5 and Engine Ground	more than 4.0 ohms	Short Test
	Socket #3 and Socket #4	1.0 to 2.0 ohms	Resistance Wire Test

SYSTEM PROTECTION

The Ford Solid State Ignition System is protected against known electrical currents such as are produced or used by any vehicle component during normal operation. However, damage to the ignition system can result from alternator output tests that are NOT performed as follows:

- Alternator output tests must be conducted ONLY by the Volt-Ohm method.
- DO NOT use the Volt-Amp method or test procedure, or any test equipment wherein a KNIFE SWITCH is used at the battery terminal.

Fig. 6-44. Summary of Ford ignition tests. (Courtesy Ford Motor Company.)

show more than 4.0 ohms. If the reading is less than 4.0 ohms, then locate and repair the short to ground at the DEC terminal of the ignition coil or in the primary wiring leading to the coil. (Refer to the wiring diagram in Fig. 6-29.) If you get a reading of more than 4.0 ohms, proceed to step 19.

19. Using an ohmmeter, test between socket No. 3 and socket No. 4. Be sure ignition is off. (See Fig. 6-43.) In this resistance test, the correct reading should be between 1.0 and 2.0 ohms. If the reading is within these figures, then substitute a known good electronic module. (If you substitute a known good electronic module as a temporary measure, the old module does not have to be removed. Simply plug in a new test module. It does not require grounding through attachment bolts or screws.) If you do not get the specified reading of 1.0 to 2.0 ohms, then replace the resistance wire in the ignition circuit. (See Fig. 6-29.) If the substitution of the module corrects the condition, reconnect the original module to assure that a repair elsewhere has not affected the correction. If the original module still fails to operate properly, then install a new module. If the new module does not correct the condition, reinstall the original module and recheck the other ignition units.

Note: The multipin connectors used by Ford and other auto manufacturers often give trouble due to poor connection, dampness, and other causes. It is good practice to apply a grease having conductive properties (e.g., *Lubriplate D.S.*) to the terminals before plugging sockets and prongs together.

A summary of the Ford ignition system tests is shown in Fig. 6-44.

Chapter 7

Replacement Transistor Ignition Systems

This chapter will explore a few of the many makes of replacement-type transistor ignition systems on the market. Insofar as practicable, systems will be listed in the order of point triggered, magnetically triggered, and light triggered. The theory of operation will be covered only to the extent necessary for explaining correct installation and efficient troubleshooting.

JUDSON ELECTRONIC MAGNETO

The Judson *Electronic Magneto* is not a magneto in the usual sense but is a point-triggered transistor ignition system. This system, shown in Fig. 7-1, is easy to install because the coil, transistor amplifier, and other parts are all in one package.

At first glance, the schematic (Fig. 7-2) looks like that of the usual point-isolating circuit. Further inspection shows that all the primary current goes through the contact points. The contact points, on opening, are protected from the inductive kick of the primary by the shunting action of the zener and the 3 μF capacitor.

When the breaker points close, the emitter of Q_1 is at ground potential, forward base bias is applied through R_1, and Q_1 conducts. Current flows through the primary of the coil, and the field reaches saturation quickly. When the points open,

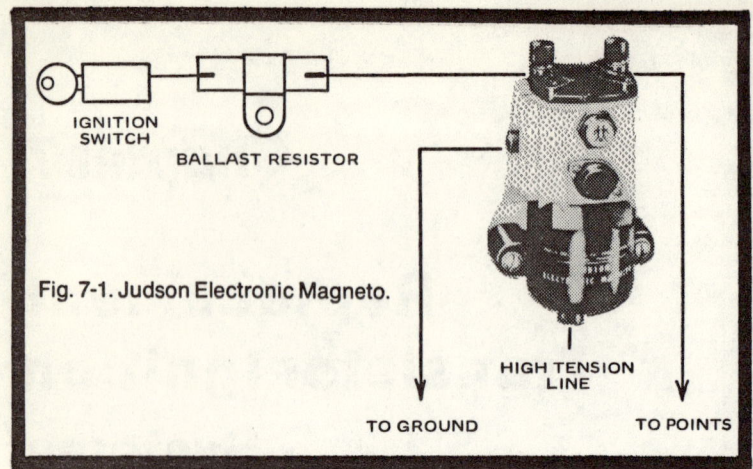

Fig. 7-1. Judson Electronic Magneto.

bias is removed and Q_1 ceases to conduct. High voltage is induced in the secondary winding and fed to the spark plugs via the rotor and distributor cap.

When the points open, the voltage across them is initially held to zero by capacitor C_1 and nonconducting zener D_2. The primary winding thus appears open and does not load the secondary winding. This allows the highest possible voltage to develop. As the voltage induced in the primary winding reaches the breakdown voltage of D_2, any excess voltage charges capacitor C_1. When the points again close, this voltage will force current through the contacts. Zeners D_1 and D_2, acting together, limit the induced primary voltage appearing between the emitter and collector of Q_1.

The advantages claimed for this system are an unusually fast spark rise time of 0.5 μsec and long point life because of the removal of induced primary voltage from the contacts at opening.

Installing the Judson Electronic Magneto

The *Electronic Magneto* is available for 6V or 12V and for negative- or positive-ground applications. Thus it can be used on nearly any American or foreign make of automobile. Installation of this system is quite simple and easy. The following procedure is recommended by the manufacturer.

1. Remove original ignition coil.
2. Mount *Electronic Magneto* in place where original coil was mounted. If this is not possible, install unit on

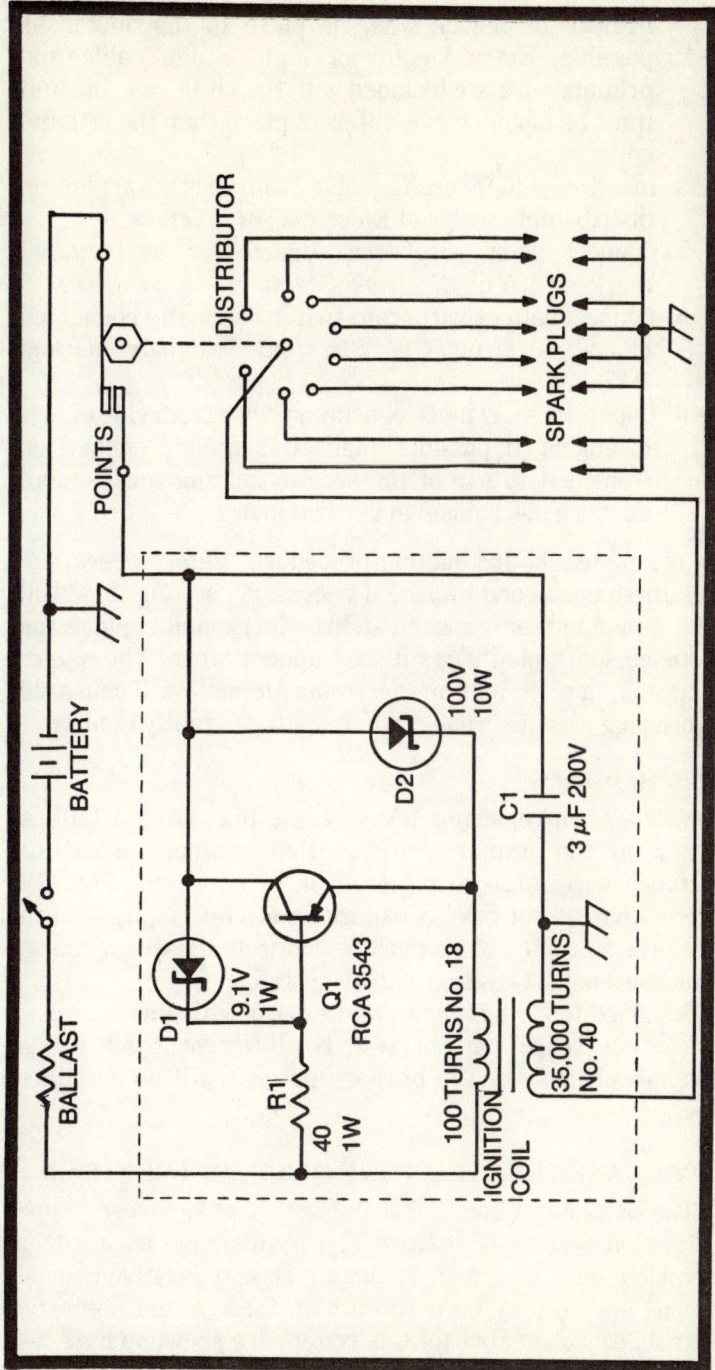

Fig. 7-2. Schematic of Judson Electronic Magneto.

firewall or fender well, as close to distributor as possible. Extra lengths of high-voltage cable and primary wire are included with the kit in case the unit must be mounted in a different place than the original coil.
3. Insert new high-tension cable from center of ignition distributor to socket of *Electronic Magneto*.
4. Connect point wire from distributor to terminal marked DIST on *Electronic Magneto*.
5. Connect battery wire from switch originally connected at coil to terminal on *Electronic Magneto* marked BAT.
6. Connect a short piece of primary wire from side of unit to engine. If possible, make this ground connection from unit to one of the screws holding the vacuum advance mechanism to the distributor.

This completes the installation procedure. Before operation, check these points and replace if necessary, setting the dwell to the manufacturer's specifications. Check and replace the resistance spark plug wires if they appear worn. The higher voltage output of the Judson *Electronic Magneto* will cause old or worn plug wires to break down, resulting in faulty ignition.

Ballast Resistor

Note: When replacing 12V systems that have a ballast resistor in the primary circuit, the original ballast or resistance wire must be replaced or reconnected. For 12V systems that do not have a ballast as original equipment, a ballast resistor of 1.3 ohms must be connected in the primary. Do not use a ballast resistor with 6V systems.

Standard test equipment can be used with this ignition; however, a scope pattern will be different than for a conventional ignition. The primary pattern will be a square wave.

DELTA MARK TEN CAPACITIVE-DISCHARGE IGNITION

The Delta *Mark Ten*, shown in Fig. 7-3, is an inverter-type CD ignition system. The *Mark Ten* is available as a kit or assembled unit. It comes in negative- and positive-ground versions and so may be used on both foreign and domestic automobiles. Schematics for this system are shown in Figs. 7-4 (negative ground) and 7-5 (positive ground).

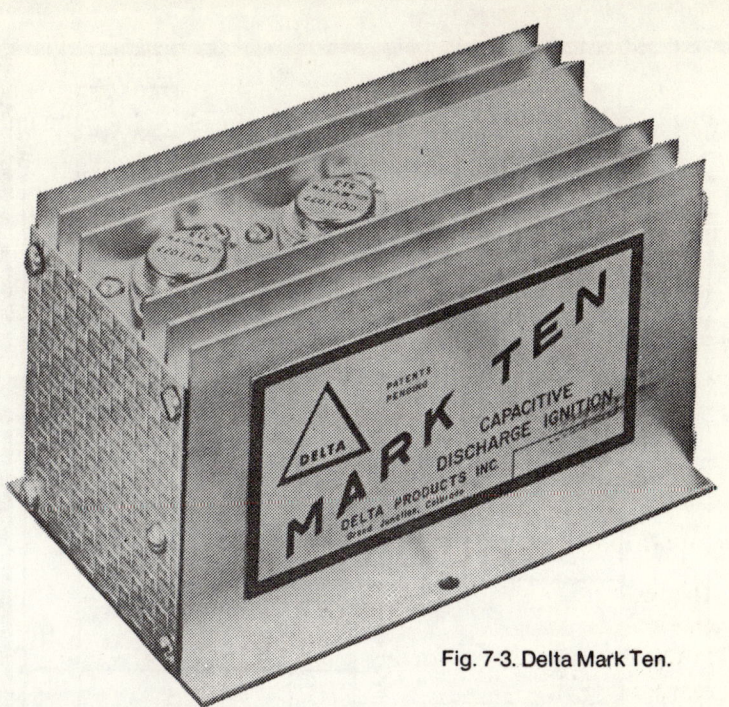

Fig. 7-3. Delta Mark Ten.

Converter Operation

The system consists of a DC-to-DC converter (to change the battery voltage to a higher voltage), a storage element (capacitor), a switching element (silicon controlled rectifier), and a high-voltage output transformer (coil) to transform the stored low-voltage DC to a level that will fire the spark plugs.

The applied battery voltage is converted from a nominal 12V to approximately 400V by the converter circuitry-transistors Q_1 and Q_2, and transformer T_1. The battery voltage applied to transformer T_1 causes current to flow through resistors R_1, R_2, R_3, and R_4. Since it is impossible for these two paths to be equal in resistance, one half of the primary winding will have a higher current.

Assuming that the upper half of the primary winding carries slightly higher current than the lower, the voltages developed in the two feedback windings (the ends connected to R_3 and R_2) tend to turn Q_2 on and Q_1 off. This increases the current through the upper half of he transformer winding. The increase in current drives Q_2 further into conduction and Q_1 into cutoff, simultaneously transferring energy to the secondary of T_1.

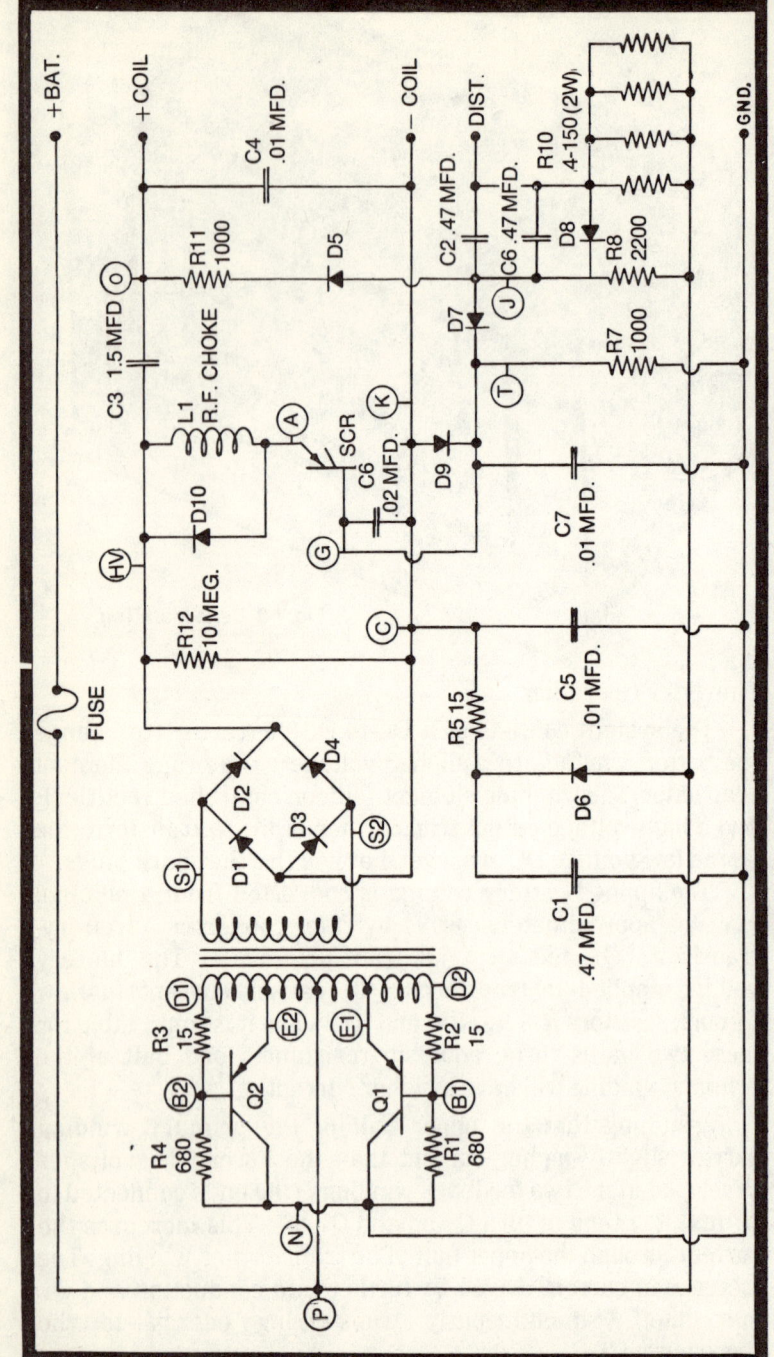

Fig. 7-4. Schematic of Delta Mark Ten (negative ground).

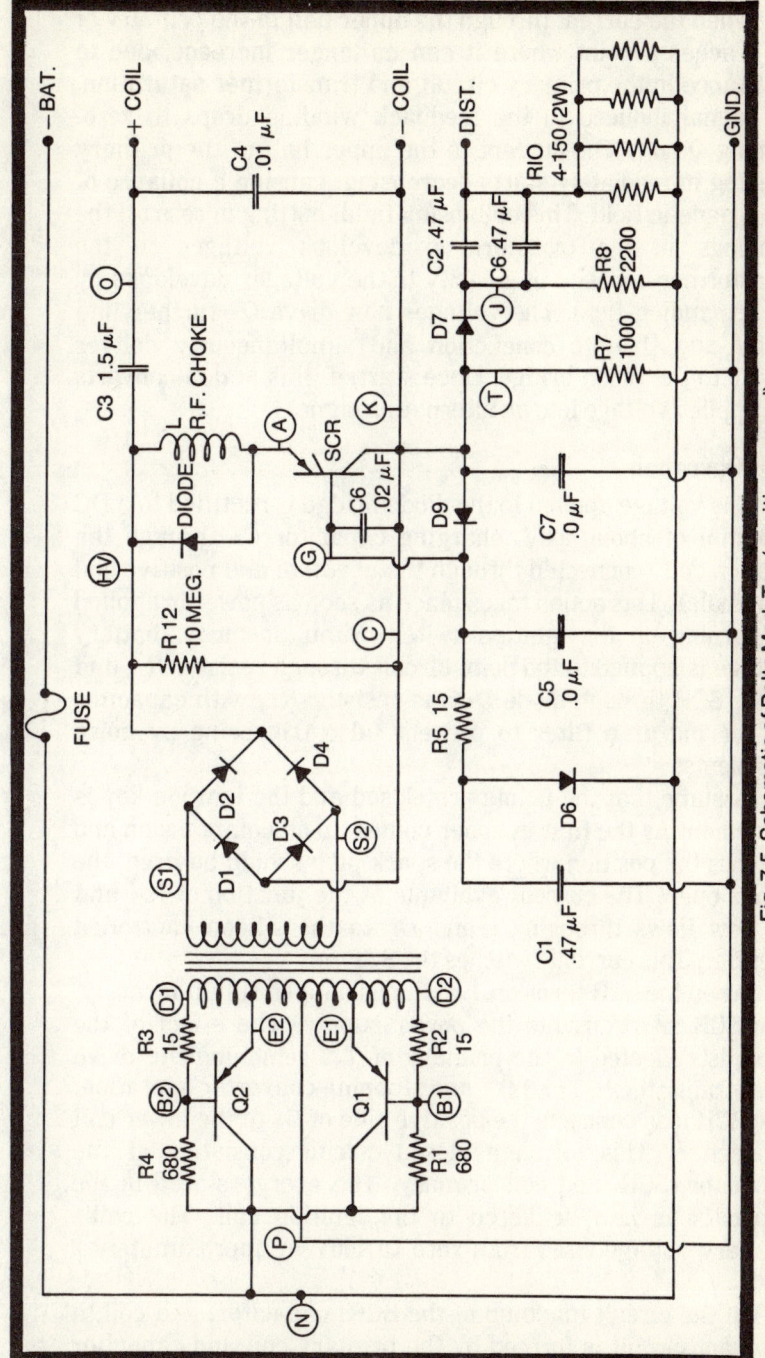

Fig. 7-5. Schematic of Delta Mark Ten (positive ground).

When the current through the **upper half of** the primary of T_1 reaches a point where it can no longer increase, due to resistance in the primary circuit and transformer saturation, the signal induced in the feedback winding drops to zero, turning Q_2 off. The current in the upper half of the primary winding immediately starts decreasing, causing a collapse of the magnetic field. This collapsing field, cutting across all the windings in the transformer, develops voltages in the transformer opposite in polarity to the voltages developed by the expanding field. The voltages now drive Q_2 further into cutoff and Q_1 into conduction and simultaneously deliver power to the diode bridge. Once started, this action converts the applied voltage into an alternating signal.

SCR Operation

The voltage applied to the diode bridge is rectified to a DC potential of about 400V, charging capacitor C_3 through the ignition coil (connected through the negative and positive coil terminals). This action takes place as soon as power is applied by turning on the ignition switch. Simultaneously, battery voltage is applied to the point circuit through resistor R_{10} and to the SCR through diode D_6 and resistor R_5, with capacitor C_1 serving as a filter to prevent false triggering by noise transients.

Assume that the points are closed and the ignition key is turned on. As the first cylinder comes up on compression and reaches the position where the spark plug should be fired, the points open. The current available at the junction of R_{10} and C_2 now flows through C_2 and D_7 to the silicon controlled rectifier. This current switches the SCR on.

When the SCR turns on, two things happen simultaneously. The SCR short-circuits the power supply. The effect of the short is reflected to the primary of T_1, removing the drive from transistors Q_1 and Q_2 and stopping converter operation. The SCR also connects the positive side of C_3 to the lower coil connection. This forms a closed circuit consisting of the capacitor, SCR, and coil primary. The energy stored in the capacitor is now delivered to the ignition coil. The coil's primary voltage rises from zero to 400V in approximately 2 μsec.

In the circuit made up of the SCR, capacitor, and coil, a resonant circuit is formed by the primary coil and capacitor

C_3. The flywheel effect of this circuit restores unused energy to the capacitor. The capacitor's discharge current flows through the SCR and coil primary, creating a magnetic field in the coil. This current continues to flow in the circuit until the capacitor is charged in a reverse direction to approximately 300V. At this point the current attempts to reverse through the SCR, causing the SCR to return to its *off* condition. The reverse voltage now causes the diode bridge to conduct as a short circuit (all diodes now conducting), discharging the capacitor to zero from its reverse direction and recharging the capacitor towards its normal state. When the current supplied by the coil again drops to zero, the bridge returns to the normal state, the load is removed from transformer T_1, and normal converter operation resumes.

Diodes D_5 and D_8, in conjunction with R_{11}, serve to discharge triggering capacitor C_2 completely when the SCR turns on. Diode D_7 and resistor R_8 prevent erratic triggering caused by point bounce. Resistor R_7 is used to reverse-bias the SCR to prevent erratic triggering by noise. Diode D_{10} and choke L_1 are used to control the turnon characteristics of the SCR.

The *Mark Ten* ignition system has been designed for use with original equipment coils. Using special coils may degrade the performance of this system.

High-Tension System

With the higher energy output of the *Mark Ten*, it is important that the high-tension system of the vehicle be in good condition. A defective or cracked distributor cap or rotor, which may cause occasional misfiring in a conventional system, will usually cause extreme roughness with this unit. Radio resistance wire, if used, must be in good condition, or poor performance and hard starting may result. Resistance of the spark plug wires must be below 30,000 ohms for satisfactory performance. For maximum reliability on all cars and optimum noise rejection on high-frequency radios (FM, CB, or amateur), an inductive type of high-tension wire should be used.

Spark Plugs. To assure proper performance, standard-heat-range plugs gapped at 0.040 in. should be used with this system. Surface-gap plugs are not recommended. Cold-range plugs may be used for operation at extremely high speeds.

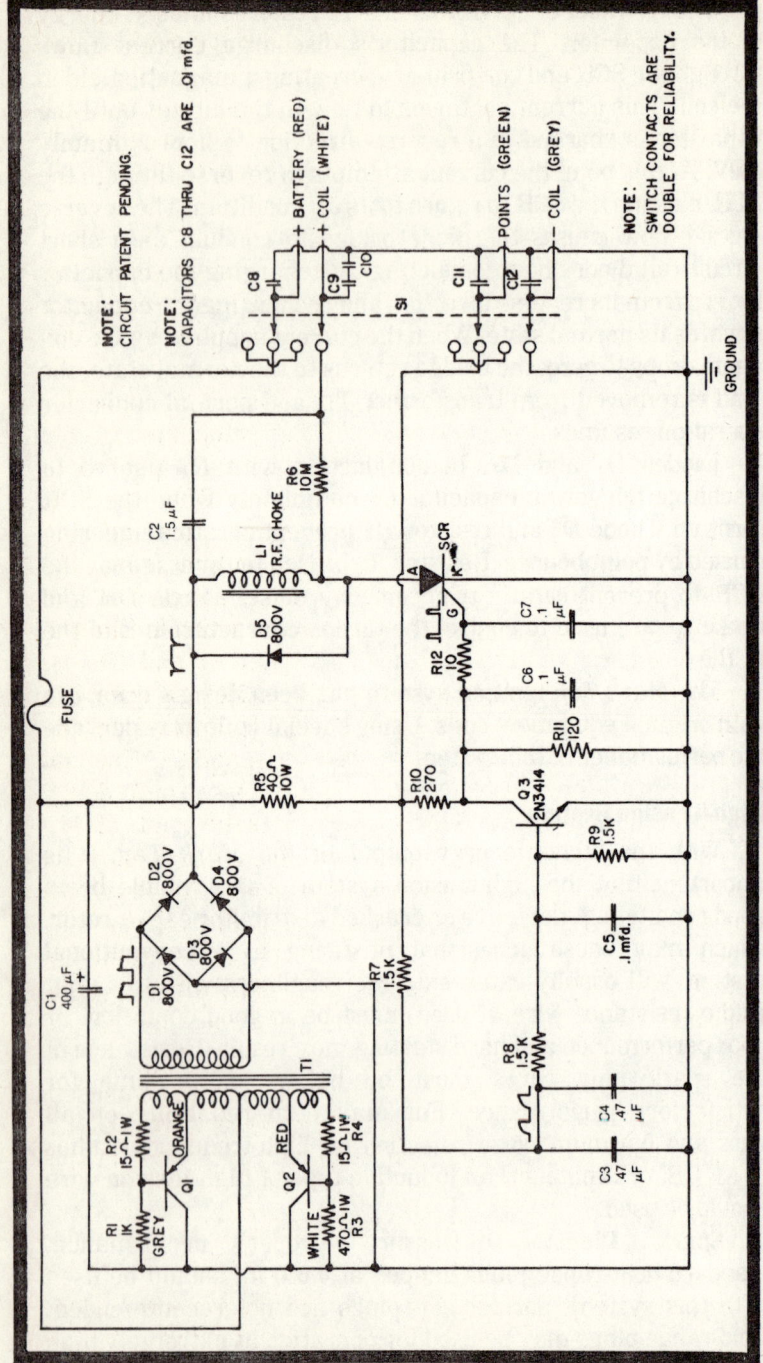

Fig. 7-6. Schematic of Delta Mark Ten B.

Ballast Resistor. The ballast resistor (or resistance wire) may be retained or bypassed at the option of the owner. The distributor point capacitor should be retained.

Radio Noise Suppression Capacitors. These may be used with the system but must not be connected to the coil terminals. Connection should be made at the ignition switch terminals on the unit.

DELTA MARK TEN B

The *Mark Ten B* is an inverter-type CD system similar to the *Mark Ten*, but having an addition primarily for aiding in emission control. This addition to the circuitry is shown in the schematic of Fig. 7-6.

Transistor Q_3, included in the trigger circuit of the SCR, is a switching transistor. When the breaker points are closed, the junction of R_5, R_7, and R_{10} is at ground potential. Transistor Q_3 is not conducting, and the SCR gate is effectively grounded through R_{10}. During this period, capacitor C_2 is charged to the rectified output from the inverter. As the points open, a positive pulse appears at the junction of R_{10} and R_{11}. This positive pulse—which is filtered by the low-pass network consisting of C_6, R_{12}, and C_7—is coupled to the SCR gate, causing the SCR to conduct. Meanwhile, however, forward base bias is applied to Q_3 through a delay network consisting of R_7, C_3, and C_4. Thus, a brief time after the SCR conducts, Q_3 saturates and pulls down the gate of the SCR. The cycle then repeats as the points close.

The purpose of the switching transistor in the gate circuit is to prevent false triggering and to insure that the SCR will not be turned on a second time after it has dumped a charge and turned off. This makes the circuit relatively immune to contact bounce and reduces the possibility of misfiring, which would adversely affect the emissions of the engine.

MARK TEN TEST PROCEDURES

Poor engine performance with this ignition can be caused by defects in the original equipment of the car as well as in the CD unit itself. The following table will help you pinpoint the trouble.

Symptoms
No hum in unit

Possible Causes
1. Shorted bridge diode
2. Shorted transformer
3. Shorted discharge capacitor
4. High-voltage short (due to corrosion)

Symptoms	Possible Causes
Continous discharge at all times.	1. Defective SCR 2. Shorted SCR gate diode 3. Open SCR gate diode 4. Shorted SCR gate capacitor 5. Open SCR gate resistor 6. High-voltage leakage path (due to corrosion)
Continous discharge after warmup.	1. Defective SCR
Hum normal; unit will not fire.	1. Open transformer secondary 2. Open input diode 3. Shorted SCR collector diode 4. Defective SCR 5. Open discharge capacitor 6. Open RF choke
Erratic hum; poor high-speed operation.	1. Shorted or intermittent bridge diode 2. Poor transistor-to-socket contact 3. Cold-soldered transistor leads 4. Leaky discharge capacitor
Blows fuse wire.	1. Defective transistor
Poor low-speed operation.	1. Defective high-tension harness 2. Plug gaps too wide 3. High point resistance 4. High secondary resistance
Poor light-load performance.	1. Spark advanced too far 2. Plug gaps too close 3. Idle mixture too lean

TRI-STAR TIGER 500 CD IGNITION SYSTEM

The *Tiger 500* (Fig. 7-7) is a compact, ruggedly built inverter type of capacitive-discharge ignition system. This system employs the original coil, contact points, and capacitor of the automobile, and has a built-in switch to switch back to the original ignition should the occasion arise.

As the schematic of Fig. 7-8 shows, the *Tiger 500* is an SCR controlled CD unit. The important difference between this and other CD units is the increased spark repetition of the *Tiger*

500. This difference stems from the construction of the inverter transformer.

The inverter transformer has a ferrite core and operates at a frequency of 8000 Hz, while most inverters operate at 1000 Hz or less. This high-frequency design reduces the number of windings required and hence the circuit losses. It also eliminates a condition in some CD systems called *sync miss*. Sync miss occurs when the engine speed corresponds to the inverter frequency or a strong harmonic thereof. The spark demand occurs at a poor time in the charging curve of the storage capacitor, causing misfiring. With the high repetition rate of this inverter, the capacitor will have many cycles to recharge even at the highest engine speed.

The rise time for this system (discharge pulse) is about 2.5 μsec. The period of spark discharge is of the order of 350 μsec.

STEVENS IGNITION SYSTEM

The Stevens ignition (Figs. 7-9 and 7-10) is a highly sophisticated capacitive-discharge system. This system is said to offer improved fuel economy, unlimited point life, 40,000 to 50,000 miles between tuneups, easier starting, and better performance.

Circuit Operation

Some of the unique design features of this system are discussed in the following paragraphs with reference to the

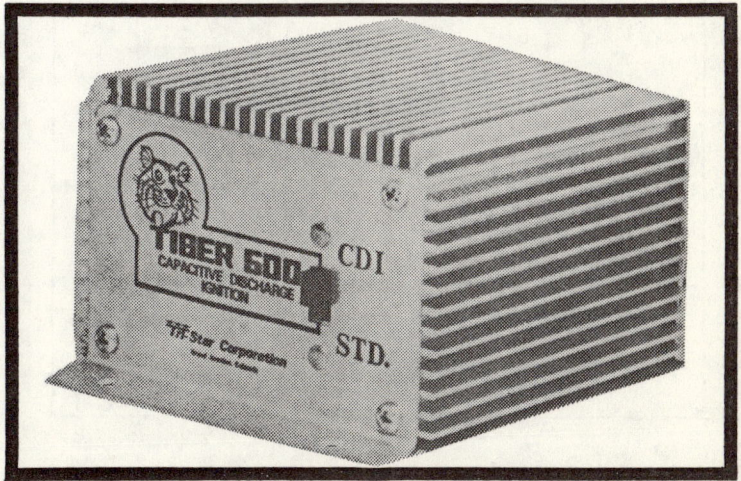

Fig. 7-7. Tri-Star Tiger 500 ignition.

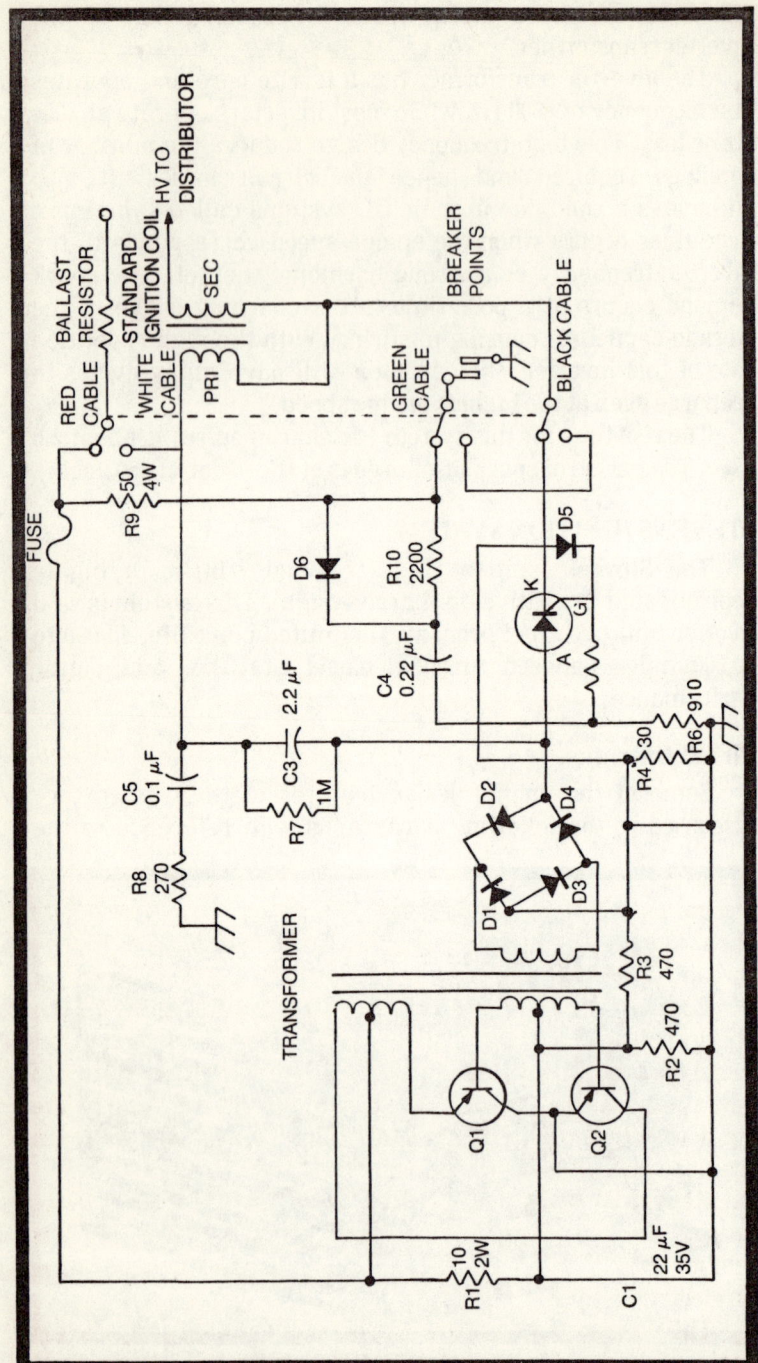

Fig. 7-8. Schematic of Tri-Star Tiger 500.

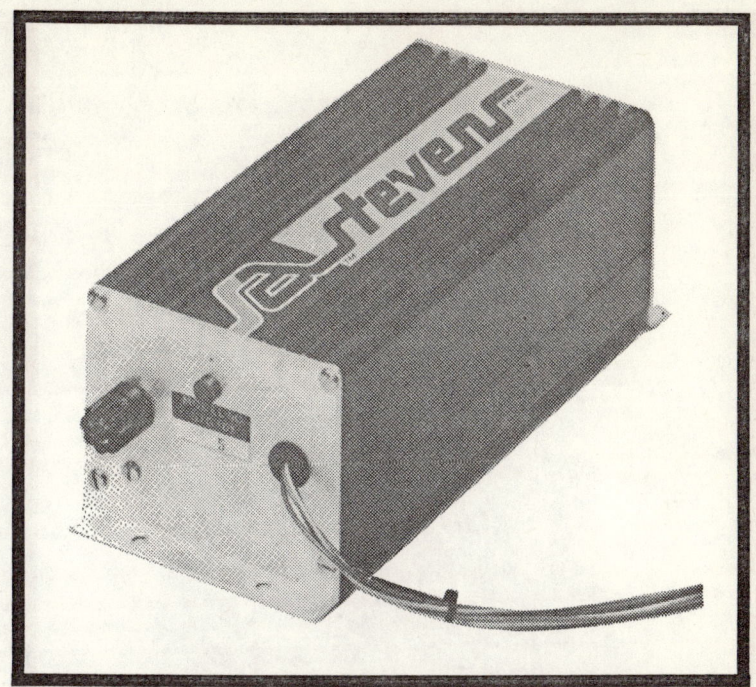

Fig. 7-9. Stevens electronic ignition.

schematic of Fig. 7-11. The circuit is divided into sections for ease of explanation. Reference letters are used to designate the various sections.

Basic Operation. Energy storage capacitor C_{10} (section N on the diagram) is charged to the proper energy level and then discharged through the ignition coil every time the points open. The coil, in turn, transfers the accumulated energy through the distributor to the spark plugs.

Energy Storage Capacitor. In the Stevens ignition, the energy storage capacitor is three to four times larger than that found in other CD units. As a result, it pumps more energy to operate more efficiently. It also lengthens the duration of the spark to between 400 and 600 μsec, which guarantees optimum ignition under all conditions.

Regulated Charging Circuit. To make sure the large energy storage capacitor performs properly, the Stevens ignition uses a highly efficient charging circuit incorporating an electronic voltage regulator.

The voltage regulator compensates for the large variation in the car's electrical system voltage during the operation of

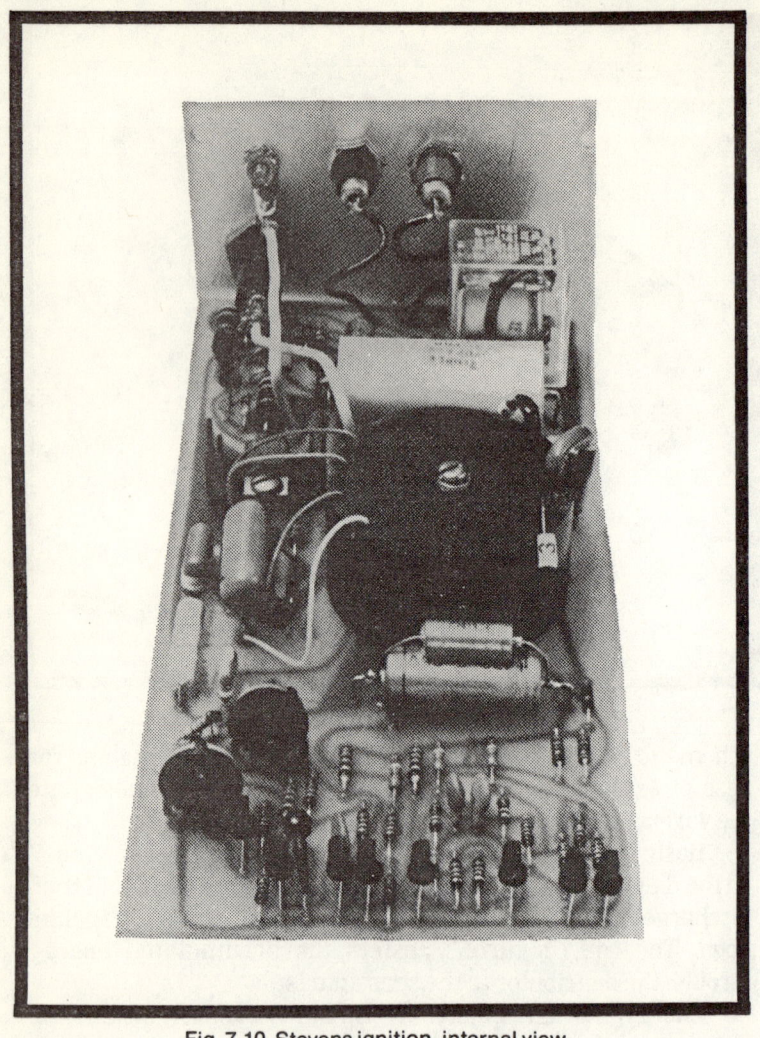

Fig. 7-10. Stevens ignition, internal view.

the engine. The voltage can vary from 8V to 16V. This means that any system without regulation has to produce excessively high voltages to insure an adequate voltage when the electrical system's voltage is at the low end of this range. Such high voltages put undue stress on the engine's electrical system, and should a spark plug wire become dislodged, the wiring harness, distributor cap, or coil could be severely damaged. To prevent such damage, the Stevens ignition produces a constant 28,000V output, controlled by the voltage regulator.

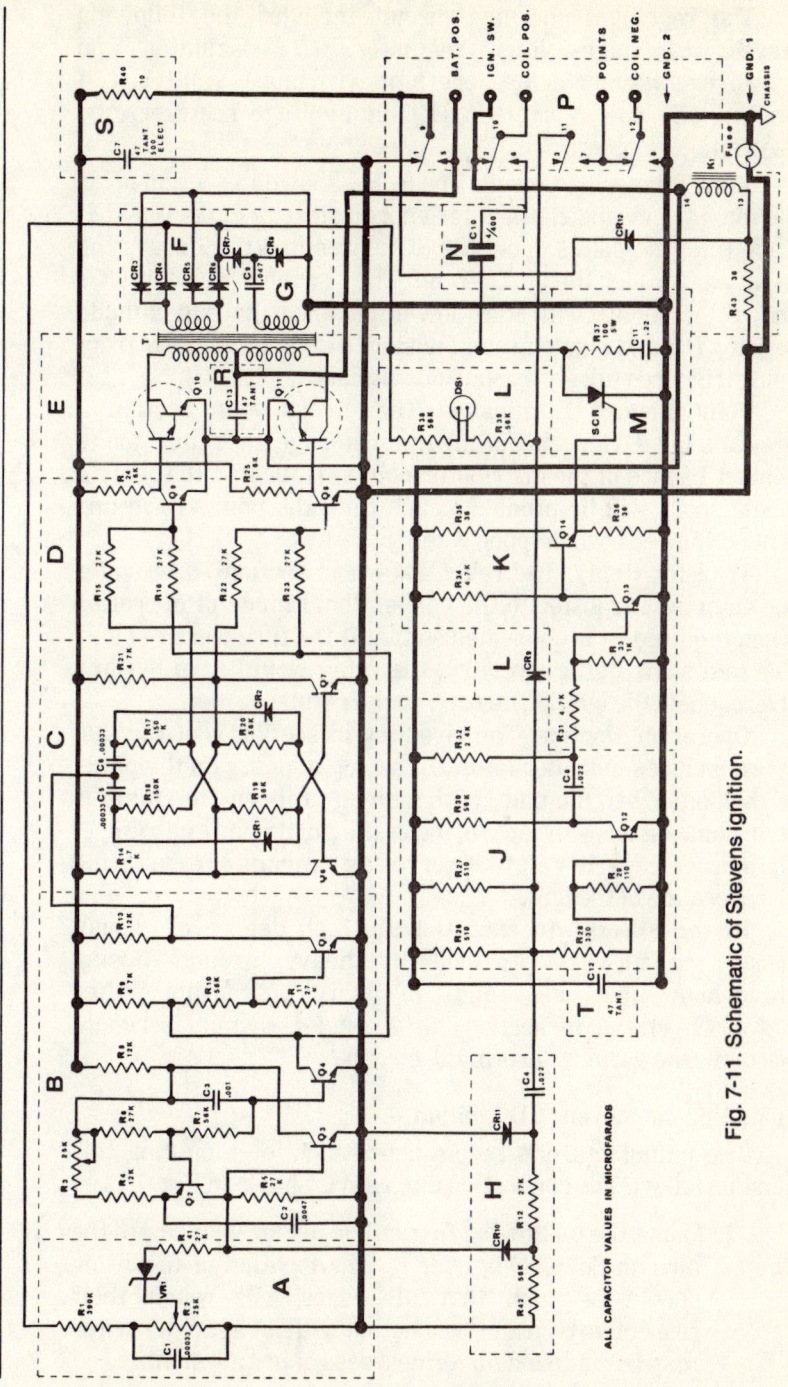

ALL CAPACITOR VALUES IN MICROFARADS

Fig. 7-11. Schematic of Stevens ignition.

The regulated charging circuit includes the following stages: (*A*) high-voltage regulator, (*B*) oscillator and crossover-switching-delay generator, (*C*) phase splitter, (*D*) drivers, (*E*) power inverter, (*F*) high-voltage rectifier, and (*G*) voltage doubler.

Main Triggering Circuit. The SCR , shown in section *M*, is the main triggering element for energy storage capacitor C_{10}. Each time the points open, the SCR fires and discharges the capacitor through the ignition coil. The "snubber" circuit (R_{37} and C_{11}), along with the low-impedance gate-to-cathode resistor R_{36} and heavy ground busing, prevents the SCR from being triggered falsely by spurious signals.

Point Bounce Eliminator. The circuitry in section *J* prevents false triggering of the main storage capacitor due to contact bounce of the distributor points. It insures that only a single spark will be produced each time the points open and that nothing else will happen when they close.

Transfer Relay. The relay, shown in section *P*, provides for automatic transfer to the conventional mode of operation when required. It is connected so that if the fuse were to blow, due to a short in the circuitry, the relay would drop out and thus connect the ignition directly to the points.

Operation Monitor. The circuitry in section *L* of the diagram includes indicator lamp D_1, which appears on the panel of the unit. When the unit is functioning properly, the lamp is lit in coincidence with the closing of the points and charging of the storage capacitor. It thus serves as a means of monitoring the operation of the unit.

Power Filters. An exceptionally high degree of overall noise immunity is provided by heavy ground busing throughout the unit and by three separate filter networks—shown in sections *S*, *T*, and *U*—which serve to decouple the various parts of the circuit.

Installing the Stevens CD Ignition

The manufacturer's recommendations for mounting this ignition follow. The connection diagram is shown in Fig. 7-12.

1. Mount the unit on the firewall or fender well where the air can flow freely over it. The location of mounting should be such that all wires will reach their respective points of connection without splicing. Wires may be cut to length for neatness of installation.

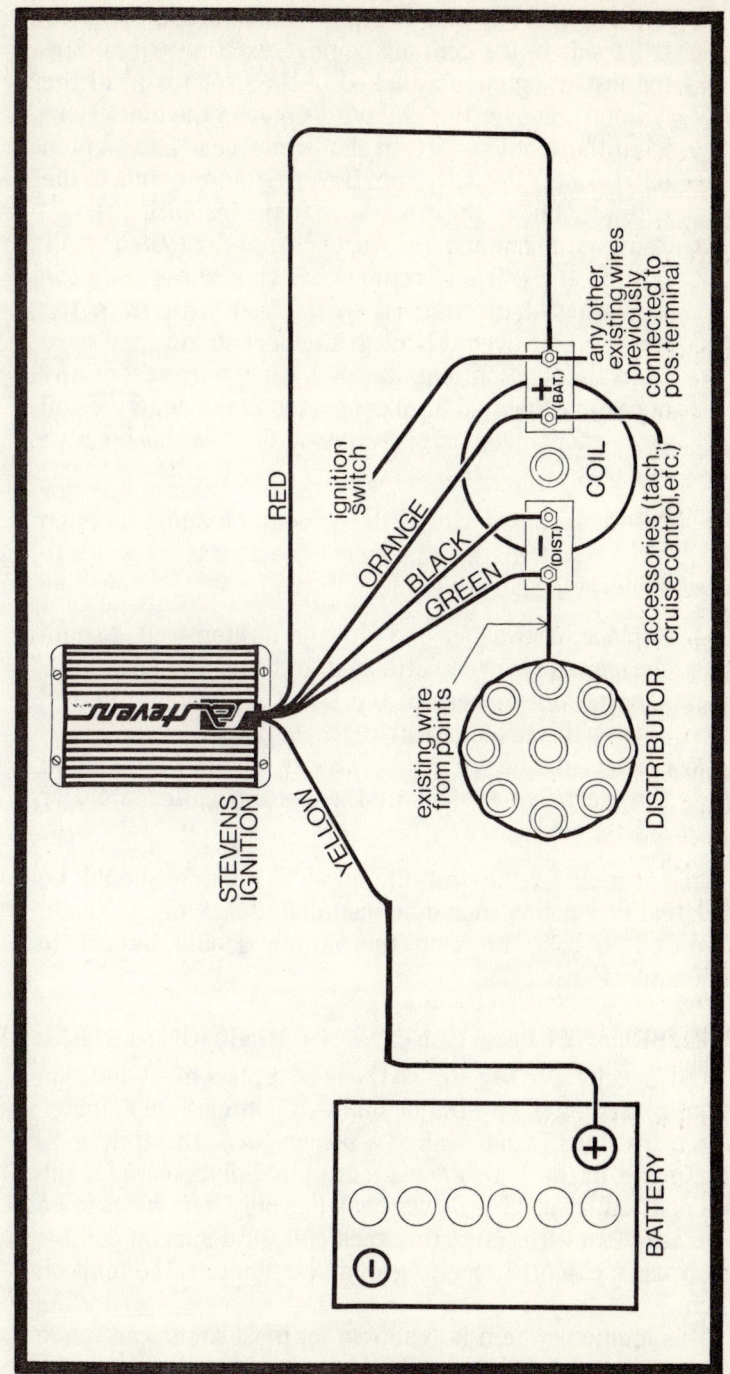

Fig. 7-12. Wire connection diagram—Stevens ignition.

2. Remove the nut and lockwasher from the NEG or DIST side of the coil and remove existing wires. Slip the insulating strip attached to the green wire of the ignition unit over this coil post. Connect the black wire from the ignition wire to this same post and tighten nut. Connect the wire from the distributor points to the screw that holds the green wire to the insulating strip.
3. Remove the nut and lockwasher from the POS or BAT post on the coil and remove existing wires. Slip the insulating strip attached to the red wire from the ignition unit over this post. Connect the orange wire from the ignition unit (and all other wires from any accessory that had been connected to the negative coil post—tachometer, cruise control, etc.) to this positive coil post.

Note: To avoid interfering with the point-cleaning function of the Stevens ignition, do not connect the accessory wires to any terminals at the negative side of the coil.

4. Replace lockwasher and nut and tighten well. Locate the wires previously attached to the positive coil post. Connect *all* of them to the screw that holds the red wire on the insulating strip.
5. Connect the heavy yellow wire to the positive side of the electrical system at the battery, alternator, or starter solenoid.

This completes the installation. The engine should be tuned, and new points should be installed. Spark plugs should be gapped to 0.050 in., and the timing should be set to specifications.

ACCEL BREAKERLESS ELECTRONIC IGNITION SYSTEM

The Accel *BEI* (see Fig. 7-13) is a replacement ignition system consisting of two major units—a complete distributor and a transistor CD unit, called a *power pack*. Installation is quite simple, as the distributor is a drop-in replacement for the stock distributor, and the power pack has only four wires to be connected. Two wires go to the stock coil (or a special coil for performance engines), one to ground, and one to the ignition switch.

This ignition system is available for most American-made engines, for boats, and even for some racing engines. Its performance features include: 41,000V output through 10,000 RPM ; extremely rapid rise time to prevent plug fouling; precise timing accuracy, with variation guaranteed not to exceed plus or minus one-fourth degree at 10,000 RPM; and completely maintenance-free operation.

The distributor is a precision-machined device with lubricated and sealed ball bearings. The trigger mechanism consists of an LED and perforated plate and cannot get out of adjustment. All distributors have a built-in mechanical

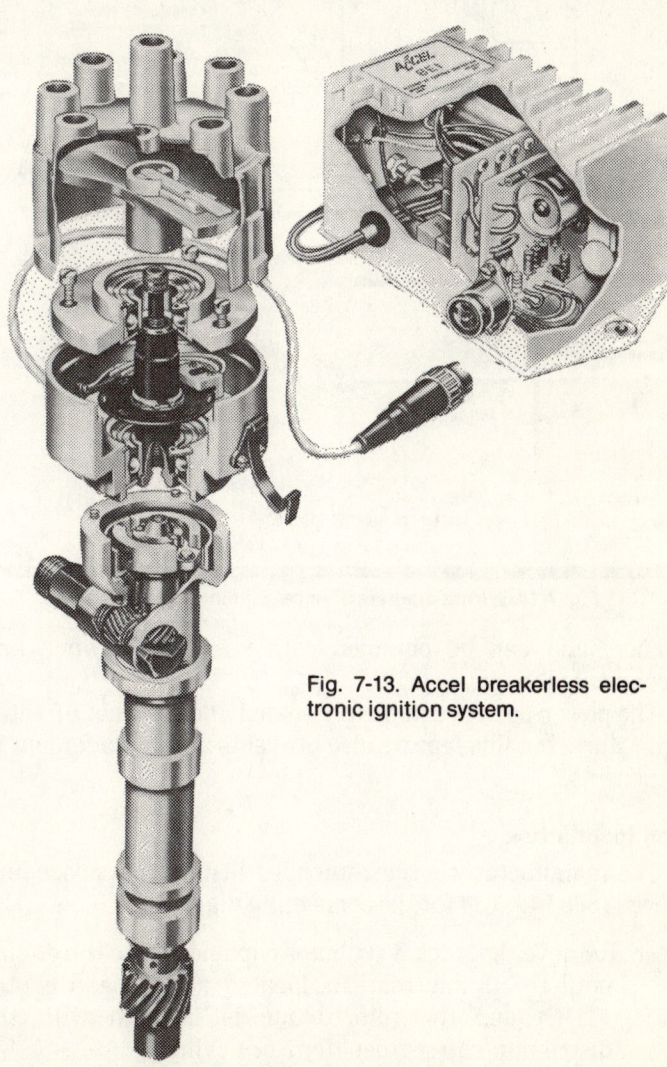

Fig. 7-13. Accel breakerless electronic ignition system.

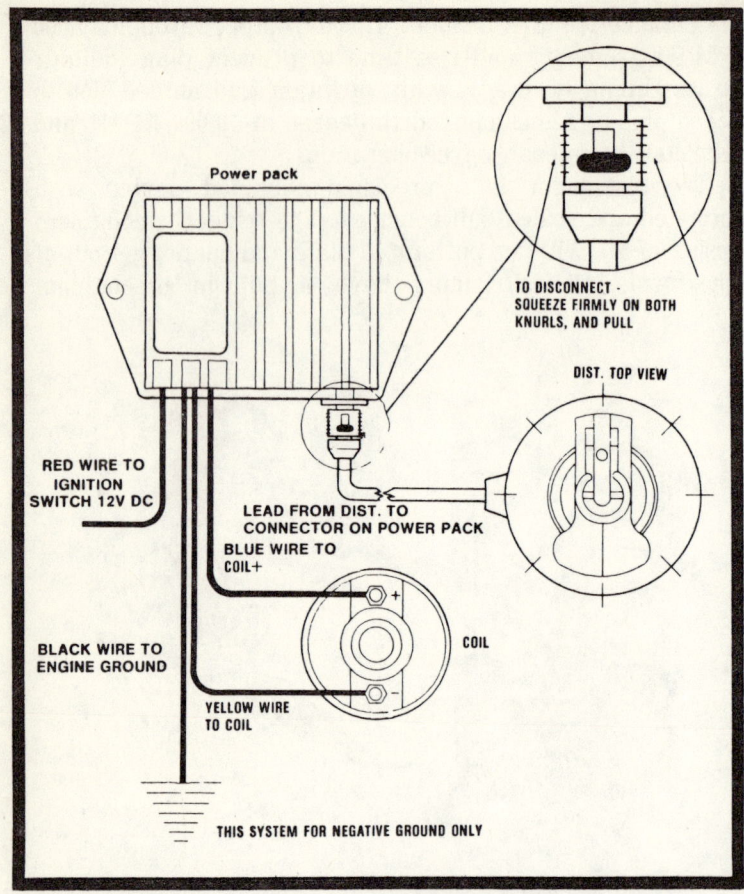

Fig. 7-14. Wiring diagram of Accel Eliminator ignition.

advance, and can be obtained with vacuum advance and mechanical tachometer drive.

The power pack is completely sealed and so is not affected by moisture, but this feature also prevents any replacement of components.

Accel Installation

The manufacturer's recommended installation procedure follows. (See Fig. 7-14 for the connecting diagram.)

1. Remove the stock distributor cap and rotate the engine until the timing mark is located at top dead center (TDC) and the rotor blade is indexed with the distributor cap segment for No. 1 cylinder.

2. Disconnect the battery.
3. Remove the stock distributor from the engine.
4. Install the Accel distributor in the engine with the gasket and rotate the housing to a position that eliminates interference with the power pack lead (and the mechanical tach if so equipped).
5. Adjust the distributor rotor. Remove the rotor and loosen the $\tfrac{3}{16}$ in. socket-head cap screw under the rotor (see Fig. 7-15A). (Those rotors that rotate in the counterclockwise direction have right-hand threads. Those that rotate in the clockwise direction have left-hand threads.) Replace rotor and rotate until the rotor tip is aligned with the mark desired for the No. 1 cylinder (see Fig. 7-15B). When it is aligned, remove rotor and tighten the $\tfrac{3}{16}$ in. socket-head cap screw to 5 to 6 ft-lb torque. Replace rotor and cap and install spark plug wires.
6. Mount the electronic power pack where it will avoid engine heat and be exposed to as much cool air as is possible. Do not mount the power pack near the exhaust system or on the engine. The power pack must be mounted so the connector cable from the distributor can be connected without splicing.
7. The wires coming from the power pack are attached as follows (Fig. 7-14):

> **Red Wire**—Connect to ignition switch (12V DC). (This system is designed to operate best without a ballast resistor or resistor wire in the circuit. If used with a resistor, a slight loss of performance may occur.)
> *To operate without a resistor,* connect red wire directly to ignition switch.
> *To operate with a resistor,* remove originl wire or wires connected to coil (+) or BAT; connect to red wire with a splice and wrap with electrical tape.
> **Black Wire**—Ground to engine, being sure to make a good connection.
> **Blue Wire**—Connect to coil (+) or BAT.
> **Yellow Wire**—Connect to coil (−) or DIST.

8. Connect the cable from the distributor into the connector on the side of the power pack. *Do not splice*

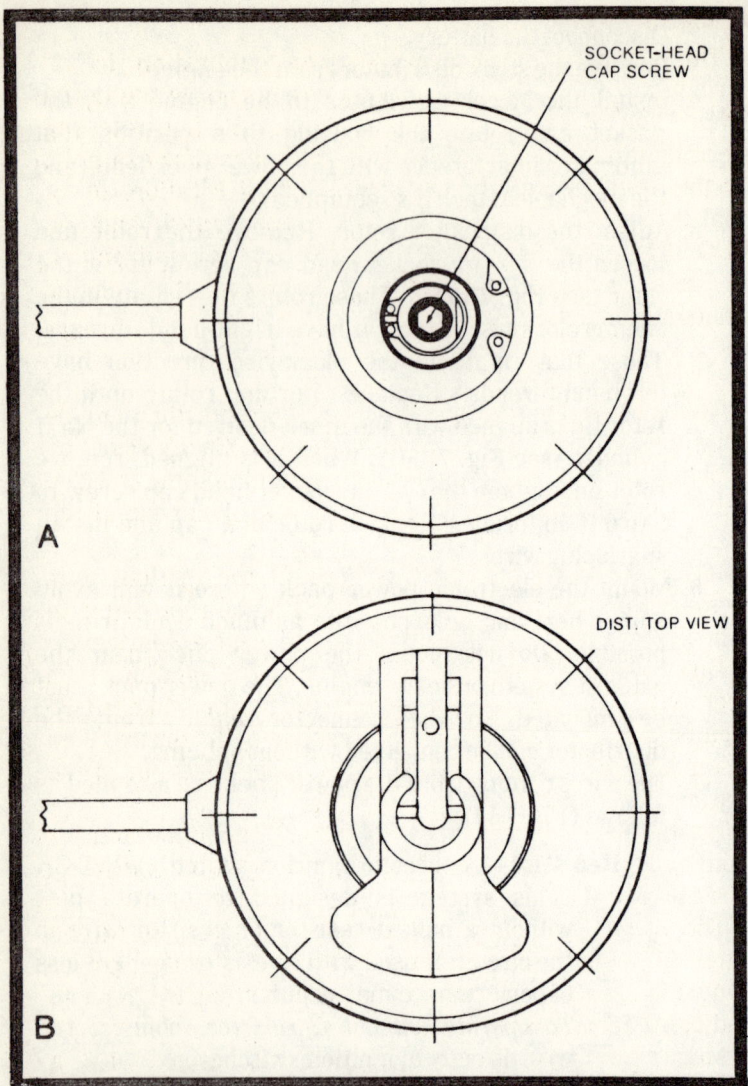

Fig. 7-15. Rotor adjustment of Accel ignition.

cable. Make sure that the connector lugs on the cable line up with the lugs on the power pack terminals (see Fig. 7-14).
9. Reconnect battery.
10. Set ignition timing by rotating the distributor housing while using a standard timing light as for conventional ignition systems.

Mechanical Advance Calibration

The standard mechanical advance calibration is 12° distributor or 24° crankshaft rotation. When setting the initial advance, the total mechanical advance plus the initial setting determines the number of degrees of spark lead. For example, with the standard calibration 24° crankshaft rotation, 10° of initial setting would make 34° total crankshaft spark lead (34° BTDC). The actual lead is determined by engine requirement, and total advance should not exceed the engine manufacturer's specification.

Special Notes for Accel Ignition

To avoid damage to the power pack, do not turn engine over with the spark plug wires disconnected. Check spark by removing coil wire from distributor cap and holding it ¼ in. from ground. When cranking engine to adjust valves, check compression, and so forth. *Disconnect red wire.*

If a steel billet camshaft is used in the engine, it is necessary that the cast-iron distributor gear be replaced with a bronze gear; otherwise, the iron gear will wear excessively.

Due to the high energy developed by the ignition, it is imperative that the spark plug wires be in "like new" condition, as crossfiring and misfiring will occur with substandard plug wires. Also, spark plug wires must be separated from each other.

For peak efficiency of the Accel system, the manufacturer recommends Accel coil No. 140002 for competition and Accel *Super Coil* No. 140001 for street use.

The Accel ignition eliminates spark scatter. If timing scatter still appears on the harmonic balancer during power timing, the timing chain, oil pump, or cam buttons will have to be adjusted to correct the problem.

Many electronic tachometers will not work with a breakerless capacitive-discharge system. Should you desire to use an electronic tachometer, check with your tachometer supplier.

If you are using an RPM limiter with three terminals, connect the normally closed terminal to the (+) wire from the ignition switch and the red wire from the power **pack** to the common terminal of the lmiter.

To take advantage of the increased output energy of the ignition, the spark plugs should be gapped at 0.040 to 0.060 in.

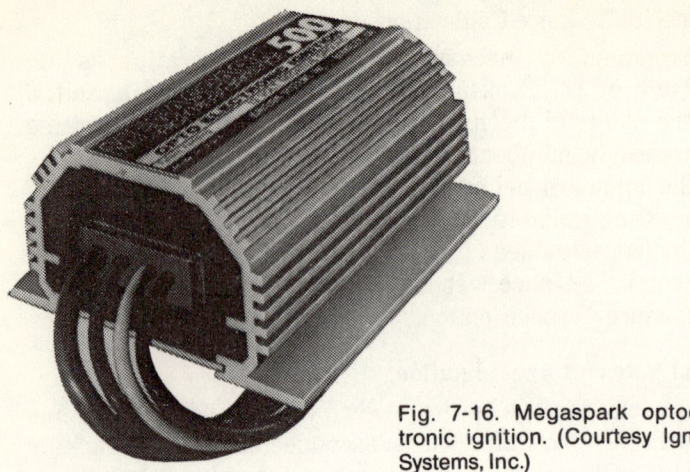

Fig. 7-16. Megaspark optoelectronic ignition. (Courtesy Ignition Systems, Inc.)

MEGASPARK OPTOELECTRONIC BREAKERLESS IGNITION

The *Megaspark* ignition (Fig. 7-16), manufactured by Ignition Systems, Inc., is a light-triggered capacitive-discharge system with output voltage to 50,000V, spark duration of 2000 μsec, and a minimum trigger voltage of 3.5V.

The CD unit consists mainly of a pulse-shaping network controlled by light beam triggering; a monolithic Darlington amplifier with output to the coil primary; and reverse-polarity, transient, open-output, and shorted-output protection circuits. The assembled unit is sealed against moisture and dirt in an extruded aluminum case.

The CD unit is available for 6V or 12V negative- or positive-ground electrical systems. It can be used without the light trigger, using the original points and capacitor of the automobile and serving as a CD *point*-triggered system.

The optical triggering unit for this system is available to fit most American and foreign distributors. The timing disk presses onto and is held in place by the distributor cam. The trigger source is an infrared LED.

Theory of Operation

Basically, the standard automotive ignition and the optoelectronic ignition (Fig. 7-17A) perform the same function: They both switch the current in the primary windings of the ignition coil on and off. The standard ignition does it by means of mechanical breaker points; the *Megaspark* unit does it by means of electronic circuitry and an infrared beam.

The triggering signal that causes the electronic switch to turn on and off is generated by the optical sensor (Fig. 7-17B). As the light-beam control disk (LCD) (Fig. 7-17B) passes through the optical sensor, it causes the infrared beam to be interrupted periodically. The solid portion represents the dwell; the slots represent the firing of the spark plugs.

The aim of the installation is therefore to produce a spark whenever the rotor is pointing at any one of the park plug terminals in the distributor cap. A spark will be produced whenever a slot in the disk is passing through the center of the optical sensor.

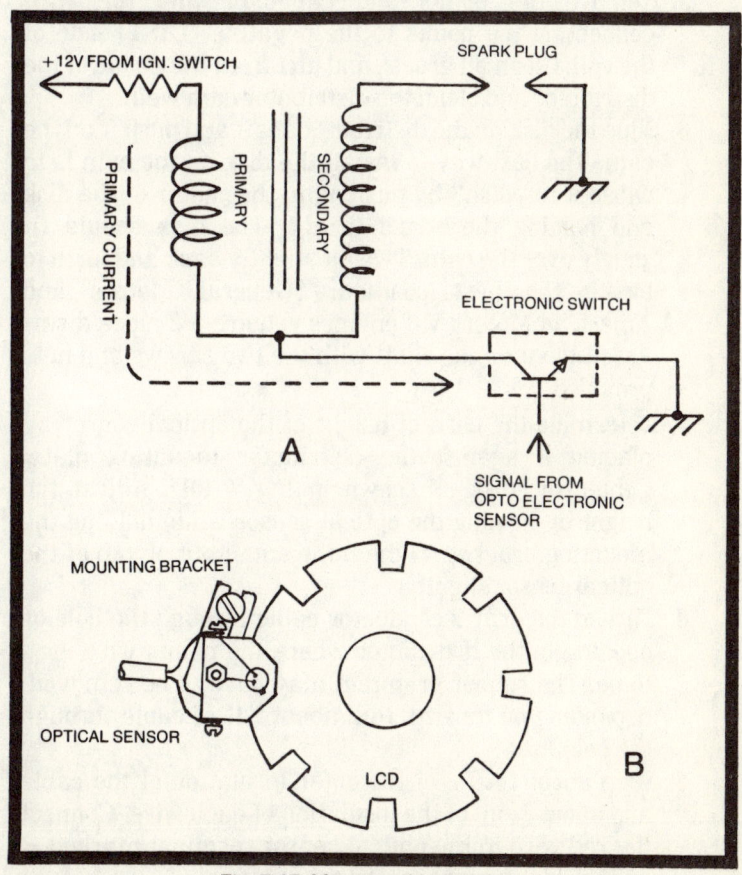

Fig. 7-17. Megaspark operation.

Installation of the Megaspark System

1. Using a soft pencil, felt tip pen, or scribe, make a line on the distributor body (not on the cap) directly below the center of any spark plug terminal (Fig. 7-18A).
2. Remove the distributor cap.
3. Crank the engine until the rotor is pointing exactly at the line drawn in step 1 (see Fig. 7-18B).
4. Remove the rotor. Locate the disk supplied with your unit and make a preliminary visual inspection to determine if it will fit your distributor. The disk should slip over the distributor shaft and fit snugly over the cam. Do not install the disk at this time. (If the disk does not fit the distributor cam, it must be exchanged for the correct one.)
5. Remove the points and capacitor and the wire connecting the points to the negative (DIST) side of the coil. Clean all grease and dirt from the inside of the distributor and clean the distributor cam well.
6. Slide the disk on the distributor shaft and push it on the cam. The best way to install the disk on the cam is to cause it to "dish" by pushing in the center of the disk and holding the edges firmly. The disk should fit snugly over the cam. Twist it slightly back and forth to locate the best position. (General Motors and American Motors V-8 engines require a 2-piece disk.) Assemble it on the shaft with the two screws and nuts provided.
7. Determine the correct height of the optical sensor by placing it against the distributor mounting plate. Center the disk as shown in Fig. 7-18D. Adjust the height by turning the optical sensor while holding the mounting bracket. Tighten the small nut on top of the optical sensor slightly.
8. Thread the gray 2-conductor cable through the hole or opening in the distributor where the points wire used to be. The rubber grommet may have to be removed, depending on its size. Pull about 2 ft of cable through the hole.
9. Strip about 1¼ in. of the outer insulation of the cable and about ⅜ in. of the insulation of each wire. Connect the red wire to the optical sensor terminal marked R and the black wire to the other terminal.

10. Mount the optical sensor in the distributor, using one of the screws that previously held the points. The disk should be placed in position at the same time. On some small distributors it will be necessary to insert the disk and optical sensor simultaneously.

The exact location of the optical sensor is not important; that is, there may be more than one possible position. What is important, however, is the relative position of the rotor to the optical sensor and a slot in the disk. The optical sensor should be mounted in such a way that a slot in the disk is centered through the optical sensor as the rotor is pointing at any spark plug terminal. (The rotor was previously adjusted in step 3.) Make sure the disk is positioned as shown in Fig. 7-18D. Crank engine to check that all clearances are satisfactory.

11. Make sure the ground wire—usually a bare copper braid that used to ground the points or distributor plate—is solidly grounded inside the distributor.
12. Replace the rotor and distributor cap. Make sure the rotor does not interfere with the optical sensor.
13. Mount the *Megaspark* unit inside the engine compartment, making sure the wires will reach the coil. Mount the unit as far as practicable from the exhaust manifold.
14. Connect the black wire to a solid ground, such as a water pump screw, thermostat housing screw, or any other suitable place. *Do not loosen head screws.*
15. (Perform for models 500 and 400 only.) Connect the red wire to the positive side of the coil, where the ignition switch connects. Connect the yellow wire to the negative side of the coil, where the points lead was connected. (See Fig. 7-18E.)
16. (Perform for model 300 only.) Connect the red wire to the battery–ignition lead (Fig. 7-18F). Connect the white wire to the place where the points lead was connected. If the CD unit is equipped with a changeover switch, the *Megaspark 300* will not operate when the CD unit is switched for standard operation.

Starting Engine

Crank the engine. If it does not start, rotate the distributor in either direction until the engine starts. If the engine still

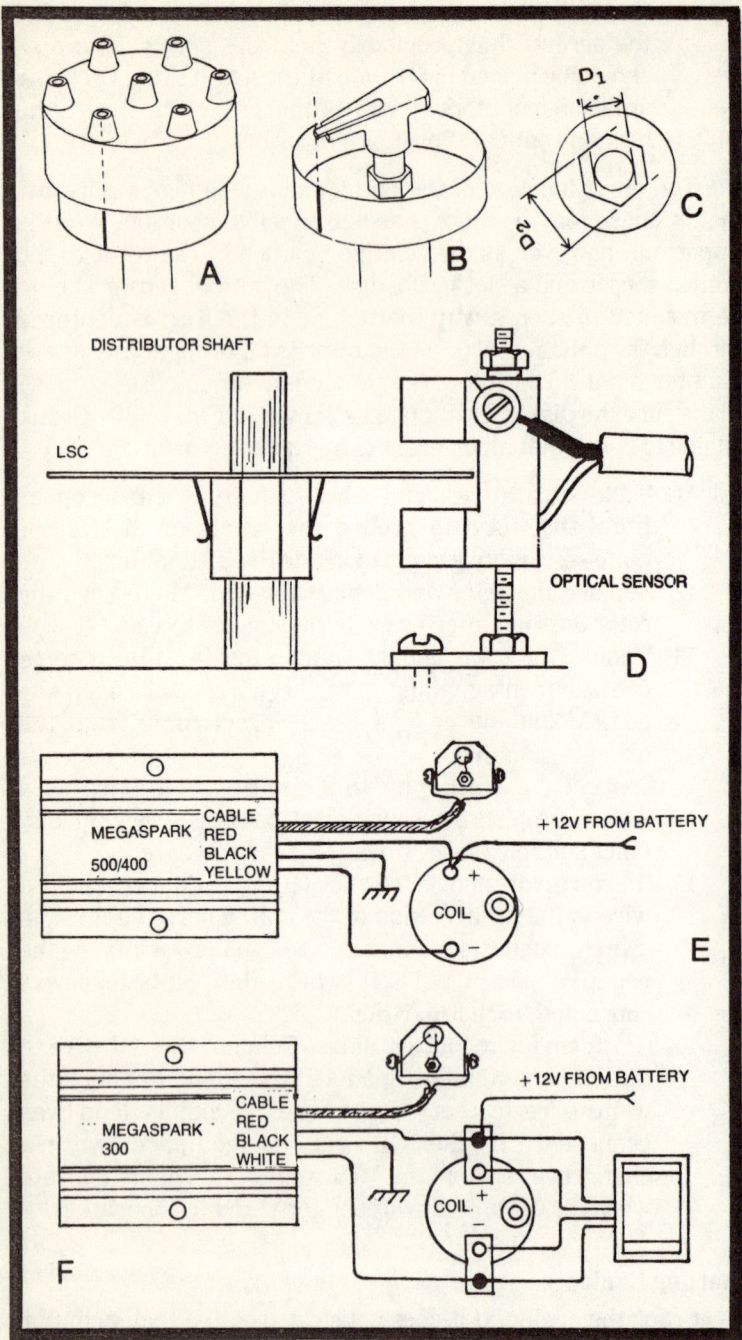

Fig. 7-18. Megaspark installation.

refuses to start, check for spark by removing the center wire from the distributor cap, placing it close to a good ground, and cranking the engine. If a spark is produced but the engine will not start, the position of the optical sensor is incorrect. After the engine is started, it should be timed in the conventional way.

Special Notes

For Honda Civic, Subaru, and certain Datsun installations with small distributors, the following procedure will insure adequate clearance between the rotor and sensor. If you suspect spark leakage to the sensor mounting screw, cover the top of the sensor with some good insulating material.

1. Cut off the top of the screw on which the optical sensor is mounted once the height of the sensor is correct.
2. File the nut on top of the screw on which the optical sensor is mounted to about one-half its present thickness.
3. File about 1/4 in. from the underside of the distributor rotor arm, but do not expose the underside of the metal portion of the arm. If you suspect spark leakage to the sensor mounting screw, cover the top of the sensor with some good insulating material.

PIRANHA ELECTRONIC IGNITION

The Piranha ignition uses a photocell light-pulsing unit and a scanning disk (Fig. 7-19) to energize the primary circuit of

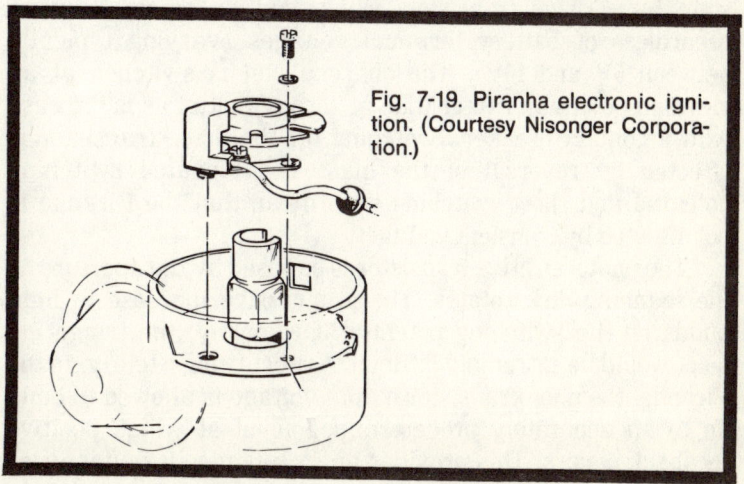

Fig. 7-19. Piranha electronic ignition. (Courtesy Nisonger Corporation.)

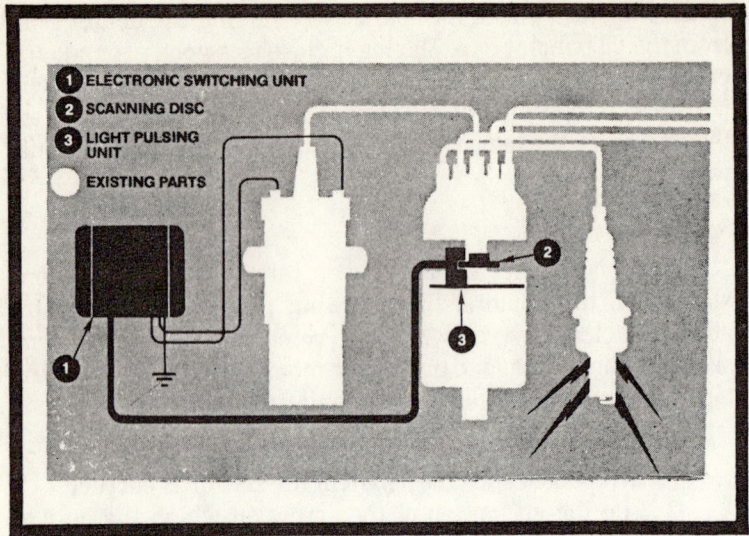

Fig. 7-20. Piranha wiring diagram.

the coil. Also included in the kit is an electronic switching module. The Piranha is manufactured in England and distributed in this country by Nisonger Corporation. It uses the car's existing ignition system, eliminating only the points, capacitor, and primary wiring from the coil. Kits are manufactured for both 4- and 6-cylinder engines.

A simplified installation diagram is shown in Fig. 7-20. The contact points are replaced by a high-speed optically pulsed electronic switch. The ignition coil is held in the energized state by a drive transistor, which can be biased fully on regardless of battery terminal voltages (varying typically between 6V and 16V). The charged coil is switched at an elevated potential, rather than at zero potential as is the case with a contact breaker. Switching off the drive transistor is effected by reversal of the bias. The elevated switching potential and short switching time mean that the Piranha is not affected by transient voltages.

The photosensitive transistor is exposed by the aperture as the scanning disk rotates. The progressive increase in light builds up the switching potential. Ordinarily, the triggering point would be extremely difficult to repeat consistently. In the Piranha, the phototransistor output voltage is allowed to build up to an accurately predetermined level at which positive feedback occurs. This provides an instantaneous voltage rise that switches the drive transistor off, insuring minimal leakage from the primary of the coil.

When the power transistor is fully conducting, there is a voltage drop across it of approximately 1V. However, the speed of switching not only compensates for this but has been accurately measured to produce 40,000V at the secondary of a standard ignition coil with an engine speed of 3000 RPM.

Installation Instructions

The following procedure applies specifically to certain Lucas distributors but can be adapted to the other distributors the Piranha ignition is made for. Refer to Fig. 7-21 as you perform the steps.

1. Unclip the two distributor cap retaining clips and remove the distributor cap, leaving the plug and coil leads attached.
2. Remove the rotor arm (A). This will be required again.
3. Remove the two screws (B). These may be required again.
4. Lift the vacuum advance-retard spring (C) from the breaker plate pin.
5. Remove the contact breaker wire (N) from the grommet (E). This wire will be connected to the Piranha yellow wire during the installation.
6. Disengage the grommet (E).
7. Remove the contact breaker plate (D) and the grommet (E). These should be kept with the vehicle for reinstallation if required.
8. Take a screwdriver and insert the blade in the camshaft so that it engages the screw within. Hold the screwdriver firmly to prevent the gear backlash from having any effect and advance the cam in the direction the distributor rotates. When the cam is fully rotated and released, it should return swiftly to its original position. If it does not rotate, the counterweights are seized. If it returns slowly or not at all to its original position, the counterweight springs should be replaced.
9. Insert a pointed tool in the vacuum spring loop and pull. The spring should expand, offering resistance to the pull, and should then retract on release.

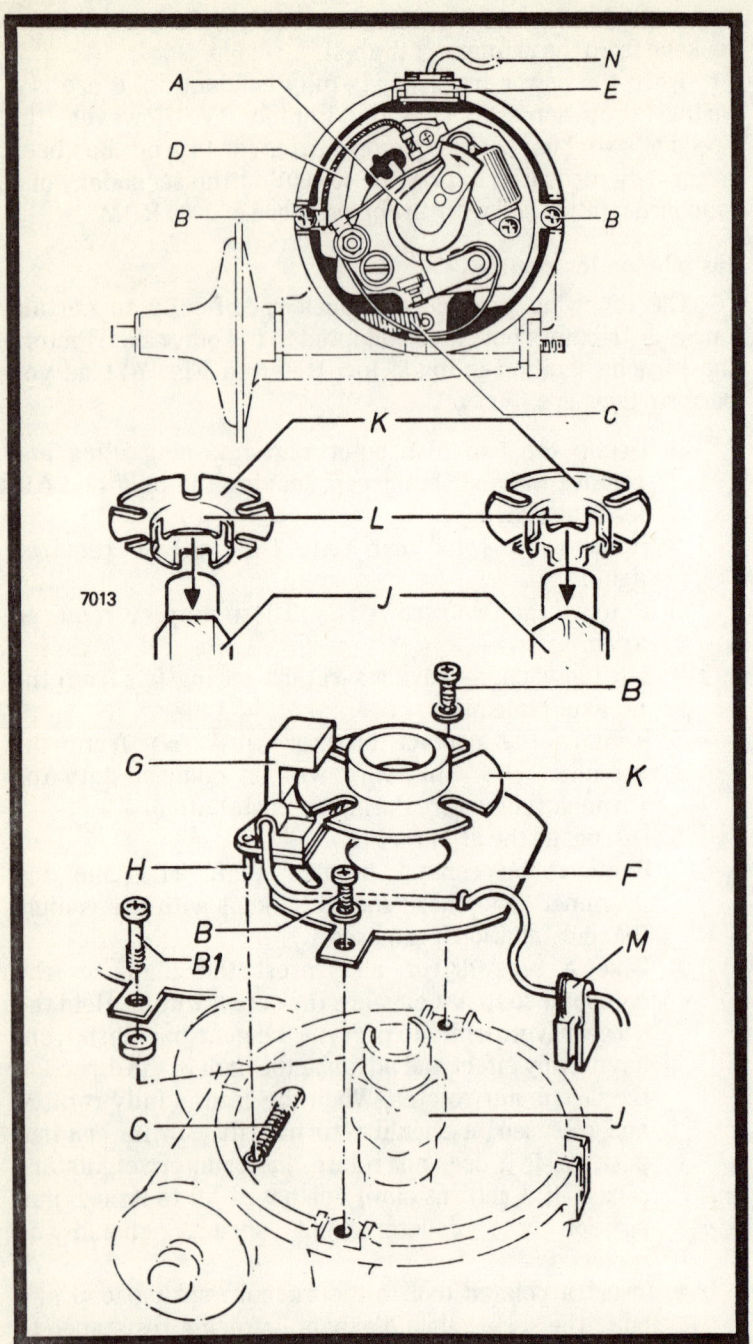

Fig. 7-21. Original distributor parts (top) and Piranha parts (bottom).

10. Examine the distributor cap and rotor arm for cracks or corrosion, which, if present, will cause the extra energy generated by the Piranha to track, producing misfiring or even stopping the engine.
11. Examine the vacuum hose for leaks. If the vacuum system is not operating correctly, poor fuel economy will result.
12. Check to see that the kit has the correct scanning disk. To check the fit of the scanning disk (K), push it onto the cam (J). There are two ways for disk 7001 to go on. The correct way is for the castellations to grip the cam angles. Once fully home the disk should be a tight fit, allowing no movement relative to the cam. If the disk is too tight to go on, it should be placed in a solution of salt water, brought to a boil, and fitted while hot.
13. Check that the lamp housing (G) is free to move on its base plate (F) along the crescent-shaped slot. The two retaining nuts are preset and sealed. It is important that the screws are not loosened, as damage may result.
14. Hold the base plate (F) over the distributor body and align the lamp housing (G) so that the pin (H) is approximately in line with the advance-retard spring (C).
15. Remove the scanning disk (K) from the cam (J) and place the rim in the mouth of the lamp housing (G). Keeping it parallel to the base plate (F), lower them both over the cam (J) until both are firmly seated. Insure that the pin (H) engages the advance-retard spring (C).
16. Check that the scanning disk does not touch either of the lamps in the lamp housing. If fouling can occur, the base plate height must be adjusted. Two tapped pillars and undercut screws ($B1$) are provided for this purpose. To avoid the pillars dropping into the distributor well, they should be threaded to the screws under the plate before installation.
17. Replace the two screws (B) or the screws and pillars ($B1$) and tighten.
18. Secure the grommet in its slot.
19. Insure that the trigger lead is clear of the scanning disk.

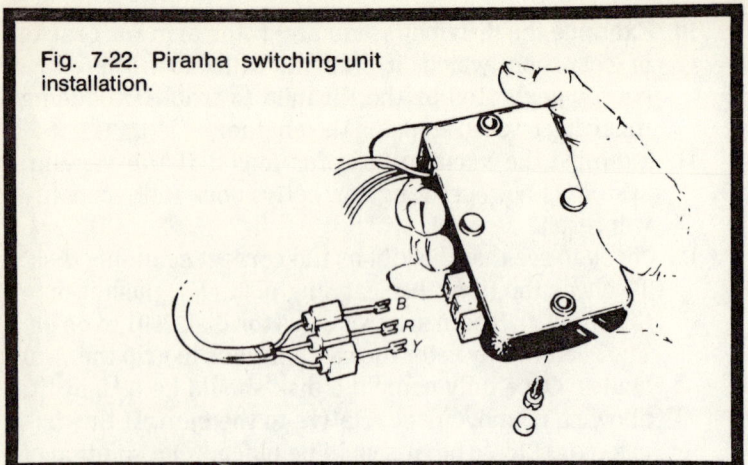

Fig. 7-22. Piranha switching-unit installation.

20. Replace the rotor arm (*A*).
21. Replace the distributor cap, lock the spring clips, and insure that all wires are securely anchored in the cap.
22. To select a suitable mounting site for the Piranha switching unit, leave slack in the trigger wire to allow for engine movement. Then drill two holes at appropriate centers and affix the unit with two screws.
23. Take the switching unit in one hand and use a screwdriver to push out the two screw stops. (Fig. 7-22.)
24. Thread the three boots onto the trigger wire terminals and connect the terminals to plug positions R , Y, and B. The red-black wire goes to the R terminal, the yellow wire to Y , and the blue wire to B . Insure that the terminals are fully home, and push the boots onto the terminal blocks (Fig. 7-22).
25. Turn the unit over, screw it to the body, and push the screw stops back in place.
26. To secure the trigger wire, drill a hole so that the terminals are insulated from vibration when the P-clip is secured. If the same hole is a suitable position for affixing the ground terminal, scrape the paint from the body metal and place the ground terminal (blue wire) directly on the metal. (See Fig. 7-23.)
27. The yellow and red leads should then be suitably connected. Any connection made to these two wires must be insulated to prevent leakage or shorting.

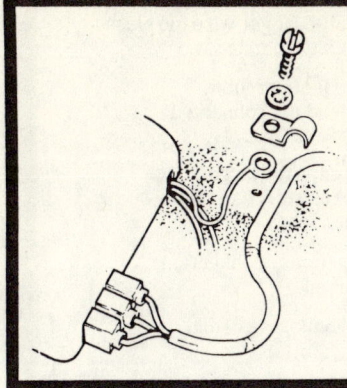

Fig. 7-23. Securing trigger wire on Piranha ignition.

28. It is not possible to time the Piranha by using the car maker's static or dwell figures. Nor should it be set stroboscopically at low engine speeds. This is because the loss of friction previously exerted on the cam by the contact breaker causes the undertensioned counterweight spring to give erratic readings under 1500 RPM. Therefore, to time correctly, disconnect the vacuum hoses and set the timing against the manufacturer's advance figures for some engine speed *above* 1500 RPM. Reconnect the vacuum hoses after timing.

Engine Malfunctions and Causes

Symptoms	Possible Causes
Poor starting.	1. Red lead not connected directly to 12V supply. 2. Inadequate ground. 3. Radio suppression capacitor connected to wrong side of coil. 4. Vacuum spring not operating. 5. Lamp housing advance mechanism stuck. 6. Timing too far advanced. 7. High resistance in ignition leads. 8. Ignition switch failing.
Engine starting on release of key only.	1. Ignition switch failing. 2. Red lead connected to circuit cut out when starter energized. 3. Red lead connected to wrong side of ballast resistor.

Symptoms	Possible Causes
Poor starting and misfiring in damp conditions.	1. Piranha trigger wire too close to high-tension leads.
Misfiring when electrical accessories on.	1. Inadequate ground. 2. Red lead not connected directly to 12V supply.
Misfiring under load.	1. Plug gaps too large. 2. High resistance in high-tension leads.
Misfiring at high RPM.	1. Coil primary connections reversed.
Engine stopping after ignition key released from start.	1. Open ballast resistor.
Engine cutting out after 2 or 3 miles.	1. Hairline crack in distributor cap or rotor arm.
Complete engine cutout at intervals.	1. Coil terminals loose.
Engine will not reach high RPM.	1. Scanning disk fouling lamps in lamp holder. 2. Counterweights seized. 3. Timing incorrect.
Poor performance below 3000 RPM.	1. Counterweight springs not functioning.
Preignition.	1. Ignition idling speed too high.
Poor fuel economy.	1. Timing retarded. 2. Vacuum system not operating properly. 3. Lamp holder mechanism (advance) jammed.
Radio interference.	1. Poor ground. 2. High-tension leads leaking to ground.

Note: For optimum performance with this ignition system, use spark plugs of the heat range recommended by the engine or plug manufacturer. Set the gap to the plug manufacturer's specifications.

BORG-WARNER ELECTRONIC IGNITION

The Borg-Warner electronic ignition kit (Fig. 7-24) consists of just four easily installed parts, and is designed to replace the ignition systems of most domestic cars and trucks. It is available for both 6- and 8-cylinder applications. This light triggered system uses the original engine coil and distributor; only the contact points and capacitor are discarded.

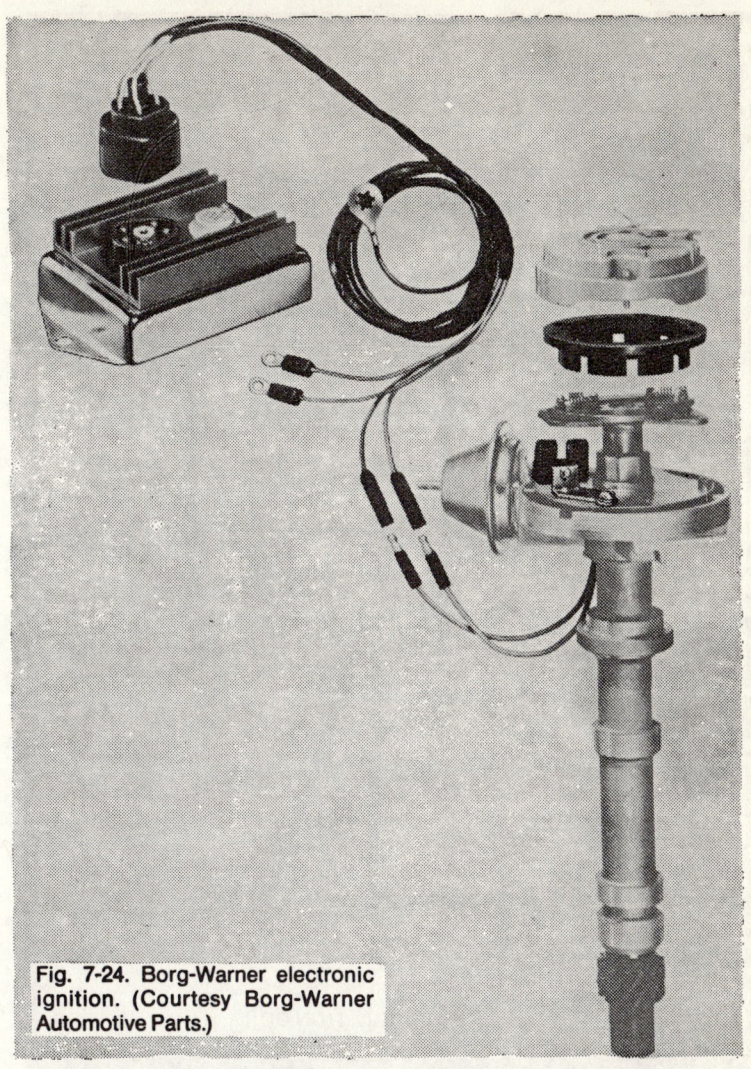

Fig. 7-24. Borg-Warner electronic ignition. (Courtesy Borg-Warner Automotive Parts.)

The triggering, or signaling device, consists of an infrared LED and a phototransistor receiver mounted on the distributor plate. The light chopper rotates with the distributor shaft, and its blades pass between the infrared sending unit and phototransistor receiver. As each opening between the chopper blades passes the sending unit, a signal is sent to the power-switching transistor in the solid-state control box.

On receiving this signal, the control box breaks the coil's ground connection to interrupt the current in the primary

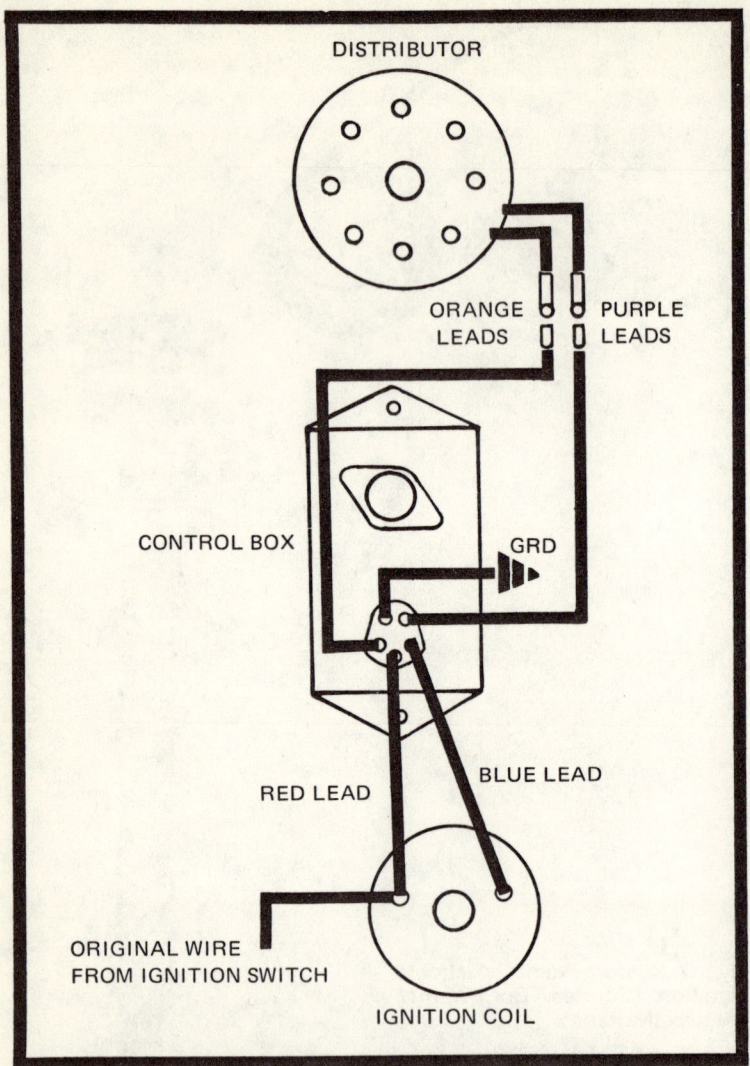

Fig. 7-25. Wiring diagram of Borg-Warner electronic ignition.

winding. This induces a high voltage in the secondary winding to fire the spark plugs. The length of time the primary is broken is determined by the slot width of the chopper. The dwell is built into the chopper and is always correct.

Installing the Borg-Warner Ignition

The installation procedures are very similar for all makes of distributors, so only the procedure for the 8-cylinder

Delco Remy distributor will be given here. Refer to the wiring diagram of Fig. 7-25 and perform the installation steps in the following order.

1. Remove distributor cap. Check for cracks or burnt electrodes; replace if necessary.
2. Remove rotor holddown screws and remove rotor. Check for burnt or oxidized contacts; replace if necessary. Discard old holddown screws and use new screws and flat washers supplied for reassembling.
3. Disconnect distributor lead from contact points. It may be necessary to crank engine to position centrifugal advance to permit removing holddown screws. Remove capacitor and bracket screw.
4. Remove distributor lead from negative terminal on the ignition coil and pull it out of distributor completely.
5. Insert orange and purple wires individually through distributor housing hole.
6. Position trigger light on base plate of distributor. *Do not* align trigger light in its proper place at this time.
7. Slide light chopper at least halfway over centrifugal advance mechanism and align the light chopper in the opening on trigger light (Fig. 7-26). Let light chopper fall over centrifugal advance mechanism and lay on base of distributor.
8. Position trigger light into place previously occupied by contact set and replace and tighten holddown screws.

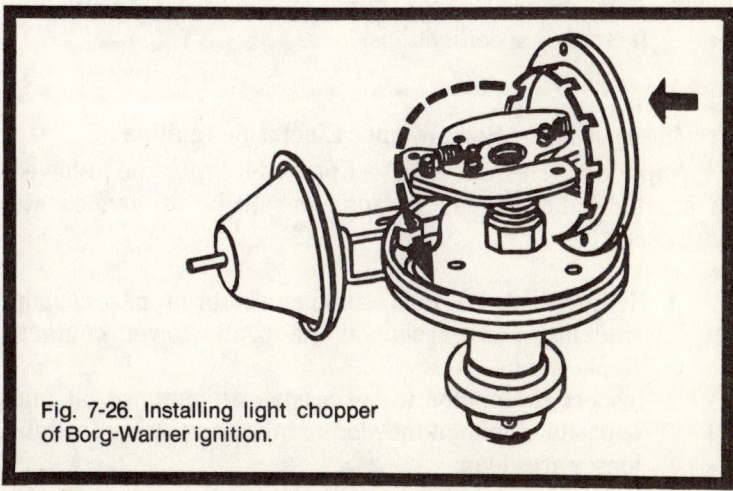

Fig. 7-26. Installing light chopper of Borg-Warner ignition.

9. Using a good rotor, position it into its proper place. Insert two screws and flatwashers provided in package. Lift light chopper up and align screw holes to rotor holddown screws.

    Important: Visually check to insure that light chopper is seated inside of rotor skirt. Then tighten screws, *but do not overtighten.*
10. Before reinstalling a good distributor cap, make sure that an ample amount of wire is provided to allow the vacuum advance chamber to work freely. Position rubber grommet in distributor housing.
11. Install a good distributor cap.
12. Before mounting control box, make sure wire harness will reach from distributor leads to control box location, and that it is subjected to the least amount of heat possible. A fender well may be best suited for this location.
13. Drill mounting holes and mount control box with screws provided.
14. Plug wire harness into control box, insert screw provided, and tighten.
15. Connect orange wires together and purple wires together. Connect black wire to good body ground. Connect red wire to positive terminal on coil. Make sure that original source of battery voltage is also still on this terminal (see Fig. 7-25). Connect blue wire to negative terminal on coil.
16. Start engine, check timing, and reset to manufacturer's specifications.

Troubleshooting the Borg-Warner Electronic Ignition

Important: The following test procedure must be followed in order. Failure to do so may result in an inaccurate diagnosis.

1. Remove distributor cap and inspect for cracks, carbon tracking, and carbon on the center-tower contact. Replace if necessary.
2. Inspect distributor for excessive amounts of oil and deposits. Clean if needed. Make sure trigger light lenses are clean.

3. Inspect light chopper for any gashes or knicks on the opening of the chopper slots. If any damage is noticed, replace light chopper.
4. Check battery voltage at battery and connections. Make mental note of battery voltage.
5. Check wiring diagram to make sure system is properly wired.
6. Using an ohmmeter, make sure control box or black ground lead is securely grounded. If it's not, ground it.
7. Disconnect orange and purple wires at bullet connectors. Remove coil wire from center of distributor cap and place it about ¼ in. away from a good engine ground. Turn ignition switch to ON position. Using a jumper wire, jump the orange and purple wires at the female ends of the bullet connectors intermittently. If spark jumps from the coil wire to ground, replace trigger light. If no spark occurs, insert coil wire in distributor cap and proceed with step 8.
8. Using a voltmeter, check available voltage at purple female bullet connector coming from wiring harness (Fig. 7-27A). If a zero voltage reading is obtained, proceed with step 9. If approximately one-half of the battery voltage reading is obtained, proceed with step 11. If normal battery voltage reading is obtained, proceed with step 12.
9. With ignition in ON position , use a voltmeter to check available voltage at positive, or battery, terminal of the coil (Fig. 7-27B). Red wire should be on this terminal. If a zero voltage reading is obtained, proceed with step 15. If approximately one-half of battery voltage reading is obtained, proceed with step 10. If normal battery voltage reading is obtained, replace wire harness.
10. Remove wire harness plug from control box and turn ignition switch to ON position. Use voltmeter to read voltage at red-wire cavity on wire harness (Fig. 7-27C). If a zero voltage reading is obtained, replace wire harness. If normal battery voltage reading is obtained, proceed with step 14. Turn ignition switch off, plug wire harness back in, and tighten down.

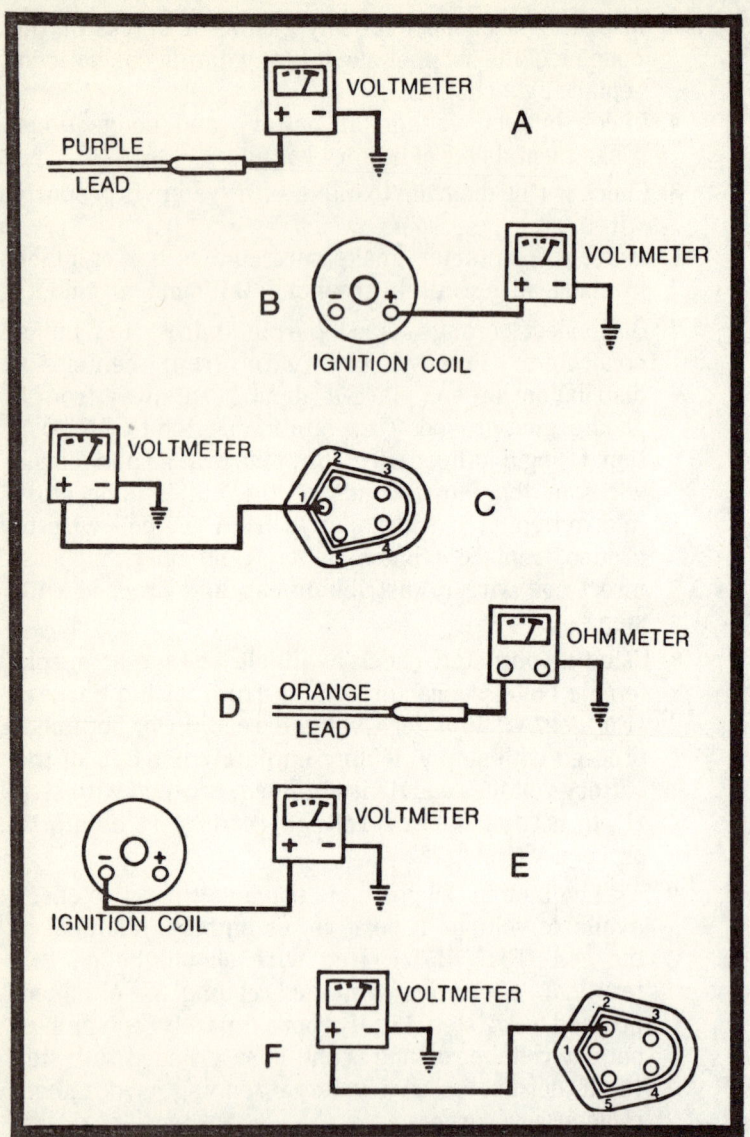

Fig. 7-27. Voltmeter checks of Borg-Warner ignition, discussed in text.

11. When doing this step, make sure that ignition switch is off. Using an ohmmeter, check resistance at orange female bullet connector coming from wire harness (Fig. 7-27D). Normal reading is about 2500 ohms. If a zero reading is obtained, replace control box. If an open-circuit reading is obtained, replace wire harness.

12. Turn ignition switch to ON position. Using a voltmeter, check available voltage at negative terminal of coil (Fig. 7-27E). If battery voltage reading is obtained, proceed with step 13. If near zero voltage reading is obtained, turn ignition switch off and replace coil.
13. Remove wire harness plug from control box and turn ignition switch to ON position. Using a voltmeter, check available voltage at blue-wire cavity on wire harness (Fig. 7-27F). If battery voltage reading is obtained, replace control box. If zero voltage reading is obtained, replace wire harness. Turn ignition switch to OFF.
14. When doing this step, make sure ignition switch is off. Using an ohmmeter, check resistance at purple female connector coming from wire harness (Fig. 7-27A). Normal reading is about 250 ohms. If zero resistance is read, replace control box. If an open-circuit reading is obtained, replace wire harness.
15. Remove wire harness plug from control box. Turn ignition switch to ON position and check voltage at positive terminal at coil (Fig. 7-27B). If battery voltage reading is obtained, replace control box. If zero voltage reading is obtained, check ballast resistor or ignition switch wire, using normal procedures. Turn ignition switch off, plug wire harness back in, and tighten down.

For optimum performance with this or any transistor ignition system, spark plugs of the correct heat range and gapped to manufacturer's specifications must be used.

ALLISON OPTOELECTRONIC SYSTEM

This breakerless electronic ignition kit (Fig. 7-28), made by Allison Automotive Company is available for passenger cars, light trucks, boats, and industrial engines. The triggering unit can be used to fire most any CD ignition system.

The Allison triggering unit utilizes an infrared LED and a phototransistor installed in the distributor (Fig. 7-29) to control a transistor amplifier, which in turn loads and fires the original coil of the vehicle. The triggering unit consists of a control rotor, detector, and small power module to which the point lead of the CD unit or negative coil lead of the conventional ignition is connected.

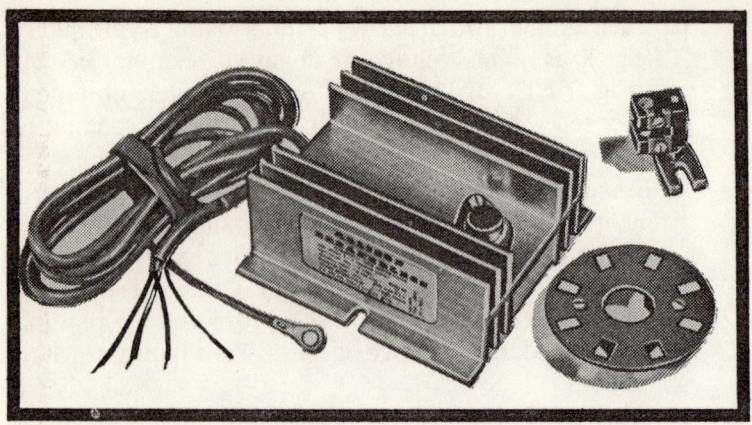

Fig. 7-28. Allison optoelectronic ignition system. (Courtesy Allison Automotive Company.)

The circuit of the Allison system is shown in Fig. 7-30. Capacitor *1*, in parallel with zener *2*, acts to limit and suppress spikes and transients in the incoming line voltage. Together with resistor *3* and transistor *4*, they function as a regulated

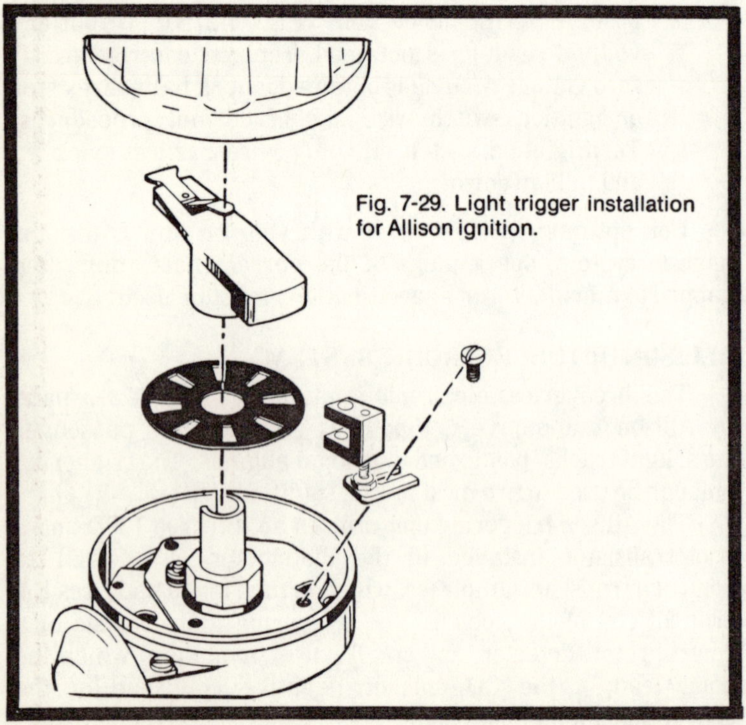

Fig. 7-29. Light trigger installation for Allison ignition.

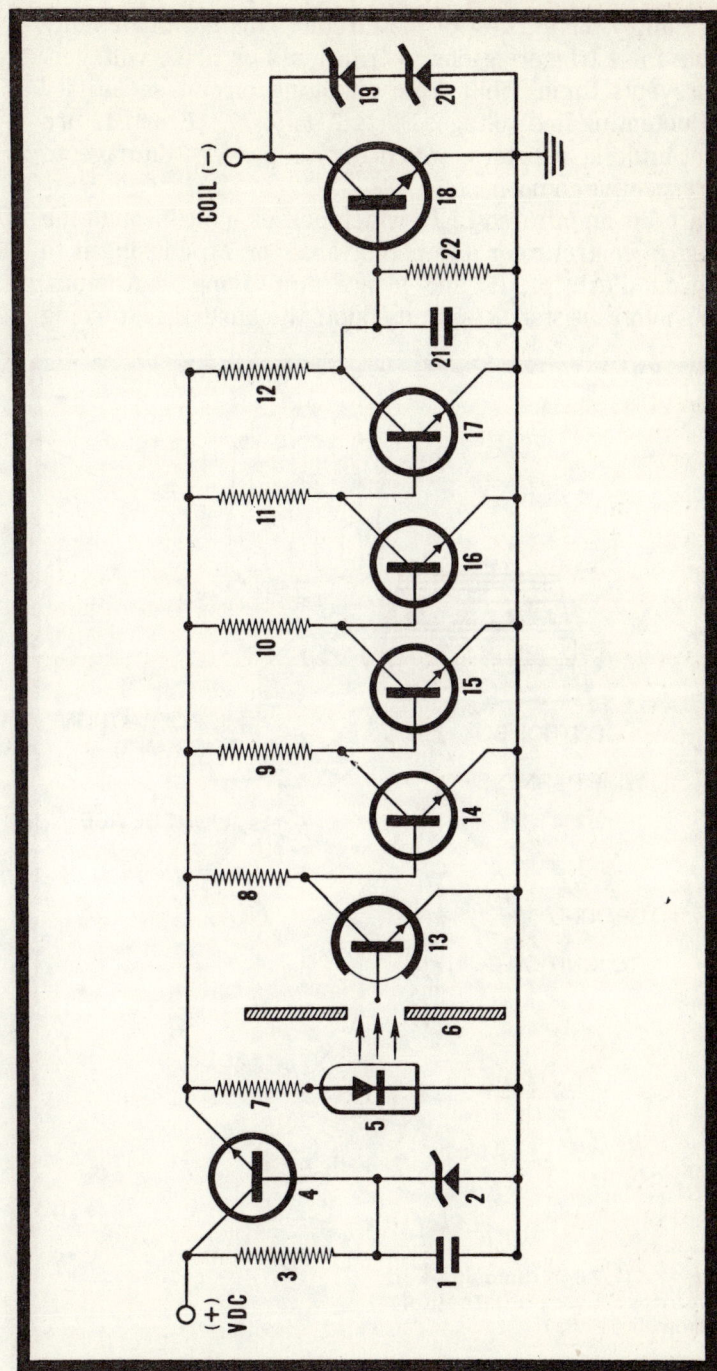

Fig. 7-30. Circuit of Allison optoelectronic ignition system.

power supply for the rest of the circuit. This eliminates any possible false triggering due to transients or noise voltages, and prevents timing shift from changing circuit sensitivity with fluctuating line voltage. Parts 7, 8, 9, 10, 11, and 12 are current-limiting resistors, which act to prevent damage to their respective components.

Part 5 is an infrared LED, which passes light through the opening in control rotor 6 to phototransistor 13, causing it to switch on. Parts 14, 15, and 16 are amplifying transistors. When phototransistor 13 is on, it shunts the base of 14, turning

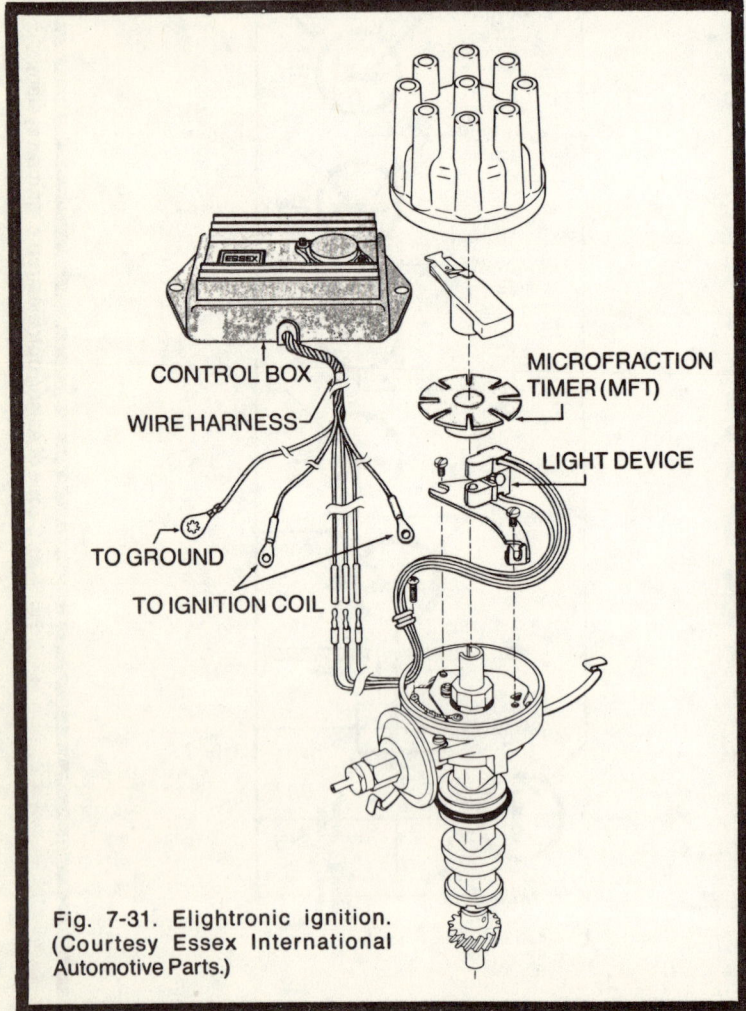

Fig. 7-31. Elightronic ignition. (Courtesy Essex International Automotive Parts.)

it off. The base of *15* is no longer shunted, and it comes on, turning *16* off. This turns driver transistor *17* on, shunting the final transistor, *18*, off. This stops the flow of current in the coil primary extremely fast, causing a very high induced voltage on the primary. This, in turn, causes a much higher than normal secondary voltage to be delivered to the spark plug.

Parts *19* and *20* are zeners, which protect power transistor *18* from damage by voltage spikes. Part *22* is a base—emitter resistor, which aids in fast switching and increases the voltage rating of power transistor *18*. Capacitor *21* prevents noise from entering the circuit through radiation across the collector—base junction of power transistor *18*.

ESSEX ELIGHTRONIC IGNITION

The *Elightronic* ignition system, manufactured by Essex International, consists of a light device, a control box with a wire harness, and what is called a *microfractional timer* (MFT). It can be fitted on most vehicles having a conventional single-point ignition system without removing or replacing the original distributor or ignition coil. Figure 7-31 shows how this works with a Ford 8-cylinder engine.

This system, triggered by an infrared LED and phototransistor receiver, utilizes the stock coil, ballast resistor, cap, and rotor. Dwell is fixed by the width of the slots of the MFT and cannot get out of adjustment. Installation of the *Elightronic* system is quite easy and very similar for all makes of distributors.

Elightronic Installation

Refer to the wiring diagram of Fig. 7-32 for connections and follow this procedure.

1. Remove distributor cap. Check for cracks or burnt electrodes and replace if necessary.
2. Remove rotor and check for burnt electrodes or oxidized contacts. Replace if necessary.
3. Remove distributor lead from negative terminal on ignition coil and pull it out of distributor completely.
4. Remove points and capacitor and relocate braided ground strap to capacitor mounting hole, using capacitor mounting screw.
5. Take light device and insert orange, purple, and black wires individually through the distributor housing hole.

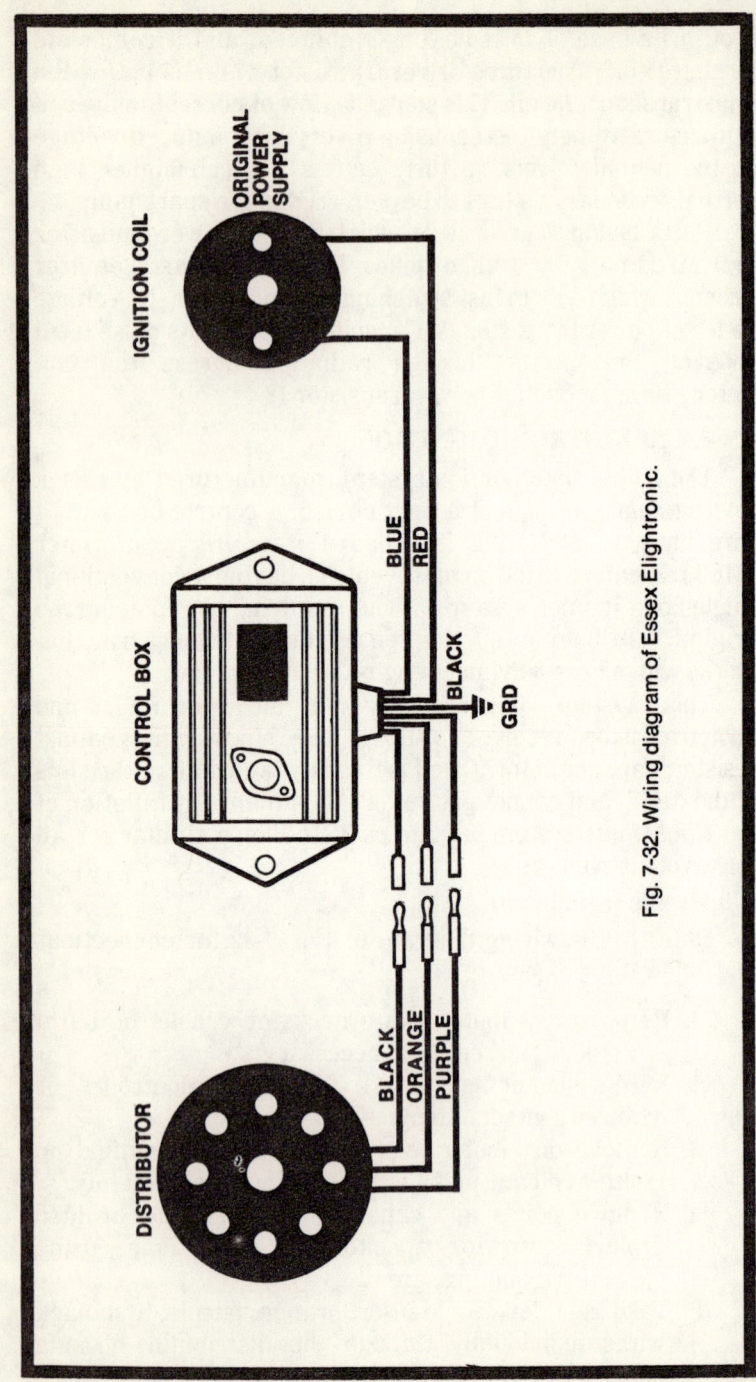

Fig. 7-32. Wiring diagram of Essex Elightronic.

6. Place MFT over distributor cam and rotate MFT until you feel index to cam. Push MFT about one-third of the way down on the distributor cam.
7. Replace point holddown screws about one or two turns into the holddown plate.
8. Slide light device onto MFT so that its opening straddles the MFT. Position light device on base plate of distributor in place previously occupied by contact set.
9. Push MFT down on distributor shaft until it bottoms. Visually check to insure that MFT clears both top and bottom of the light device. Now tighten screws.
10. Before installing a good distributor cap, make sure that an ample amount of wire is provided to allow the vacuum advance chamber to work freely. Position rubber grommet in distributor housing. Also make sure that the orange, purple, and black wires are in the light device bracket.
11. Install a good rotor.
12. Install a good distributor cap.
13. Make a bright area for the control box to contact ground.
14. Before mounting control box, make sure wire harness will reach to distributor leads and that it is subjected to the least amount of heat. A fender well may be the best location. Drill two 1/8 in. holes, using the control box as a template.
15. Mount control box with screws provided.
16. Connect orange wires together, purple wires together, and black wires together. Connect black wires to good engine ground. Connect remaining red wire to battery terminal on the coil. Make sure that the original source of battery voltage is also on this terminal.
17. Connect blue wire to negative (distributor) terminal on coil.
18. Start engine, check timing, and reset to manufacturer's specifications.

For maximum performance, check the condition of all spark plug wires and spark plugs, and replace as necessary.

Troubleshooting The Essex Elightronic Ignition

The following test steps must be followed in order. Failure to do so may result in an inaccurate diagnosis.

1. Check wiring diagram to be sure system is properly wired.
2. Check battery voltage at battery and battery connections. Make mental note of battery voltage.
3. Remove distributor cap. Inspect for cracks, carbon tracking, and carbon on center-tower contact. Replace if necessary.
4. Inspect distributor for excessive oil and deposits. Clean if necessary. Make sure light device lenses are clean.
5. Inspect MFT for any gashes or nicks in the slots. If any damage is noticed, replace the MFT.
6. Make sure that black ground lead is securely grounded to engine. If it is not, ground it.
7. With purple leads separated and still connected, use voltmeter to check voltage to ground (Fig. 7-33A). If approximate battery voltage is read, replace both light device and control box at the same time.
8. Disconnect orange and purple wires at bullet connectors. Remove coil wire from center of cap and place it about ¼ in. away from a good engine ground. Turn ignition switch to ON. Using a jumper wire, intermittently jump the orange and purple wires together at the female ends of the bullet connectors. If spark jumps from coil wire to ground, replace light

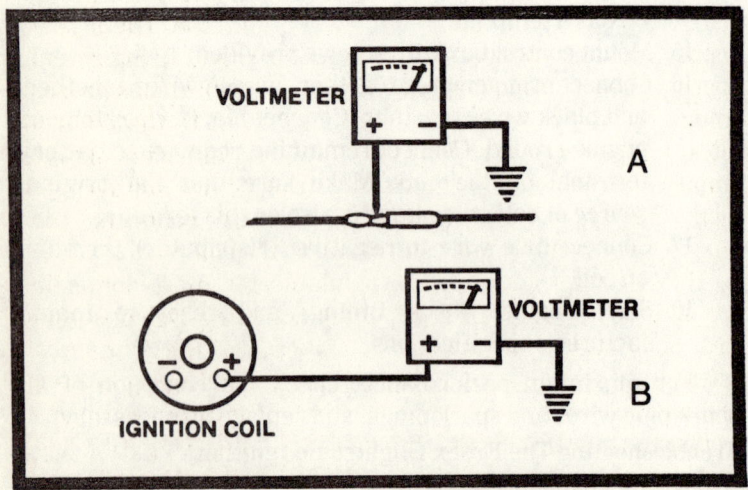

Fig. 7-33. Elightronic voltage checks.

device. If no spark occurs, insert coil wire in distributor cap and proceed with step 9.
9. With ignition switch off, check ballast resistor and coil.
10. With ignition switch on, use voltmeter to check for voltage at positive side of coil (Fig. 7-33B). If voltage reading is approximately one-half of full battery voltage, replace the control box.

SORENSEN MAGNITION IGNITION SYSTEM

The Sorensen *Magnition* (Fig. 7-34) differs from other transistor ignition systems in the triggering method it uses. The *Magnition* trigger operates on a principle named the *Hall effect*, which, simply stated, is the ability of a circuit to detect the presence of metal.

Theory of Operation of Magnition

The Hall device used in the Sorensen *Magnition* is simply an electronic switch actuated by an interrupter, or signal chopper. The Hall device is mounted on the distributor base plate. The signal chopper rotates with the distributor shaft to actuate the Hall device.

The *Magnition* system as shown in Fig. 7-35, consists of four parts: (1) The firing-signal generator (Hall device) is a U-shaped solid-state device which mounts on the breaker plate where the point set used to go. This device detects the presence or absence of metal, and is used as a solid-state point set to break the primary circuit in the control unit. (2) The signal chopper rotates between the sides of the firing-signal generator. As each opening between the chopper blades passes through the signal generator, a signal is sent to the control unit. (3) The control unit receives the signal and shuts off the primary current, developing a high secondary voltage for firing the plugs. (4) The wire harness connects the firing-signal generator and control unit to the coil.

The Sorensen *Magnition* is available for most domestic cars and trucks of six or eight cylinders using Delco Remy, Ford, or Chrysler distributors. Installation of the *Magnition* system is quite simple and straightforward, differing only in the mounting of the parts in the distributor for different makes of engines. Installation instructions for General Motors and American Motors 6-cylinder engines with Delco Remy distributors are given as an example.

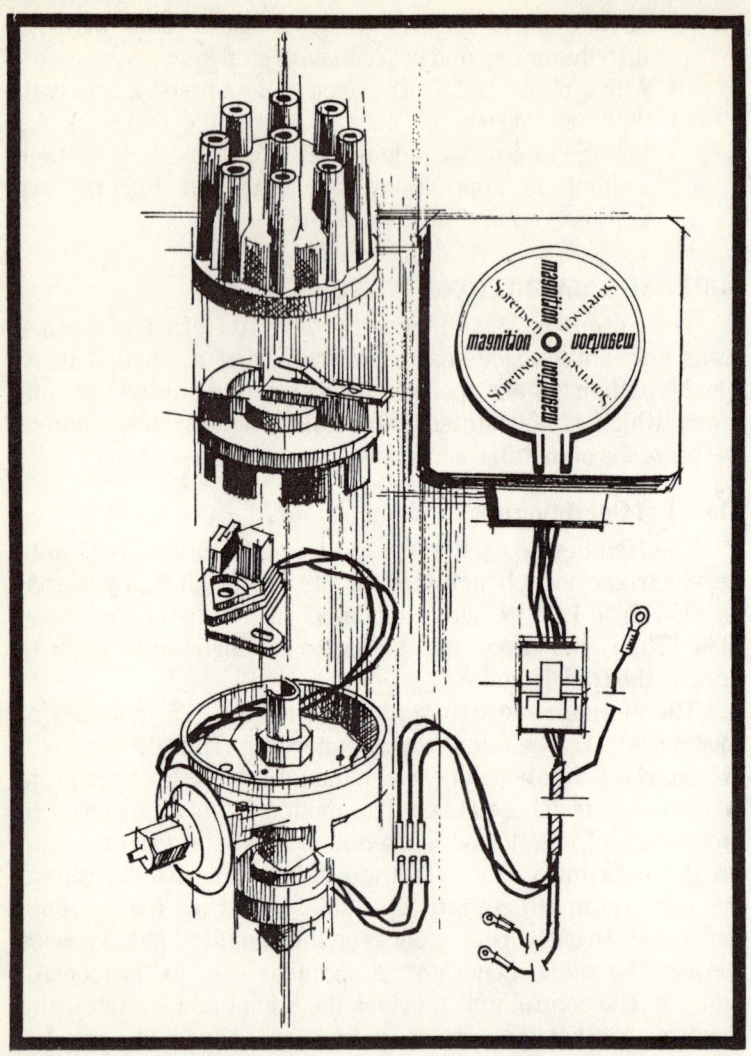

Fig. 7-34. Sorensen Magnition. (Courtesy Sorensen Manufacturing Company.)

Installing the Sorensen Magnition

1. Disconnect the negative battery terminal at the battery. This is not a requirement for installation of the system, but it is a good safety practice when changing wiring, working on the charging system, etc.
2. Remove the air cleaner assembly to obtain working room.

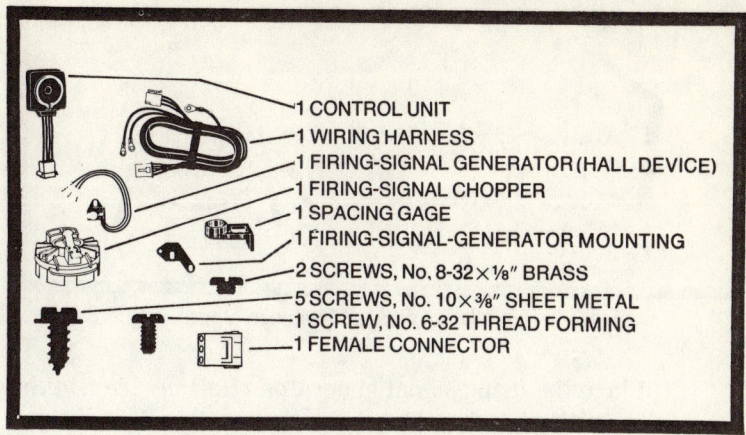

Fig. 7-35. Major parts of Sorensen Magnition.

3. Remove the distributor cap, noting the location of the black and silver cap screws before removal. It is not necessary to remove the spark plug wires from the cap.
4. Check the distributor cap for hairline cracks and burnt or corroded electrodes. Replace if necessary.
5. Remove the rotor (not used).
6. Remove the points and capacitor (not used).
7. Remove the negative points-to-coil lead from the points and coil (not used).
8. Test-mount the firing-signal generator on its mounting bracket. The two small pins on the mounting bracket should fit snugly into the two small holes on the signal generator. Separate the parts for now.
9. Thoroughly clean the distributor cam and base plate and place the firing-signal generator's mounting bracket in the base plate of the distributor in the space formerly occupied by the point set.
10. Place the spacing gage on the distributor shaft and directly over the firing-signal generator's mounting bracket. (Refer to the illustrations of Fig. 7-36 when doing this and various subsequent steps.)
11. Slide the spacing gage into the slot on the firing-signal generator's mounting bracket. Tighten the screws on the bracket, making sure the spacing gage stays in the slot. This correctly locates the bracket.
12. Remove the spacing gage from the distributor shaft.

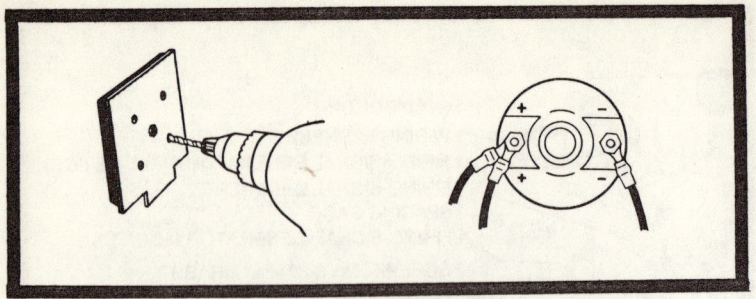

Fig. 7-36. Installation aids for Sorensen Magnition.

13. Place the firing-signal generator (Hall device) on the mounting bracket. Make sure the two small pins on the bracket fit into the two small holes in the signal generator. This will securely hold it in place while the new brass screws are installed.
14. Insert the wires from the firing-signal generator into the existing rubber grommet that fits the slot in the side of the distributor.
15. Arrange the wires of the firing-signal generator so that they will not be cut by the signal chopper. Route the wires flat against the inside of the distributor housing and base plate. The length of wire coming out of the grommet should be 5¼ in.
16. Insert the three pin terminals from the firing-signal generator into the female connector. Hold the female connector with the latch tap on top and to the left. Insert the red wire into the top slot, making sure the aligning guide tab is on top. (See illustration in Fig. 7-36.) Carefully push the pin terminal into the female connector until you feel it snap into the locked position. Pull lightly back on the wire to make sure the pin has locked. Next, insert the green wire in the center slot, followed by the black wire in the bottom slot.
17. Inspect the breaker plate to be sure it is not raised and that the pin is still connected to the vacuum advance arm.
18. Seat the signal chopper on the distributor shaft. Rotate it and push it down until you feel it index on the shaft. Make sure the signal chopper blades do not touch the sides of the firing-signal generator.

19. Replace the distributor cap. Make sure the cap fits snugly and that the black and silver screws are properly located and tightened.
20. Replace the coil wire snugly into the cap.
21. Connect the wire harness by pushing the male connector together with the female connector installed in step 16. They only go together one way. Make sure the connectors are fully engaged and the latch is properly hooked. Be sure the color code of the wires is correct—that is, red to red, green to green, and black to black.

    Note: If it becomes necessary to disconnect the firing-signal from the wiring harness, first press the latch on the wiring harness connector and gently separate it from the generator connector. Insert a very small screwdriver or sharp tool under the terminal lock in each of the generator connectors, one at a time. Raise the terminal lock to clear the terminal pin and pull gently on the wire. It should slide out easily. *Do not force the wire.* If it does not come out easily, you have not fully released the terminal lock. Follow this procedure with all three pins. To reconnect, follow step 16.
22. Connect the blue wire to the positive (battery) side of the coil. Make sure the original wires also stay attached.
23. Connect the yellow wire to the negative (distributor) side of the coil.
24. Select a spot for the control unit. The best spots will be metal fender wells or the firewall. Do not mount on the fender well if it is made of plastic or fiberglass. Select an area which will not be subject to extreme heat.
25. Test-route the wiring harness to the spot selected for the control unit. Make sure the harness reaches the spot without touching or coming too near moving parts or exhaust manifolds. Make sure the harness can flex freely between the engine and the spot selected.
26. Locate the control unit. Start by unscrewing the center screw and removing the backplate. Use this as a template and drill four $1/8$ in. holes in the surface on which the control unit is to be mounted. Attach the backplate with four $3/8$ in. No. 10 sheet metal screws.

Make sure the side of the plate with the raised area goes against the mounting surface selected.

27. Remount the control unit to the backplate, put the screw in, and tighten. Make sure the control unit fits flush against the plate. There is a notch in the mounting plate that fits into the notch on the back of the control unit where the wires come out. *Match these two notches*, even though the control unit may have to be mounted upside down or on its side to fit the area selected.
28. Connect the wiring harness to the control unit. The connections are designed to fit one way only. They will snap together when properly lined up.
29. Mount the black ground wire by drilling a ⅛ in. hole in some nearby sheet metal. Scrape away the paint from around the hole to insure good contact and attach the ring terminal with a ⅜ in. sheet metal screw.
30. Arrange the wiring harness over the previously selected route. Tape the harness in place and fold any excess wire back over itself. Take care to keep the harness away from moving parts or excessive heat. Leave enough slack in the wire to allow for engine movements.
31. Replace the air cleaner and any vacuum hoses that may have been removed for the installation.
32. Reconnect the negative battery terminal if it was disconnected.
33. Start the engine. The engine should start immediately. In some cases, the timing may be off and the engine may run roughly. If the engine has not started, go back to the beginning and check out each step. If the engine will not start, refer to the troubleshooting procedures, which follow these installation instructions.
34. Check the timing and reset to the manufacturer's specifications. Dwell is permanently set by the design of the signal chopper and need not be checked.
35. For maximum economy and performance, check the condition of all spark plugs and plug wires. Replace plugs and wires in sets when replacement is indicated.

Troubleshooting the Magnition—Preliminary Steps

Before performing any service checks on this system, make the following preliminary checks.

1. Check the wiring diagram (Fig. 7-37) to insure that the system is properly wired. Make sure black control unit ground wire is properly grounded. Many cars are equipped with fiberglass fender wells; make sure the ground wire is on clean metal ground.
2. Check battery condition and cable connections.
3. Check spark plug cables.
4. Check vacuum hoses.
5. Check belt tightness.
6. Remove distributor cap, inspect for cracks, carbon tracking, and the condition of the carbon on the center-tower contact. Replace if necessary.

Spark Test

1. Remove coil wire from distributor. Crank engine, hold wire ¼ in. from good ground, and check for spark. If spark occurs, reinstall coil wire into cap. If no spark occurs, follow the recommended procedures in the *no-spark condition* section.
2. Remove a spark plug wire from a spark plug. Insert a screwdriver into the spark plug terminal, hold ¼ in. from spark plug, crank engine, and see if spark occurs. If spark does occur, trouble is not in electronic

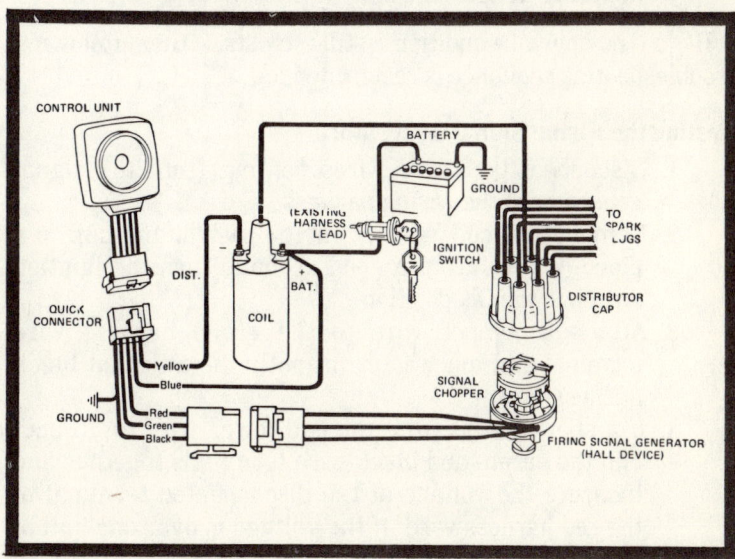

Fig. 7-37. Wiring diagram of Sorensen Magnition.

ignition. If no spark occurs, problem is in the signal chopper and it will have to be replaced.

No-Spark Condition

If you have a no-spark condition, the following procedure is recommended. You must use a voltmeter or ohmmeter to troubleshoot the system.

1. Check battery voltage at battery and battery connections. Make a mental note of battery voltage.
2. Remove distributor cap, inspect for cracks, carbon tracking, and the condition of the carbon center-tower contact. Replace if necessary.
3. Inspect firing-signal generator and signal chopper for any indication of rubbing action or nicks on the opening of the signal generator slots. If any damage is noted, replace firing-signal generator or the signal chopper.
4. Remove the spark plug wires, one at a time, and measure the resistance of each with an ohmmeter (also the coil tower wire); then reconnect each. None of these readings should be more than 20,000 ohms. If any wire shows an unusually high resistance, or if they are all old and the insulation is cracked, replace all of them with a new wire set.

If a no-spark condition still exists, the following troubleshooting sequence is recommended.

Testing the Firing-Signal Generator

1. Disconnect the three wires coming from the signal generator at the wiring harness.
2. Remove the coil wire from the distributor cap and place it ¼ in. from a good ground. Turn the ignition switch to the ON position.
3. Attach a jumper wire to the green harness wire terminal and touch intermittently the adjacent black harness wire.
4. If a spark jumps from the coil tower wire to ground, clip the green- and black-wire terminals together and measure the voltage at the disconnected terminal of the red harness wire. If the voltage is over one-half of the battery voltage, replace the signal generator in the distributor.

5. If no spark occurs at the coil tower wire to ground, proceed with the wiring harness test.

Wiring-Harness Test
1. Turn ignition switch to OFF.
2. Disconnect yellow and blue wires from coil (see Fig. 7-38). Insulate the ends of the yellow and blue wires with electrical tape to prevent false readings during the harness check.

Checking Wiring Harness for Continuity and Shorts
1. Connect one ohmmeter lead to the double black connector. Take the other lead and touch each terminal—red, yellow, blue, and green. There should be no reading on the ohmmeter. If a reading occurs, replace wiring harness.
2. Connect one end of the meter again to the double black wire and touch the ground screw of the black wire from the wiring harness. The meter should read approximately zero ohms. If it does not, or if it shows high resistance, there is a poor ground or open wire.
3. Check each individual wire by touching one ohmmeter lead to each end of the wiring harness—red to red, blue to blue, yellow to yellow, green to green, and black to black. The meter should read zero ohms.

Ignition Coil Resistance Check
1. The primary resistance (Fig. 7-39A) should be between 1.0 and 3.0 ohms.

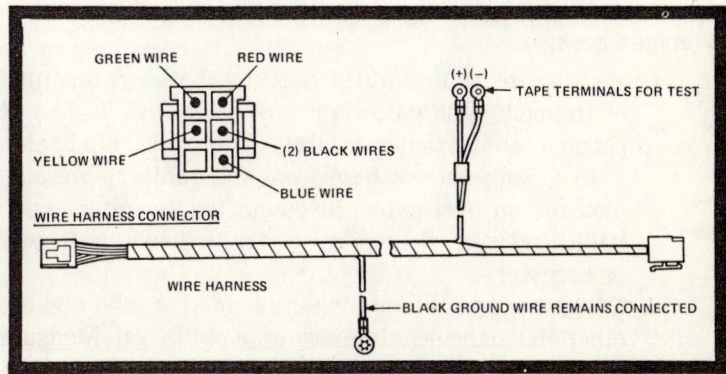

Fig. 7-38. Testing the wiring harness of the Sorensen Magnition.

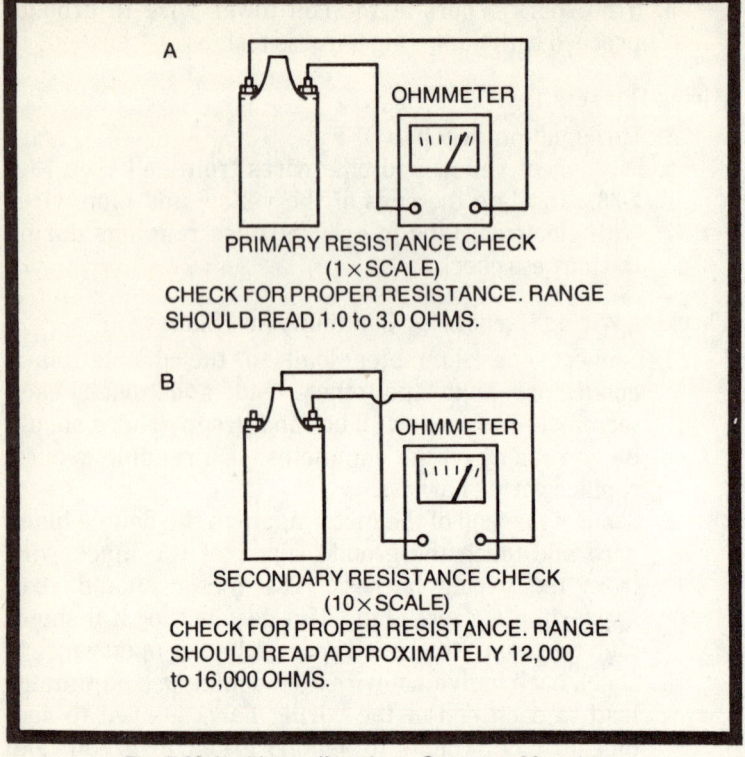

Fig. 7-39. Ignition coil testing—Sorensen Magnition.

2. The secondary resistance (Fig. 7-39B) should be from 12,000 to 16,000 ohms. If the resistance readings of the primary and secondary are within limits, proceed to the voltage check.

Voltage Check
1. Measure the voltage at the positive (battery) terminal of the coil (ignition switch on). (See Fig. 7-40A.) It should read full battery voltage. If it does, skip to step 2. If it reads zero or much less than battery voltage, look for an open wire, disconnected terminal, open ballast resistor, or inoperative ignition switch. Repair as necessary.
2. Attach one end of a clip lead to a good ground and the other end to the negative terminal of the coil. Measure the voltage at the positive coil terminal again (Fig. 7-40B). It should read about one-half battery voltage.

If it does, skip to step 3. If it reads either much higher or much lower than one-half battery potential, check for a poor connection or a shorted ballast resistor or resistance wire. Repair or replace as necessary. (Most ballast resistors measure between 1 and 2 ohms.)

3. Remove the center ignition wire from the distributor cap and place it close to a good ground. While watching for a spark between the coil tower wire and ground, lift the clip lead off the negative coil terminal (Fig. 7-40C). Touch it back on and remove it—several

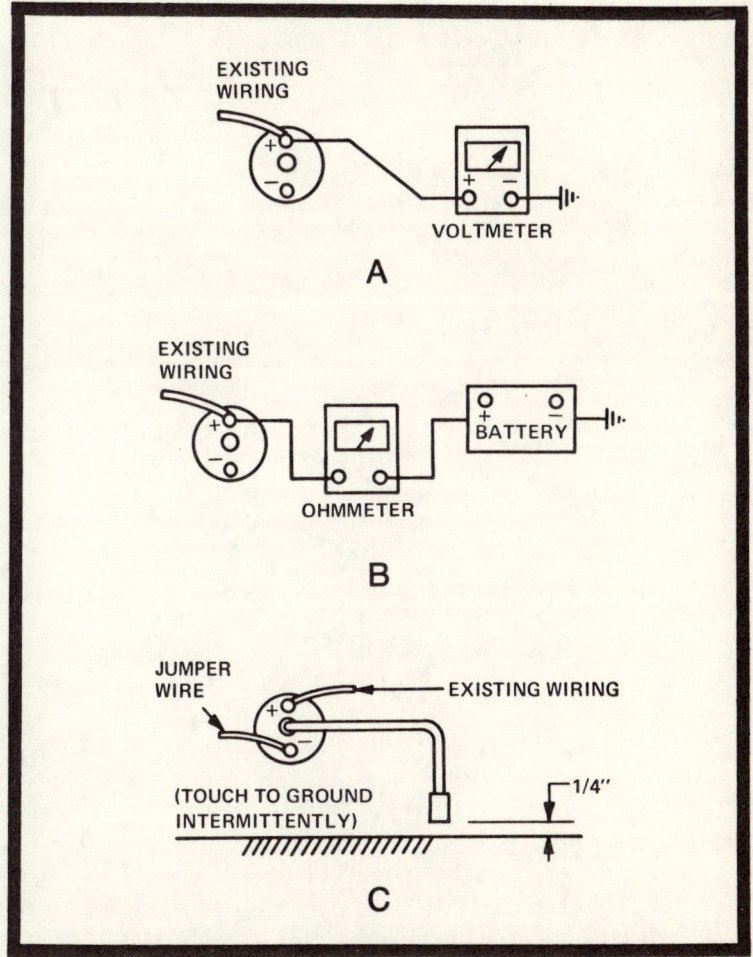

Fig. 7-40. Voltage checks of Sorensen Magnition.

times if necessary. If no spark is observed, replace the coil. If a good spark is observed, replace the control unit and reconnect the wiring harness and connections.

Due to space limitations, it is impossible to give installation and troubleshooting procedures for all of the makes of replacement-type transistor ignitions now on the market. The installation and troubleshooting procedures given, however, can serve as a guide for those systems not described in this book.

Chapter 8

Electronic Ignition

The first unit to be described is not an ignition system of any kind inasmuch as it does not replace any single item of a conventional ignition system. It is, however, very effective for the prevention of misfiring at high RPM when using a conventional ignition.

DWELL EXTENDER

The problem with conventional ignitions at high RPM is the insufficient time available for coil saturation (dwell time). This is because the time taken to mechanically open and close the points does not allow the points to be closed long enough to saturate the coil between each firing of a plug. This problem is eliminated to some extent by the dual-point distributor in which the points are in parallel, with one set opening just before the other set closes. This arrangement does, however, add to the maintenance cost (two sets of points to replace each time). Then, too, there is the difficulty of keeping two sets of points in correct adjustment.

The dwell extender does electronically what the dual points do mechanically. Connected in parallel with the contact points, the dwell extender electrically closes the point circuit about 100 μsec after the points open, and it maintains the circuit until the points mechanically close. Thus, the dwell time is said to be extended.

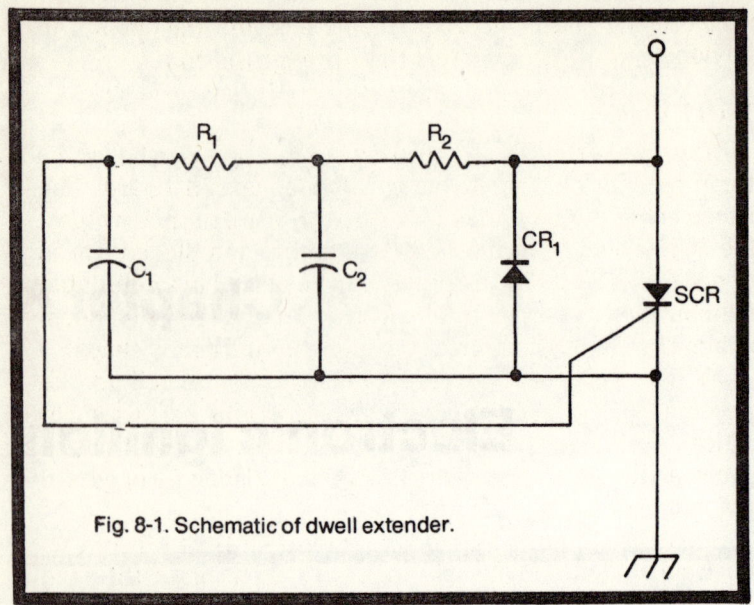

Fig. 8-1. Schematic of dwell extender.

Dwell Extender Operation

The simple circuit for a dwell extender is shown in Fig. 8-1. Point A is connected to the point side of the coil (−), and with the cathode of the SCR connected to ground, the unit is across, or in parallel with, the contact points. When the points are closed, the extender circuit is bypassed and no current flows through the SCR . During this time, current flows from ground through the closed points, then through the coil primary and back to the battery.

When the points open, the field collapses, inducing the high voltage in the secondary to fire the spark plugs. However, the instant the points open, battery voltage is applied directly to the anode of the SCR and, through the resistance-capacitance network, to the gate of the SCR. About 100 μsec after the points open, the positive voltage has built up on the gate to a value that will trigger the SCR. The SCR will stay until the voltage difference between its anode and cathode is removed. Thus, the primary current flows through the SCR until the points close and take over the job of carrying the primary current. The closing of the points short-circuits or bypasses the SCR, turning it off. It is now reset for the next point opening and plug firing. It has assisted the points in providing more time of current flow through the coil.

Dwell Extender Construction

The dwell extender is quite easy to build on a perfboard, or it can be built on a do-it-yourself printed-circuit board. The placement of the six parts is not critical, nor are their values. The SCR should be heatsinked for long life and placed where air can flow over it. The assembly can be placed in a ventilated aluminum utility box about 4 in. long × 3 in. wide × 2 in. deep, obtainable at most electronic supply stores and hobby shops.

A list of parts is given in Fig. 8-2. As stated in the preceding paragraph, the values of the various parts are not critical, but physical size obviously will have an effect on the layout and overall dimensions of the unit. Hence, suggested part numbers are given.

Parts layout for a 3½ by 2 in. perfboard is shown in Fig. 8-3. Note that it will not be necessary to insulate the stud (anode) connection from the heatsink, as the perfboard is nonconductive and the SCR does not touch any other metal part.

Wiring of this unit is straightforward, as shown in Fig. 8-4. The lead A to the negative (distributor) side of the coil should be well soldered to the soldering lug on the stud of the SCR, and brought out through the grommet on the side of the box. Be

---

C_1, C_2—CAPACITORS, 2.2 μF, 50V (SPRAGUE 502D225 OR EQUIVALENT)

R_1—RESISTOR, 2200 OHMS, 1W.

R_2—RESISTOR, 120 OHMS, 1W.

SCR—SILICON CONTROLLED RECTIFIER, 50V, 8A (MOTOROLA HEP R1220 OR EQUIVALENT.)

PERFBOARD, 3½ IN. × 2 IN., 0.2 IN. HOLES.
4¾ IN. ALUMINUM SPACERS, TAPPED 6-32 EACH END.
8 SCREWS, 6-32 × 1½ IN., WITH SHAKEPROOF LOCKWASHERS.
UTILITY BOX, APPROXIMATELY 4 × 3 × 2 IN., WITH COVER.
RUBBER GROMMET, MISCELLANEOUS SOLDER LUGS, WIRE, AND SOLDER.

Fig. 8-2. Parts list for dwell extender.

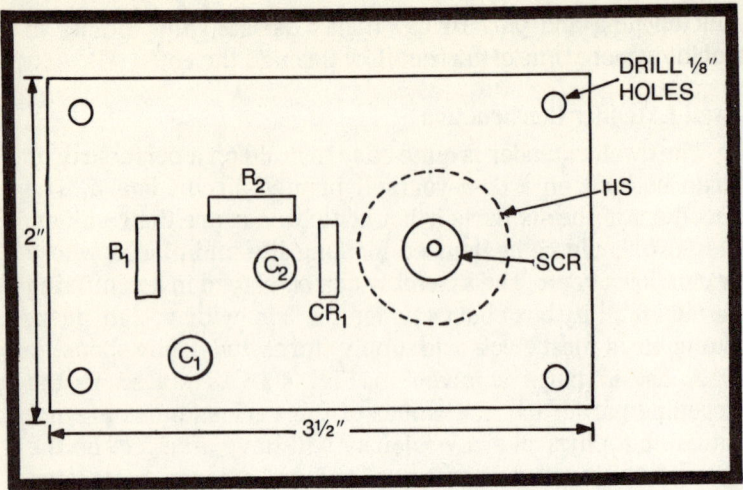

Fig. 8-3. Location of parts on dwell extender board.

sure to allow sufficient lead length to reach the coil when the dwell extender is mounted. The ground lead may be connected under one of the mounting spacers if care is taken to insure a good ground of the unit when it is mounted.

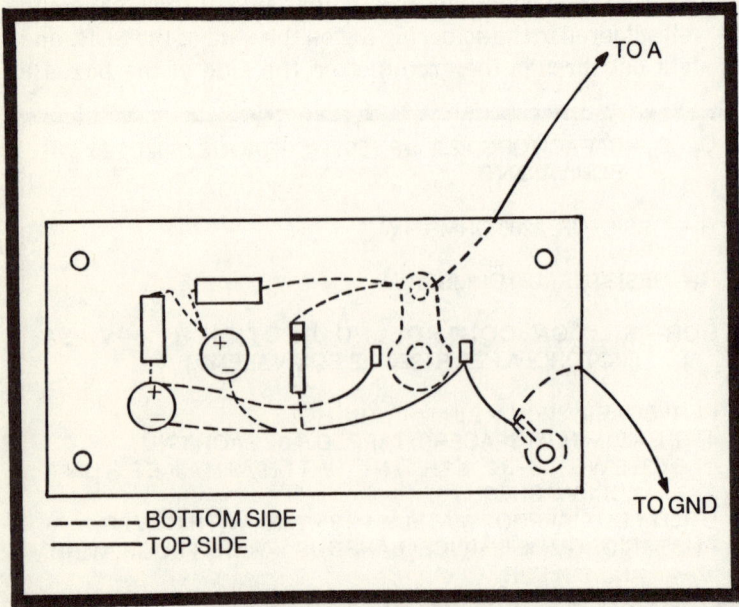

Fig. 8-4. Wiring layout for dwell extender.

Four mounting holes to match the four holes in the perfboard should be drilled in the top of the box. The four tapped spacers are then fastened inside the box by four 6—32 screws and lockwashers. Flat mounting tabs may be fastened to the top of the box by these screws, or the tabs may be fastened to the sides if more convenient.

The wired circuit board is then placed inside the box and fastened to the tops of the threaded spacers by the four 6—32 screws. The negative coil lead and ground lead, if used, should be fed through the grommet as the circuit board is placed on the spacers. The bottom (which becomes the top of the box when the box is mounted) is now fastened in place by its regular cover screws. This completes assembly of the unit, and it is now ready for mounting on the vehicle.

Mounting and Using the Dwell Extender

The unit should be mounted as close to the coil as practicable. It should not be mounted on a part of the engine that is subject to extreme heat. The leads should be long enough to allow for normal engine movement, and soldering lugs or crimpon terminals should be used at the coil and ground ends.

Before wiring the unit to the coil, the contact points should be checked and replaced if necessary, and the dwell and timing should be checked and set to specifications. When connecting the lead to the coil negative connection, remember that the coil—distributor lead is not to be removed; the lead from the dwell extender is an *added connection*. Connect the ground lead to an unpainted grounded surface, or if the lead is not used, be sure the unit itself makes a good metal contact with ground.

Once the unit is installed, no adjustments are possible. If the engine will not start, remove the extender-to-coil lead and crank. If the engine still will not start, the trouble is not in the dwell extender and will have to be searched out elsewhere. If the engine starts, the problem is in the dwell extender. Make the following checks in order.

1. Remove cover from unit and check for A-lead shorted to case.
2. Check for shorted SCR , CR_1, C_1, or C_2.

Note that any open in the wiring or components will prevent the extender from operating properly, but will not prevent the engine from running.

The dwell extender can best be checked for proper operation on an oscilloscope. Run the engine at high RPM and note the voltage spikes on the secondary pattern. If the spikes are about the same for each cylinder and do not fall below the values shown at low RPM, the dwell extender is working properly and the coil is being saturated at high RPM. Another method of checking the operation of the extender is to run the vehicle in second gear at a high engine RPM. First a run is made with the extender—coil lead disconnected and any misfiring noted. The extender is then reconnected and a run made at approximately the same throttle setting. With the extender working properly, the misfiring should disappear and a slightly higher speed should be noticed at the same throttle setting.

POINT-TRIGGERED CAPACITIVE-DISCHARGE IGNITION

The dwell extender increases the length of time for current to flow through the coil's primary and saturate the coil. By applying a many times higher than normal voltage across the primary, a CD ignition achieves improved coil saturation by forcing a higher current through the coil during the dwell period. Also, in the CD system only small SCR trigger current passes through the points, greatly increasing point life.

The home-built CD ignition system whose schematic is shown in Fig. 8-5 is not difficult to build and has several advantages compared to the conventional ignition system. It can deliver a 25,000V output from a 12V standard ignition coil. It will operate well on a 6V input for good cold-weather or low-battery starting. It works well on a 4-, 6-, or 8-cylinder foreign or domestic engine.

The original points, capacitor, and coil are used. If it becomes necessary, the system is quickly put back to the conventional mode by disconnecting the +12V, (+) coil, points, and (−) coil wires and restoring the distributor-to-coil and switch-to-coil wires to their original connections. In fact, a double-pole, double-throw switch may be connected in the output leads to accomplish this changeover and enable a comparison of the performance in both modes of operation.

Circuit Operation of a CD Ignition

The CD ignition of Fig. 8-5 contains an inverter to step up the battery voltage to approximately 400V, a bridge rectifier to

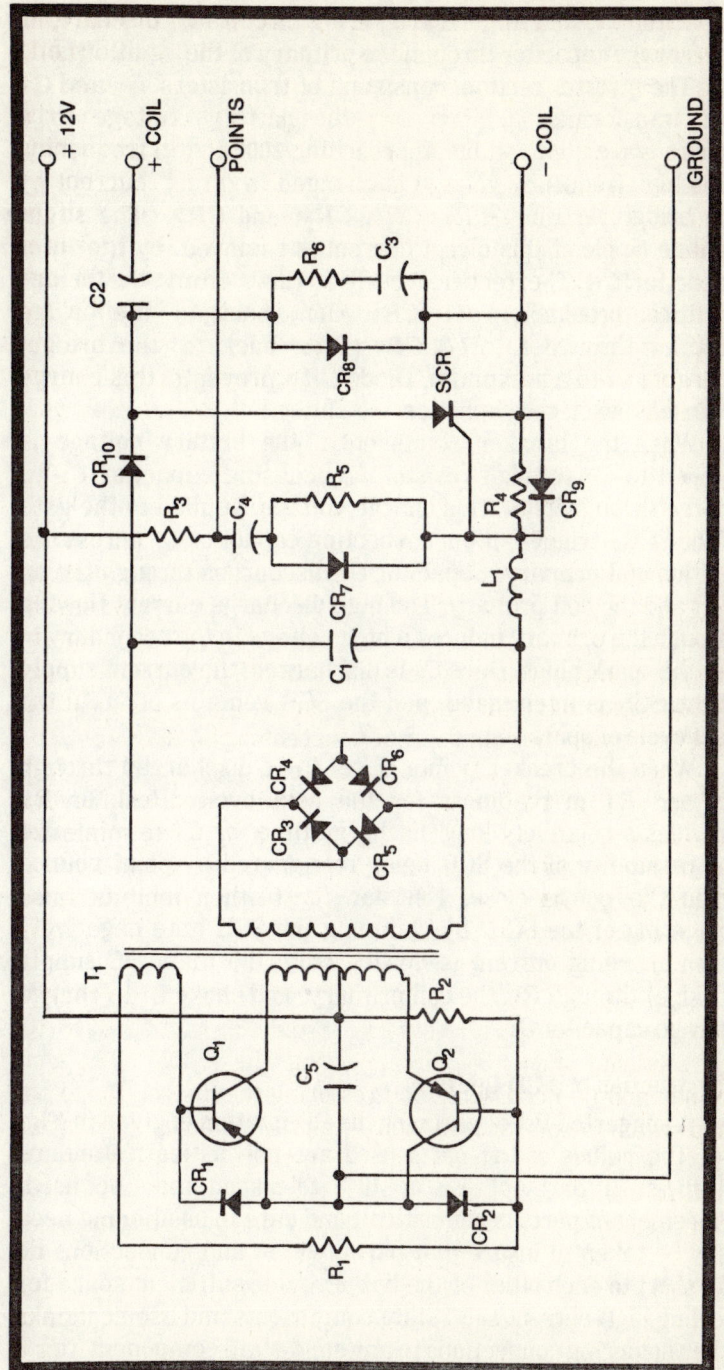

Fig. 8-5. Schematic of CD ignition.

change this voltage t a DC voltage to charge the storage capacitor C_2, and an *SCR* triggering circuit for discharging the storage capacitor through the primary of the ignition coil.

The inverter section, consisting of transistors Q_1 and Q_2 and transformer T_1, converts the battery voltage to a square-wave high voltage approaching 8000 Hz in frequency. This high-frequency voltage is changed to direct current by the bridge rectifier—CR_3, CR_4, CR_5, and CR_6. The slight voltage ripple of this direct current is removed by the filter capacitor C_1. The rectified current flows from the bridge rectifier through L_1, R_4, CR_8, CR_{10} back to the bridge rectifier through L_1, R_4, CR_8, CR_{10} back to the bridge, charging C_2 to a maximum. Diode CR_{10} prevents this charge from leaking off the capacitor.

When the breaker points open, the battery voltage is applied to C_4 through resistor R_3, causing capacitor C_4 to charge through CR_7. This charge voltage, applied to the gate of the SCR , triggers it on, connecting capacitor C_2 across the ignition coil primary. Capacitor C_2 discharges through the *on* SCR and the coil primary. The high discharge current flowing through the primary induces a high voltage in the secondary to fire the spark plugs. Once C_2 is discharged, the current supply of the SCR is interrupted, and the SCR remains off until the next cycle of operation.

When the breaker points close, C_4 is discharged through R_5 and R_4 in readiness for the next cycle. Resistor R_5 provides a relatively long discharge time for C_4 to minimize the possibility of the SCR being retriggered by point bounce when the points close. Resistor R_4 further inhibits false triggering of the SCR by clamping the SCR gate negatively when charging current is flowing from the main DC supply (bridge) through R_4, the coil primary, and choke L_1 to charge storage capacitor C_2.

Construction of a CD Ignition

A suggested list of parts for the CD ignition is given in Fig. 8-6. The values of the parts used are not critical; standard off-the-shelf parts of 5% or 10% tolerance may be used. Placement of parts is not critical, and care in positioning need only be taken to insure that parts, wires, and connections do not short to each other or the box. Provide sufficient space for cooling high-current solid-state components and use heatsinks when soldering connections to any solid-state component.

C_1—CAPACITOR, 10 μF, 600V (SPRAGUE TVA-1963).
C_2—CAPACITOR, 1 μF, 450V (SPRAGUE TVA-1700).
C_3—CAPACITOR, 0.003 μF, 600V (SPRAGUE 6TM-S33).
C_4—CAPACITOR, 0.1 μF 200V (SPRAGUE 2PS-P10).
C_5—CAPACITOR, 220 μF, 30V (SPRAGUE 600D227G).
CR_1—THROUGH CR_{10}, DIODE (MOTOROLA HEP R0054).
L_1—0.4 MH CHOKE (UTC ML2).
Q_1, Q_2—NPN TRANSISTOR (MOTOROLA HEP S5019).
R_1—RESISTOR, 180 OHMS, 2W.
R_2—RESISTOR, 5600 OHMS, 1W.
R_3—RESISTOR, WIREWOUND, 50 OHMS, 5W.
R_4—RESISTOR, 10 OHMS, 1W.
R_5—RESISTOR, 22,000 OHMS, ½W.
R_6—RESISTOR, 10 OHMS, ½W
SCR—SILICON CONTROLLED RECTIFIER, 500V, 8A (MOTOROLA HEP R1246).
T_1—TOROIDAL TRANSFORMER (TRIAD TY-86).
HEATSINK FOR POWER TRANSISTORS (MOTOROLA MS-15).
HEATSINK FOR SCR MADE FROM ¾ IN. ALUMINUM ANGLE 2 IN. LONG.
4—ALUMINUM SPACERS, ¼ × ⅝ IN. TAPPED 6−32 IN. EACH END.
4—ALUMINUM SPACERS, ¼ × 5/16 IN. DRILLED ⅛ IN. THROUGH.
4—6−32 × ⅜ IN. SCREWS WITH STAR LOCKWASHERS.
4—6−32 × ⅞ IN. SCREWS WITH STAR LOCKWASHERS.
2—0.062 IN. HOLE VECTORBOARDS, 3½ × 4½ IN.
1—4 × 5 × 2 IN. ALUMINUM BOX AND COVER (BUD AC1404 AND BPA1504).
MISCELLANEOUS MOUNTING FEET, GROMMETS, SOLDER LUGS, ETC.

Fig. 8-6. Parts list for CD ignition.

Figure 8-7 is a layout diagram of the No. 2 circuit board. This board is cut to 4½ in. by 3½ in. from 0.062 in. hole perfboard. The four mounting holes (size to pass a 6−32 screw) should be drilled first. Next, the hole should be drilled to fit the stud of the SCR. The heatsink for the SCR is made from a piece of ¾ in. aluminum approximately 2 in. long. Drill the heatsink to pass the stud of the SCR. Mount the SCR through the heatsink and vectorboard. Secure both of them in place with a flatwasher, a solder lug, a star lockwasher, and the nut that comes with the SCR. The rest of the components are mounted by inserting the leads of each component through the appropriate holes in the board, bending the leads on the

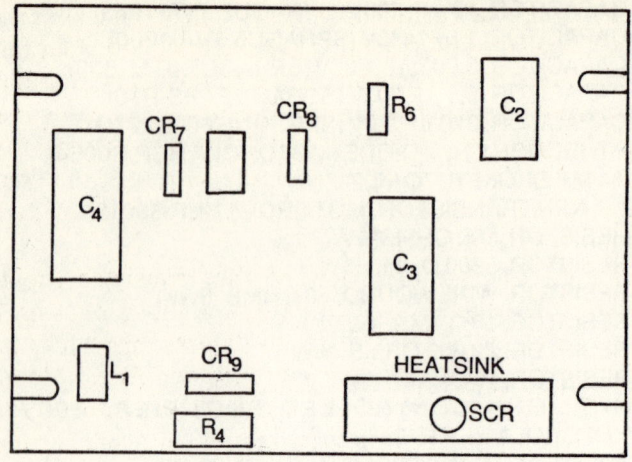

Fig. 8-7. Layout for CD ignition—circuit board 2.

underside of the board to hold the components in place, and shaping the leads in the appropriate directions for ease of connection.

Figure 8-8 is the suggested layout diagram for the No. 1 circuit board, containing the inverter and rectifier. Note that Q_1 and Q_2 are not located on this board, although they are a part of the inverter circuit. They are located on a heatsink

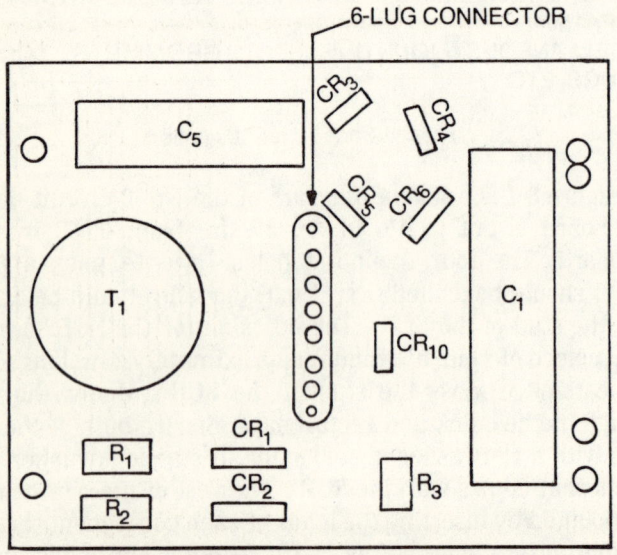

Fig. 8-8. Layout for CD ignition—circuit board 1.

mounted on the box cover; the 6-lug connector is used on the No. 1 circuit board to facilitate connection of the leads from Q_1 and Q_2. Drill the four mounting holes to match the four holes in the No. 2 board before mounting the components. Components are mounted, held in place, and connected in the same manner as with circuit board 2. One lug of the 6-lug connector can serve as the tie for the 12V lead to the outside of the box. The five remaining lugs are to be used as tie points for the leads coming from transistors Q_1 and Q_2.

Figure 8-9 is a top view of the transistor heatsink. Prepare the heatsink by drilling the eight mounting holes shown. Use one of the mica insulators provided in the transistor mounting kits as a marking template. Mount the two transistors on the heatsink, using the insulators. Place a solder lug under one mounting screw of each transistor (collector connection). Solder a 2½ in. length of No. 16 insulated copper wire to each solder lug, base terminal, and emitter terminal. Connect the two emitter terminals together with a length of No. 18 wire.

Drill four mounting holes in the cover to match the mounting holes of the circuit board. Drill five holes in the cover to pass the wires from the transistors to circuit board No. 1. Mount the heatsink to the cover, using the four $6-32 \times \mathrm{^3/_8}$ in. screws and lockwashers and inserting them into the tapped ⅞ in. spacers.

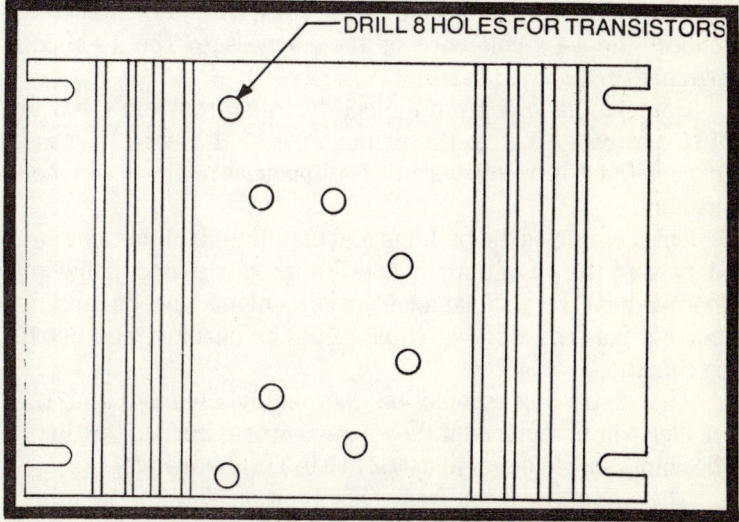

Fig. 8-9. Preparation of heatsink for CD ignition.

Make the connections between the two circuit boards, keeping the boards about ⅜ in. apart. Connect the wires to their appropriate points and form them into a harness. Solder the leads from transistors Q_1 and Q_2 to the proper lugs on the 6-lug connector, and mount circuit board 1 on the cover spacers. The components on circuit board 1 face the cover plate, and the ⅞ in. spacers provide space for them. The No. 2 board is separated from the No. 1 board by the $^5/_{16}$ in. spacer and the long threaded spacers.

Start the wiring harness through the grommet in the end of the box. Feed the harness through the grommet and lower the board assembly into the box. Fasten the cover to the box with the cover screws and the unit is complete.

Installing the CD Ignition

The box should be mounted on the fender well or firewall to avoid extreme heat or vibration.

Note: The transformer in the unit "sings" when operating and, therefore, may cause interference in the car's radio receiver if mounted too close to it.

Be sure that the box is well grounded and solidly attach the ground wire from the unit to a clean ground point. Remove the wire from the coil terminal marked (+) or BAT and connect it to the +12V wire of the harness. If there is a noise suppression capacitor connected to the (+) terminal of the coil, it too should be connected to the +12V wire of the harness. Connect the (+) coil wire of the harness to the (+) coil terminal.

Remove the wire from the coil terminal marked (−) or DIST and connect it to the points wire of the wire harness. Connect the (−) coil wire of the harness to the (−) coil terminal.

This completes the building and installation of the system. To permit the ignition to operate properly and show an improvement in performance at all engine speeds and in starting, the rest of the ignition should be checked and put in top condition.

The distributor should be thoroughly cleaned and the breaker points replaced if they appear worn, burned, or dirty. The points should be set at 0.0038 to 0.040 in. clearance.

The voltage output from this ignition system is much higher at all speeds than the output from the conventional system. To prevent shorting of the high voltage, the distributor cap must be clean and dry inside and out. Replace cap and rotor if contacts appear burned or if carbon tracks or minute cracks appear.

Inspect all high-voltage wiring (plug and coil wires) for frayed or burned insulation and loose ends. Replace if it does not appear to be in good condition. Be sure the plug wires do not cross one another and are separated as far as is practicable to avoid crossfiring of the plugs.

Clean, and replace if necessary, all spark plugs. Set plug gap at 0.040 in. Use plugs of heat range specified by manufacturer.

Recheck timing, as the widening of the breaker point gap will change it. Set the timing at the low end of the range specified by the manufacturer. *Do not advance the initial timing.*

Checking the CD Ignition

The following procedure is recommended for checking the ignition, using a voltmeter and a neon test lamp.

1. Short the breaker points by connecting a jumper wire from the (−) coil terminal to engine ground.
2. Connect the neon test lamp between the (+) and (−) terminals of the ignition coil.
3. Turn the ignition switch on but do not crank the engine.
4. Use the voltmeter to check for voltage at the +12V wire of the unit. If voltage is not present, check for a short or open circuit or blown fuse.
5. Listen near the CD unit for a telltale squeal indicating the inverter section is operating. If no sound is heard, observe the neon test lamp for a weak glow. If the lamp glows, the inverter is working. If neither sound nor glow is detected, the inverter is probably not working.
6. Block the breaker points open with a clean nonconductive material. While observing the neon test lamp, remove the jumper wire installed in step 1. The lamp should flash brilliantly, indicating the triggering of the SCR and discharge of the storage capacitor. If the unit fails to trigger, the SCR, capacitor, or trigger circuitry may be defective; the unit and the ignition coil must be removed to the bench for further troubleshooting.

Bench troubleshooting of this unit is best done by ohmmeter testing of continuity and resistance and by testing the individual components. Diodes and transistors in good condition show low resistance when connected to the ohmmeter in the forward direction and very high resistance when connected in the reverse direction. The SCR will show low resistance in the forward direction when about 3V is applied to the gate.

Small capacitors usually show infinite resistance when connected to the ohmmeter. Large-value capacitors show an initial meter drop to the low end of the scale, with a rise to the high end as the capacitor charges. The precise low and high observed on the meter depend upon the value of the capacitor. High-value capacitors should hold the charge impressed upon them by the ohmmeter voltage.

Chapter 9

Scope Testing of Transistor Ignitions

The oscilloscope method of checking an ignition system is especially valuable because it is the only method of checking with the engine running. It takes into account the effects of compression, temperature, and other operating factors and does this at all speed ranges.

For conventional ignition systems the scope is primarily a timesaver, as it takes only minutes to locate a faulty component, compared to perhaps hours to remove and test each individual component. With the advent of transistor ignition systems with extremely fast voltage rise times, high voltages, etc., and with increased emphasis on pollution control, it has become absolutely necessary to use a scope for the checking, testing, maintenance, and tuneup of ignition systems.

An oscilloscope is essentially a voltmeter that portrays the voltage reading on a screen similar to a television screen rather than on a graduated meter face. However, the important difference between the meter and the scope lies in the fact that the meter movement cannot oscillate with the rapid voltage changes occurring in ignition systems—it is damped to prevent this—so it indicates an average value over a short period of time. The oscilloscope shows voltage variations occurring during exceedingly small fractions of a second. It portrays this information as a voltage graph on the face of the scope tube.

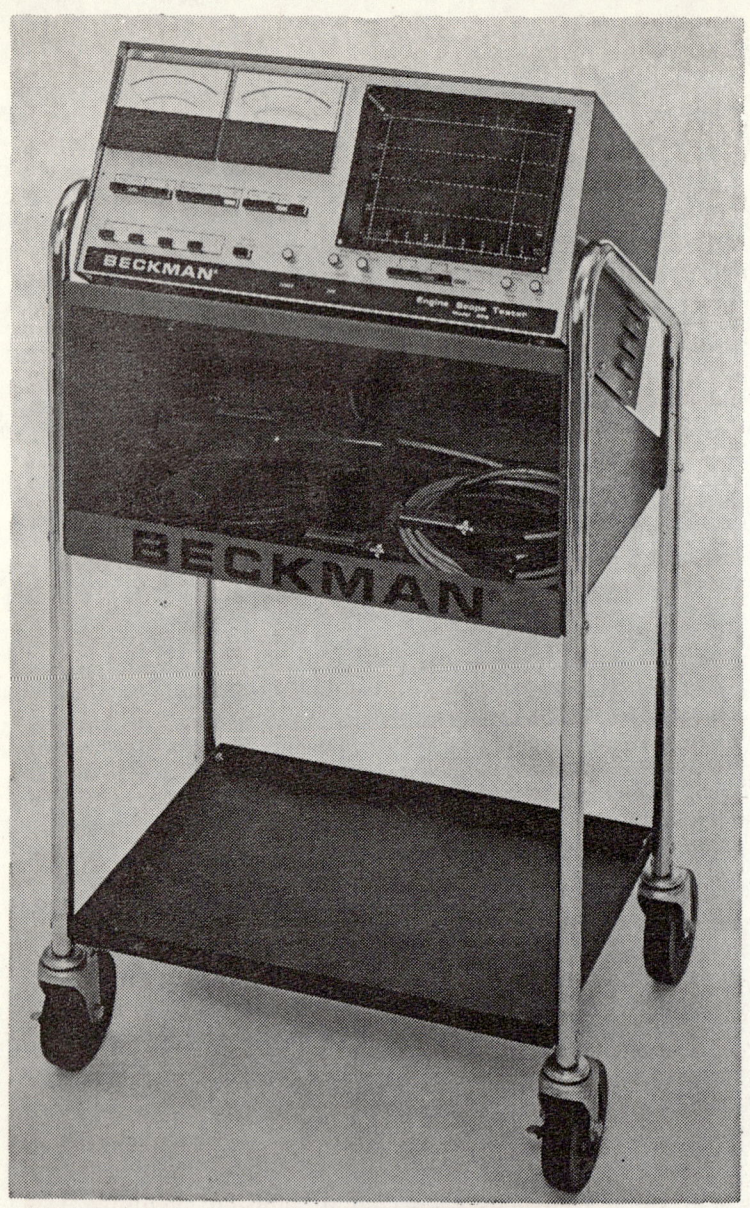

Fig. 9-1. Beckman oscilloscope Model 595. (Courtesy Beckman Instruments, Inc.)

The automotive oscilloscope, or *scope*, used with this chapter and pictured in Fig. 9-1, is the Beckman Model 595, manufactured by Beckman Instruments, Inc., Fullerton,

California. It has the capability of checking not only the conventional ignition but also the magnetic, transistorized, and other systems. All pictures of waveforms used in this chapter were obtained on this scope and are presented through the courtesy of Beckman Instruments, Inc.

BASIC IGNITION PATTERNS

For a knowledge of the basic waveforms and their interpretations, refer to Fig. 9-2. This illustration shows the normal primary pattern of a conventional ignition system. The four areas marked on the pattern should be memorized for proper and efficient scope use. This will enable you to notice any variation from the normal pattern and to recognize which primary component is at fault. With CD and transistor ignitions, the same or similar functions take place, but they do not show a pattern that is identical to the conventional ignition pattern.

The normal primary pattern as well as unsatisfactory patterns and the possible defects causing them, are illustrated in Fig. 9-3 through 9-6. Figure 9-3 shows the primary pattern of a single cylinder placed to read the dwell directly on the screen. To position the pattern for reading the dwell angle, the HORIZONTAL POSITION control is adjusted so that the firing line at the right end of the pattern is placed directly over the 0° mark. Dwell angle is then read on the screen opposite the points-closed line.

Figure 9-4 shows the normal oscillations present in the second section of a normal pattern as the coil's energy is

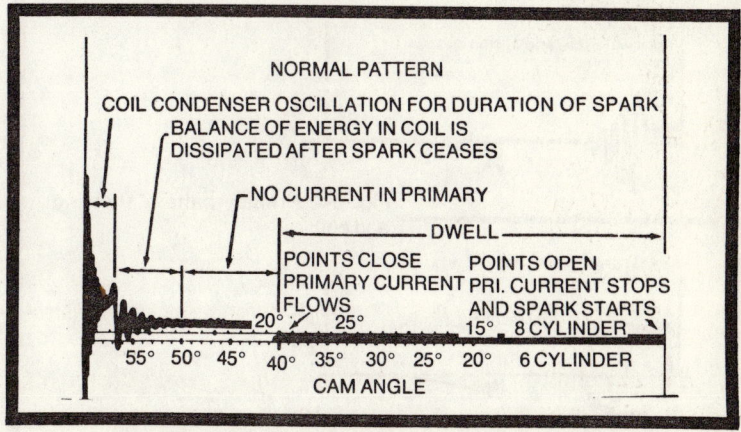

Fig. 9-2. Normal primary pattern—conventional ignition.

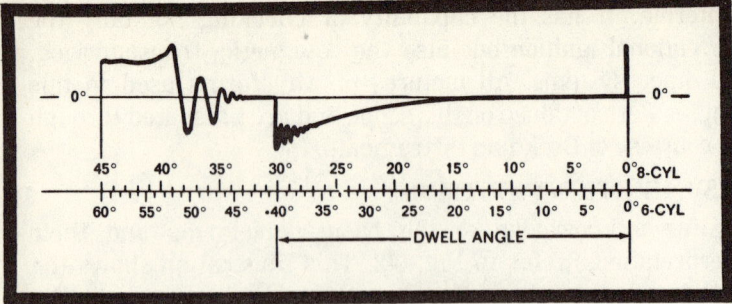

Fig. 9-3. Primary pattern to check dwell angle.

dissipated after the spark ceases. Six oscillations are considered normal—more if neither resistance plug wire nor resistance spark plugs are used. A display of fewer than six oscillations (lower pattern in Fig. 9-4) is usually caused by shorted turns in the coil.

Figure 9-5 illustrates normal and unsatisfactory actions of the breaker points as observed in the dwell section. The cause of the unsatisfactory pattern may be point misalignment, point bounce, weak spring tension, burned or dirty points, or in some cases, a faulty capacitor. Many of the point problems will show up as excessive point resistance as well.

Resistance in the secondary circuit as viewed in the primary pattern is illustrated in Fig. 9-6. Note that with systems using suppression wires or plugs the plug-firing

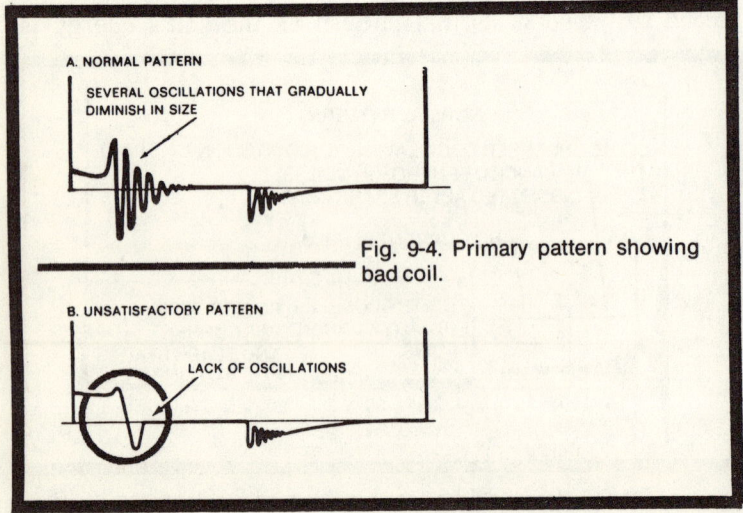

Fig. 9-4. Primary pattern showing bad coil.

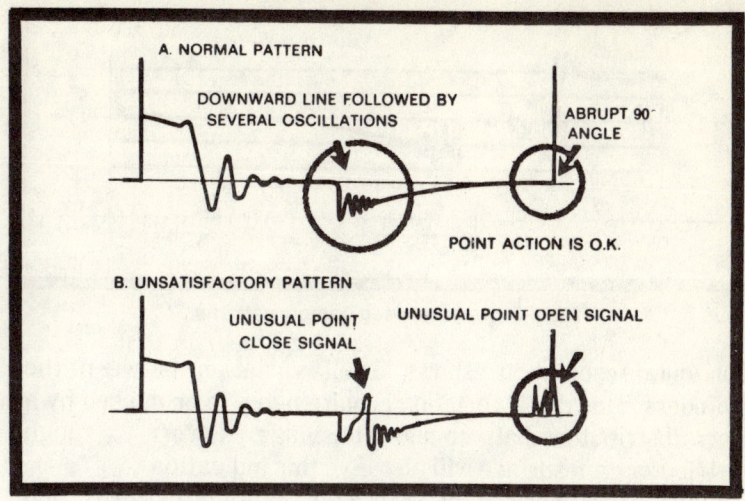

Fig. 9-5. Primary pattern showing bad point action.

(spark) line may rise at a slight angle to the point of oscillation. The downward angle of the spark line shown in the lower figure indicates high resistance in the secondary circuit. This excessive resistance may be in the rotor contact, cap tower contacts, or wires.

Figure 9-7 shows the primary patterns of all cylinders superimposed on each other. This particular pattern, with its

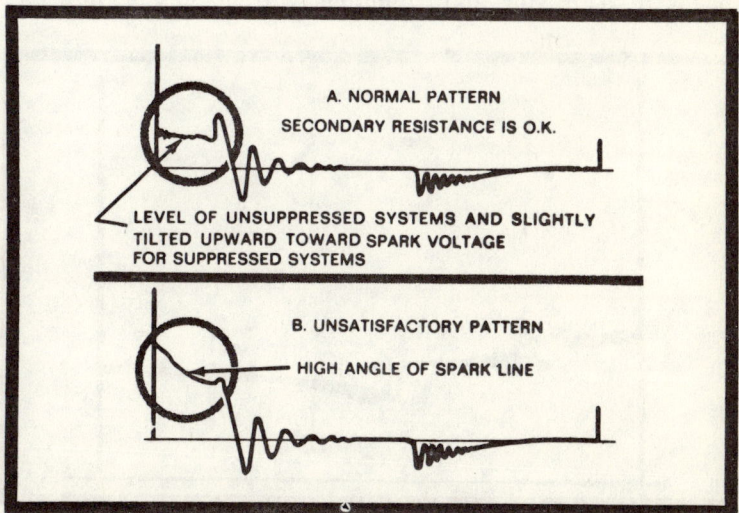

Fig. 9-6. Primary pattern showing resistance in secondary circuit.

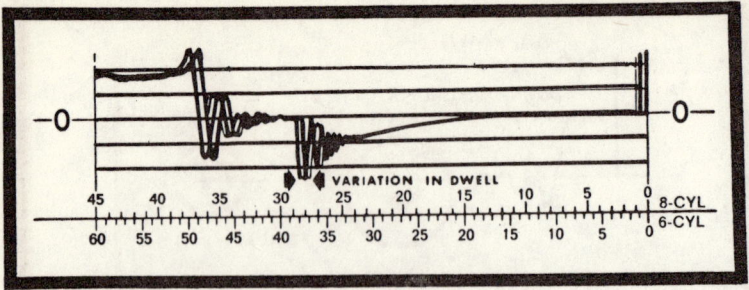

Fig. 9-7. Superimposed primary patterns.

horizontal oscillation, shows dwell variation between the cylinders. This dwell variation is quite likely to be caused by a worn distributor shaft or short bushings. A worn or rough distributor cam surface will also give this indication.

For a comparison of transistor ignition patterns and conventional ignition patterns, refer to Figs. 9-8 and 9-9. Figure 9-8 shows the superimposed primary patterns of a transistor ignition system. Note the low firing line and greatly reduced coil oscillations. Figure 9-9 shows the superimposed primary patterns of a ignition. Note the brief firing time and coil oscillations and the extremely long dwell time.

These comparisons show how the pattern of the primary of any transistor equipped ignition will vary from the accepted primary pattern of conventional ignitions. Also, different makes of transistor and ignitions will display somewhat

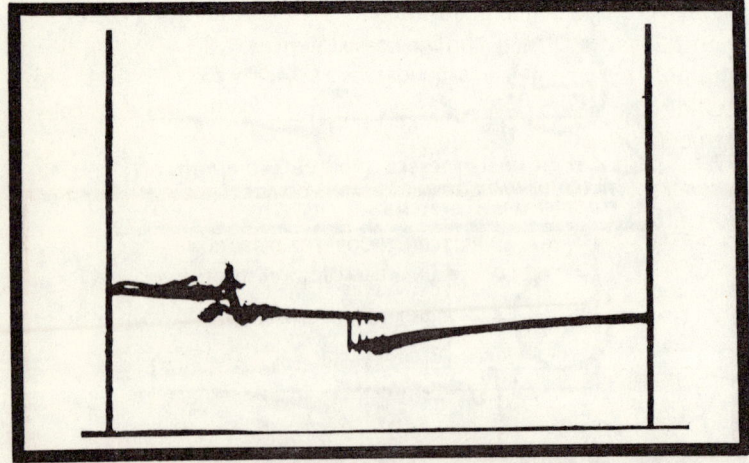

Fig. 9-8. Transistor ignition primary—superimposed.

Fig. 9-9. Capacitive-discharge ignition primary—superimposed.

different patterns, and not all scopes are capable of showing the patterns of the more sophisticated systems.

Figure 9-10 shows the secondary pattern of an 8-cylinder conventional ignition system in the *parade* mode. This pattern is useful for a comparison of the secondary and primary action among the cylinders. A visual comparison is made of the firing voltage, length of time of firing, coil oscillations, and dwell for each cylinder. The time for each action is not readable except for comparison, but the firing voltage may be read directly on the screen.

Figure 9-11 shows the superimposed secondary patterns of a transistor ignition in good working order. It is much different from the pattern of a conventional ignition. Some transistor ignitions suppress the ghost-like traces during the coil oscillations and point closure, but all will show larger-than-conventional oscillations at these places.

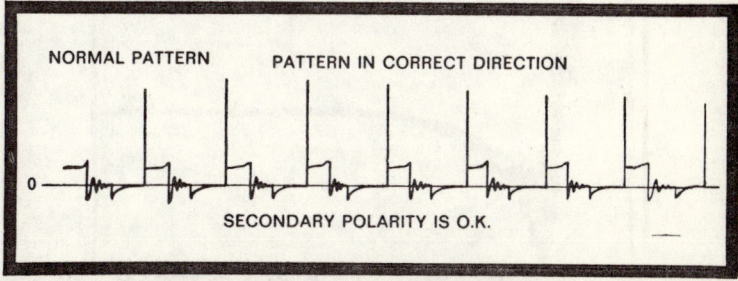

Fig. 9-10. Normal secondary pattern.

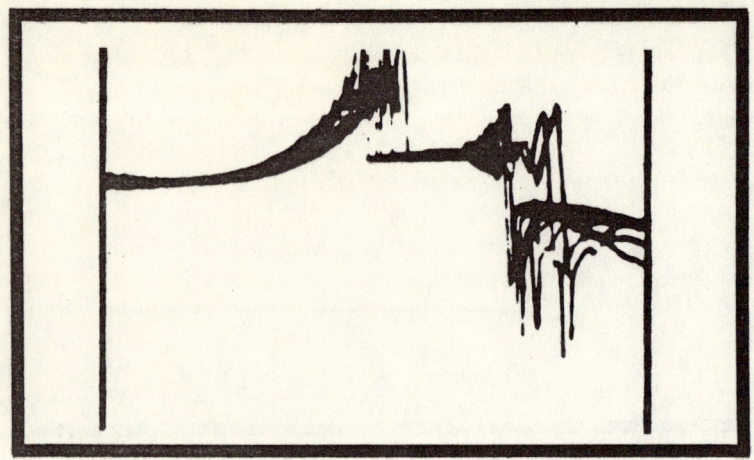

Fig. 9-11. Transistor ignition secondary—superimposed.

Figure 9-12 shows the superimposed secondary patterns of an ignition system. Note the solid, straight spark line and the clean, fast coil oscillations with a sharp return to dwell.

ADVANCED IGNITION TESTING

The patterns shown thus far are basic but valuable in revealing some major problems in the four areas of ignition systems. For a scope to be of general value in pinpointing ignition and other engine problems, and in testing and adjusting modern emission-controlled engines, it must portray engine characteristics not shown in the basic patterns. One

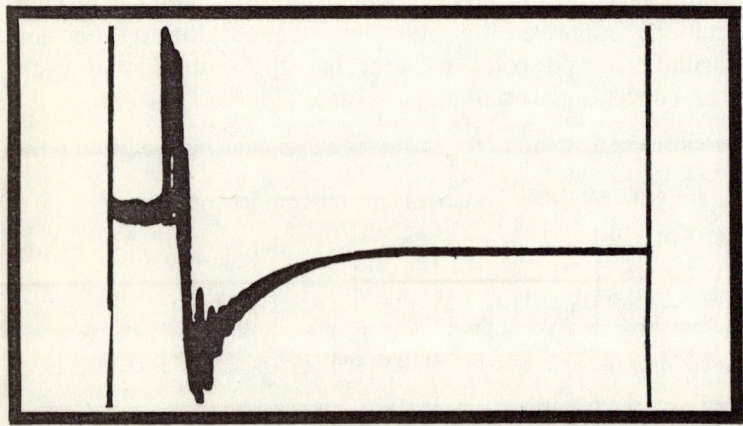

Fig. 9-12. Capacitive-discharge ignition secondary—superimposed.

scope with such capabilities is the Beckman Model 595. This instrument, with the meters and timing light that are part of it, will be used as a model for advanced ignition testing.

When a scope is in the superimposed mode, either on a primary or secondary pattern, major ignition differences among cylinders can be seen, but not small differences. Neither can the problem cylinder be pinpointed from the pattern. A scope with a SPREAD control can stretch the pattern so that small discrepancies are more easily seen; but when the cylinder patterns can be separated and stacked one above the other in firing order (Fig. 9-13), the ignition patterns of the individual cylinders can be more readily compared, and any problem cylinder can be immediately located from the firing order.

In transistor ignitions, extremely small differences between individual cylinders can cause problems. By blowing up the pattern to four times the original length, as in Fig. 9-14, the small differences in time and waveform can be more easily compared. For the really sticky problems, the pattern can be expanded to as much as eight times the original size (Fig. 9-15). These expansion capabilities are used with all patterns—parade, superimposed, and stacked.

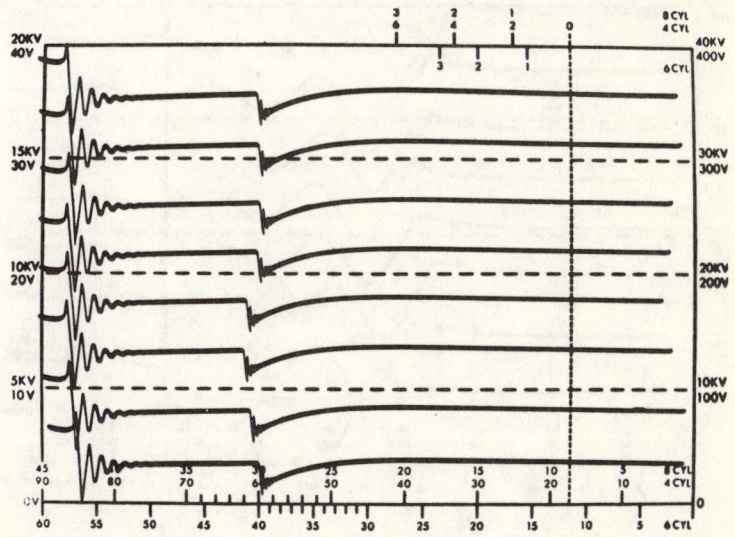

Fig. 9-13. Stacked secondary patterns.

229

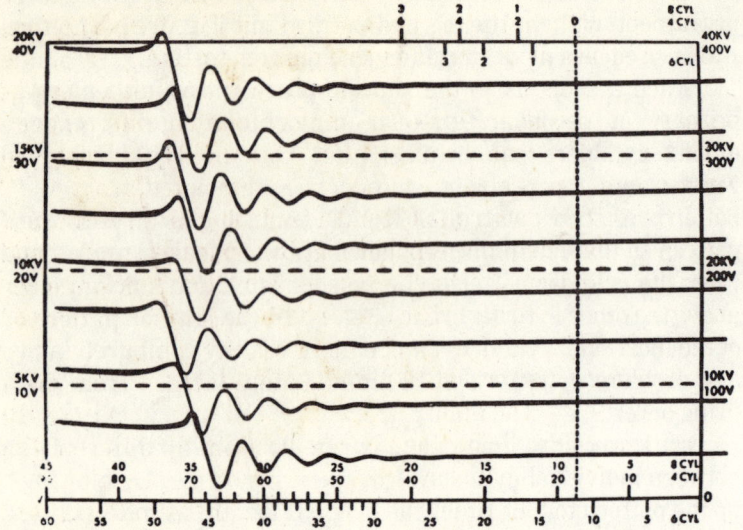

Fig. 9-14. Pattern expanded to four times original size.

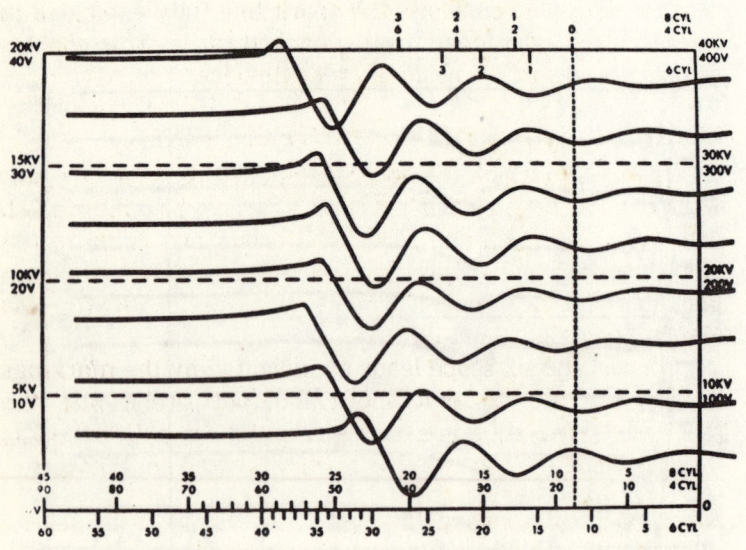

Fig. 9-15. Pattern expanded to eight times original size.

The usefulness of additional flexibility in a scope used for transistor ignition testing is illustrated in Fig. 9-16. The first pattern shown is obtained by lifting the pattern of a single known cylinder from the parade pattern and displaying it above the parade pattern. This is useful in viewing a single cylinder pattern that seems to differ from the others displayed in the parade mode.

The second pattern is obtained by lifting two (or more if desired) cylinder patterns from the parade mode and displaying them in the stacked mode. This is useful for closer comparison, especially if the pattern is expanded to four or eight times original size.

The third pattern shows 0.001 sec timing marks on a stacked pattern. The ability to read elapsed time in very small increments directly on the screen permits analysis of the action of each part of the system.

The fourth pattern shows delayed triggering of a stacked pattern. This is useful in comparing the firing action of all cylinders.

The fifth pattern shows a delayed-triggering single-cylinder pattern with timing marks imposed. This permits visual analysis of dwell time to 0.001 sec.

The sixth pattern shows the spark line fully expanded to eight times normal length in the stacked mode. This enables comparison of spark time among all cylinders.

OBTAINING AND INTERPRETING PATTERNS

The uses to which the above-mentioned patterns are put, what to look for in each pattern, and how to obtain each pattern on the Beckman Model 595 scope are given in the following paragraphs. This material has been abstracted from Beckman Instruments' Engine Scope Tester Instruction Manual (copyright Jan., 1976).

Connect the six scope leads as indicated by the markings on the leads. Note that the coil-output probe and the spark-plug-wire probe are of the inductive type. This makes the disconnection of the wires from plugs or coil unnecessary.

Superimposed Secondary Patterns

Set scope controls as follows: STACKED—pushed in; 20 kV—pushed in; VERTICAL SPREAD—fully counterclockwise; HORIZONTAL POSITION—fully counterclock-

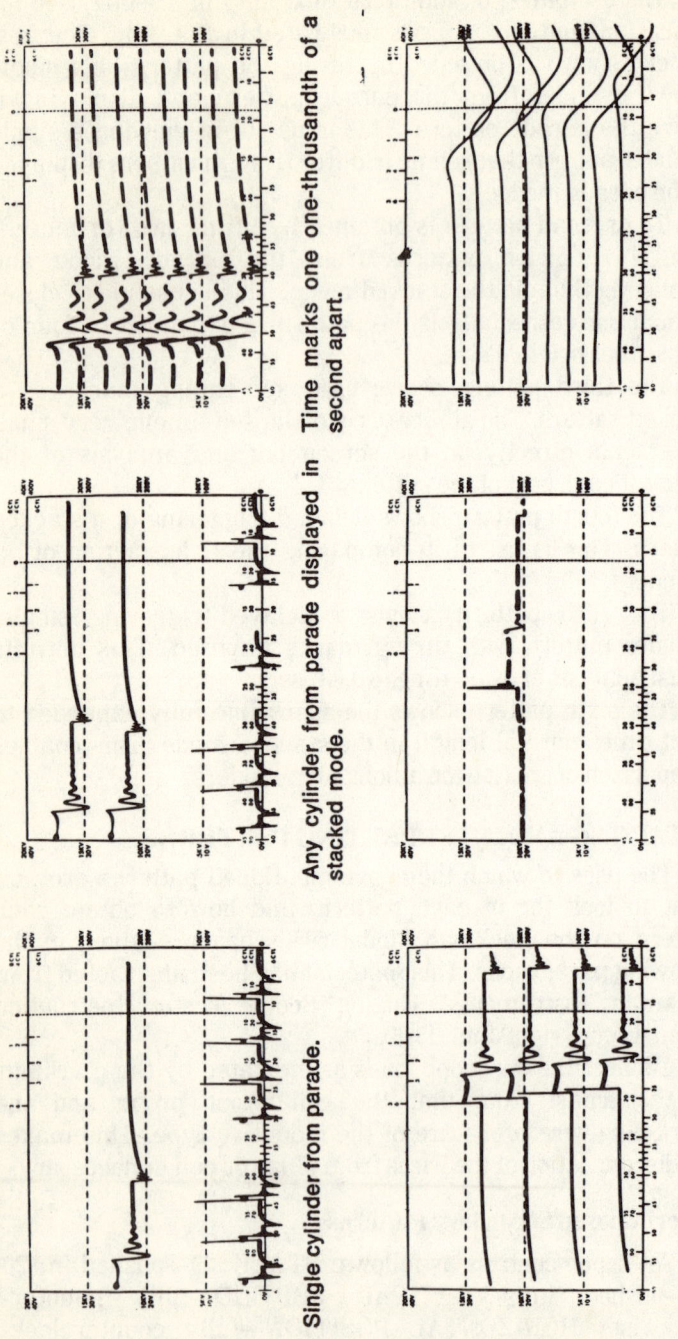

Fig. 9-16. Useful features for a scope for transistor ignition testing.

wise; 1200 RPM—pushed in; CYLINDERS—set to 4, 6, 8, or ROTARY, depending on the engine under test.

Start engine, push POWER switch in, and adjust RPM of engine to 750 as shown on tachometer. When pattern appears, adjust INTENSITY control for clear, legible trace. Use VERTICAL POSITION to adjust pattern to 0V line. Turn HORIZONTAL POSITION and align pattern with left voltage scale. Turn HORIZONTAL EXPANDED to align end of pattern with right voltage scale. The pattern should appear as shown in Fig. 9-17, but on the 0V line. The pattern in Fig. 9-17 has been raised to the 5 kV/10V line for clarity of illustration.

From this pattern, superimposed secondary, the dwell of all cylinders can be read, and the spark characteristics and coil oscillation for all cylinders can be compared. Dwell can be adjusted on point-triggered systems having a distributor with external access to the point-adjusting screw.

With the pattern placed as shown in Fig. 9-17, pull out the TIME SHIFT knob. The pattern now starts when the ignition points close, as shown in Fig. 9-18. This allows closer inspection of the firing lines of the cylinders when superimposed.

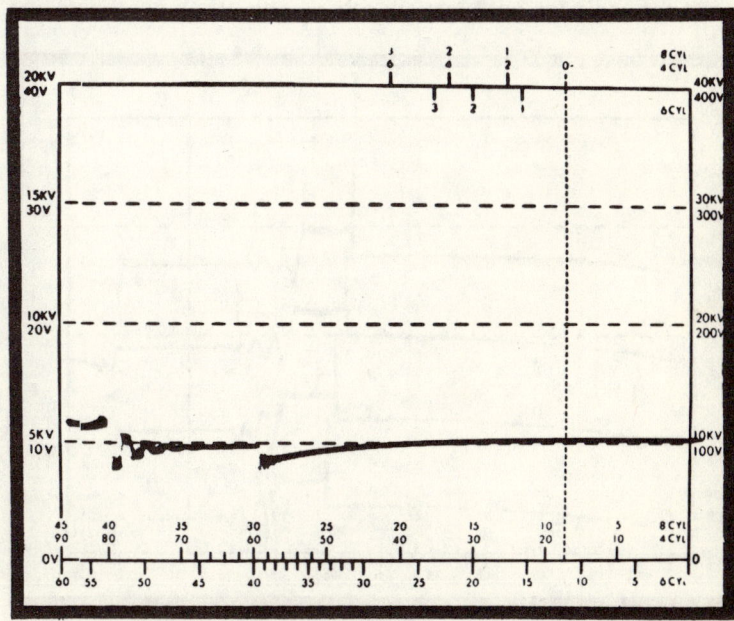

Fig. 9-17. Stacked, superimposed secondary patterns.

233

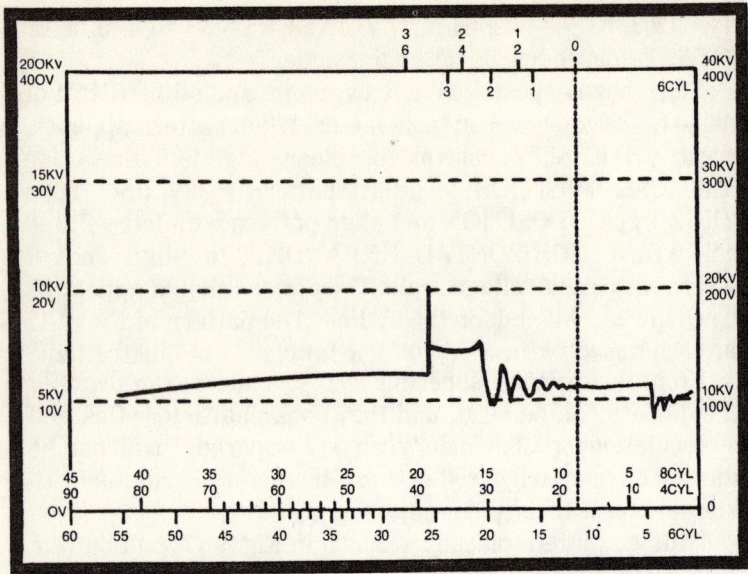

Fig. 9-18. Time-shifted, superimposed secondary patterns.

Stacked Secondary Patterns

Rotate the VERTICAL SPREAD control clockwise to stack the cylinder patterns one above the other as shown in

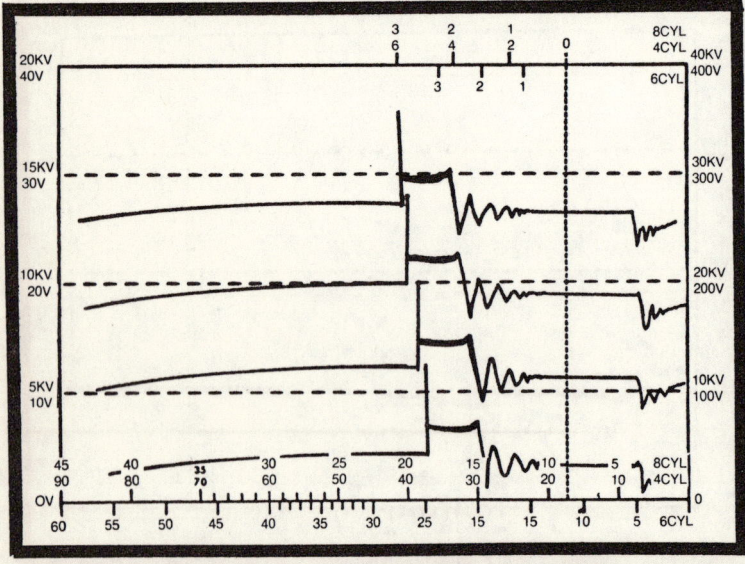

Fg. 9-19. Time-shifted, stacked secondary patterns.

Fig. 9-19. Use this display to compare all parts of the firing lines of all cylinders displayed.

Parade Display

Push in the TIME SHIFT knob and PARADE button. The pattern now displayed is that of the secondary of all cylinders in firing order (Fig. 9-20). If all cylinders do not display, rotate the HORIZONTAL controls to align the right and left sides of the pattern. This pattern is useful in comparing the firing-line spikes of each cylinder. Should the spikes appear uneven as in Fig. 9-21, a problem is indicated in the cylinders with abnormally high or low spikes.

When any of the cylinders exhibit abnormal spikes, push in the FIRING ORDER buttons of the particular cylinders to display those cylinders above the parade pattern (Fig. 9-22). Irregularities of a cylinder's pattern in a specific area usually suggest the problem.

Cylinder Balance Test

The POWER BALANCE control is used to perform a cylinder balance test. To perform the test, push in any FIRING ORDER button. Push in and hold in the POWER BALANCE button. There will be no spark line on the cylinder

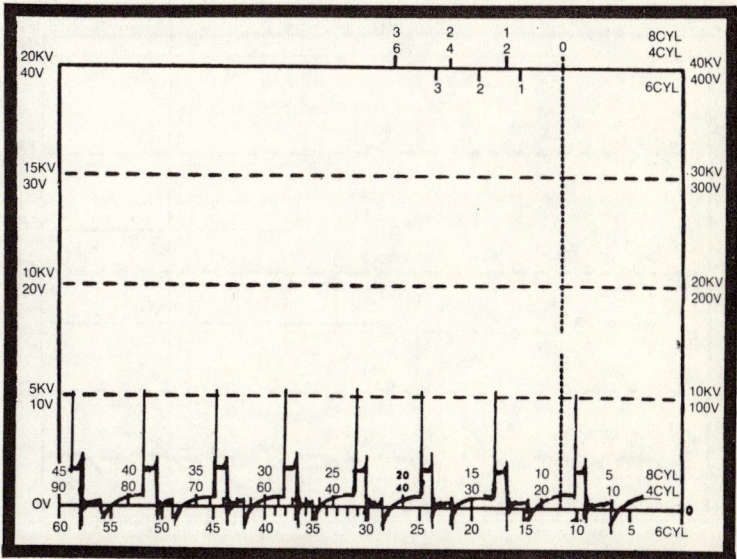

Fig. 9-20. Parade of all cylinders—normal 20 kV secondary pattern.

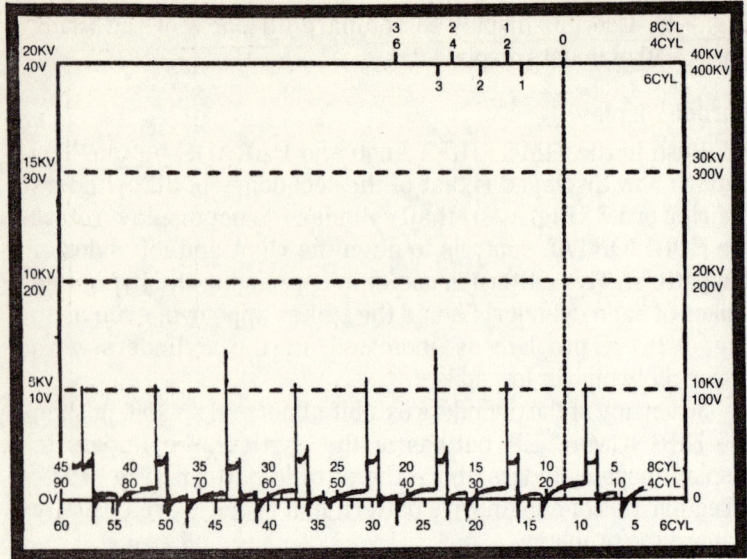

Fig. 9-21. Parade of all cylinders—uneven firing spikes.

of interest, as shown in Fig. 9-23. Observe the effect on the other cylinders when the one is shorted out. This is continued by pushing in each FIRING ORDER button in turn, holding in

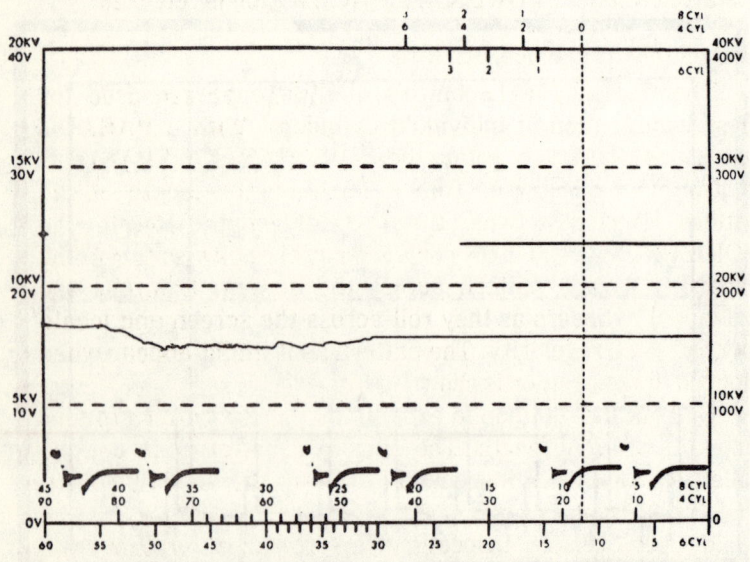

Fig. 9-22. Two cylinders stacked above parade pattern.

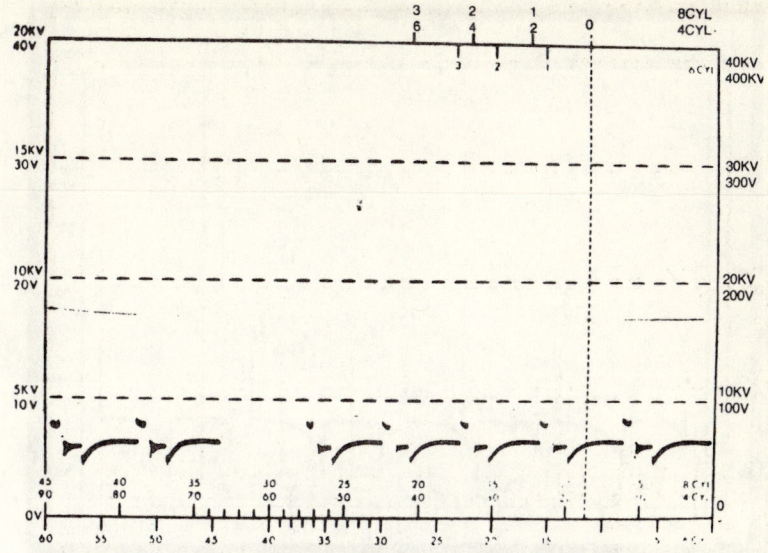

Fig. 9-23. One cylinder shorted—secondary parade.

the POWER BALANCE button and viewing the effect on the parade pattern remaining. When all FIRING ORDER buttons are all out or all are in, pushing in and holding the POWER BALANCE button will kill the engine. The engine can be restarted when the POWER BALANCE button is released.

Horizontally Expanded Displays

The HORIZONTAL controls of this scope are used for close examination of individual cylinders. With a PARADE pattern on the screen, rotate the HORIZONTAL EXPANDED control fully clockwise. This will extend the length of the pattern to nearly twice the original length. Rotate the HORIZONTAL POSITION control counterclockwise to roll the expanded parade pattern across the screen. Examine the individual cylinders as they roll across the screen and locate any pattern irregularity. The pattern as it might appear when stopped in one position is shown in Fig. 9-24.

Pull out the X4 knob to expand the parade pattern to four times its original length. The expanded pattern can now be rolled by for closer inspection by using the HORIZONTAL POSITION knob.

If yet closer inspection is required, rotate the HORIZONTAL EXPANDED knob clockwise to expand the

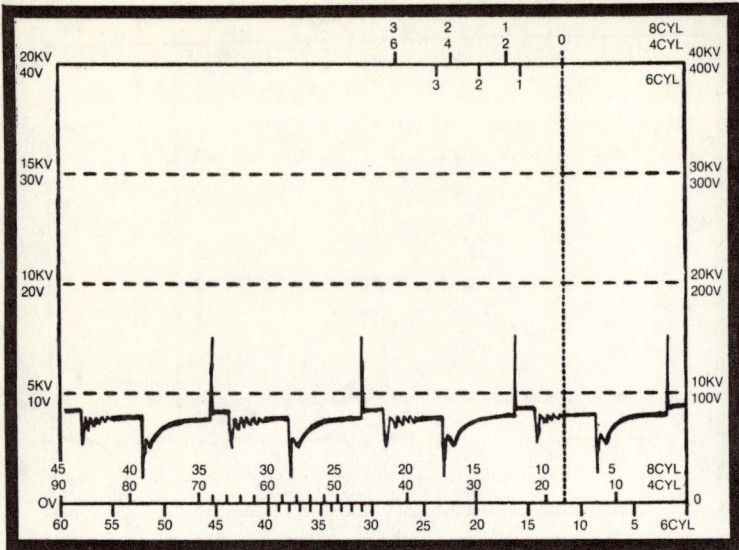

Fig. 9-24. Expanded secondary parade.

parade pattern to approximately eight times normal size (Fig. 9-25). This pattern can be rolled by for inspection by rotating the HORIZONTAL POSITION knob.

Push in the STACKED button to show a horizontally expanded display of the superimposed secondary patterns

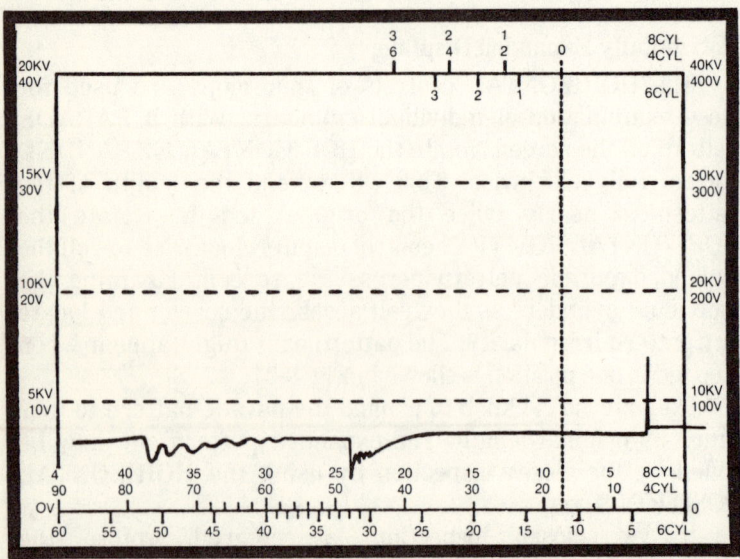

Fig. 9-25. Horizontally expanded (four times) secondary parade.

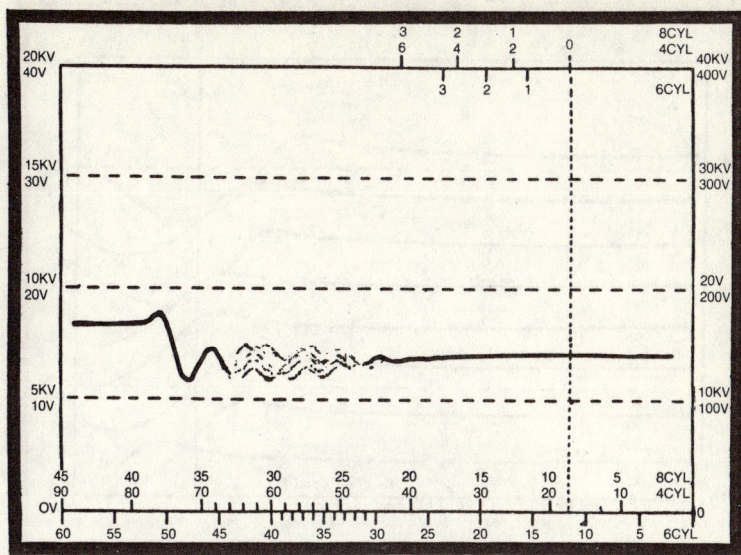

Fig. 9-26. Horizontally expanded, superimposed secondary.

(Fig. 9-26). Make a note of spark lines to see problems indicated by varying lines. If variations appear, as in Fig. 9-26, rotate the VERTICAL SPREAD knob clockwise to stack the cylinder patterns. Observation of the pattern array shown in Fig. 9-27 will pinpoint any cylinder with problems. If closer

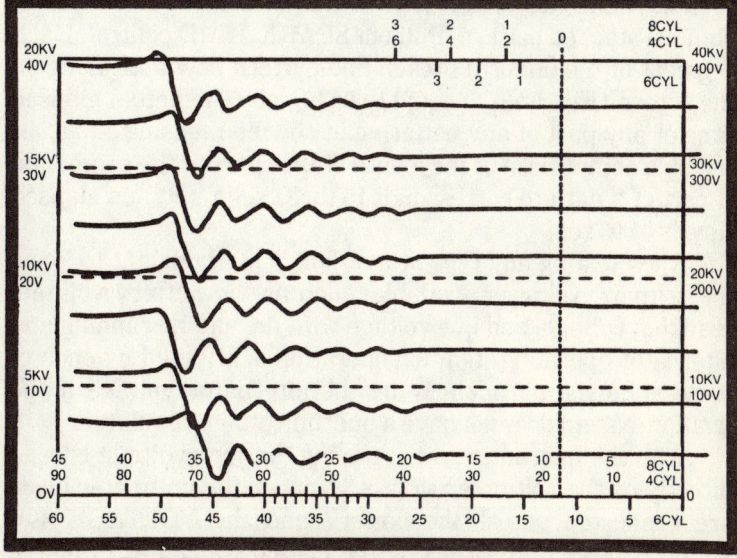

Fig. 9-27. Horizontally expanded, stacked secondary.

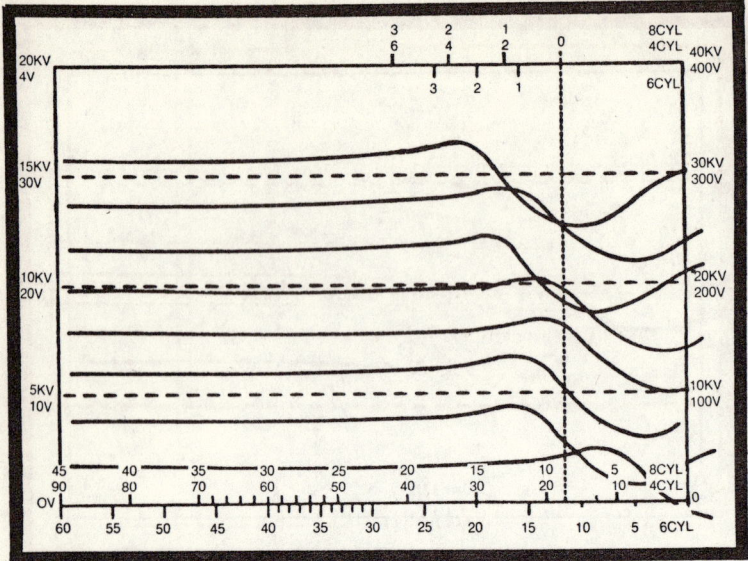

Fig. 9-28. Horizontally expanded (four times) stacked secondary.

inspection is needed, pull out X4 knob to obtain a pattern similar to that of Fig. 9-28.

Of great importance in the testing of transistor ignitions is the close measurement of elapsed time for the spark, coil oscillation, and dwell. To read these values directly on the screen, rotate the VERTICAL SPREAD control clockwise to obtain a stacked pattern. Pull out SPARK TIME control. Each segment of the uniform broken-line pattern now appearing on the screen (Fig. 9-29) is equal to 0.001 sec. The actual elapsed time of any part of any pattern can now be measured to 0.001 sec by a comparison of the length of that part to the segments. If part of a pattern corresponds to three segments, its elapsed time is 0.003 sec.

When testing any type of ignition, it is important to know the primary voltages available, such as the battery voltage, cranking voltage, and line voltage with the engine running and alternator operating. Ignition operation is affected by each of these voltages, particularly by the alternator voltage if the ignition system does not have a built-in voltage regulator.

With the instrument we are using, battery voltage is read directly on the voltmeter (Fig. 9-30) when the voltmeter leads are connected across the battery and the VOLTAGE 40V button is pushed in. Cranking the engine will allow cranking

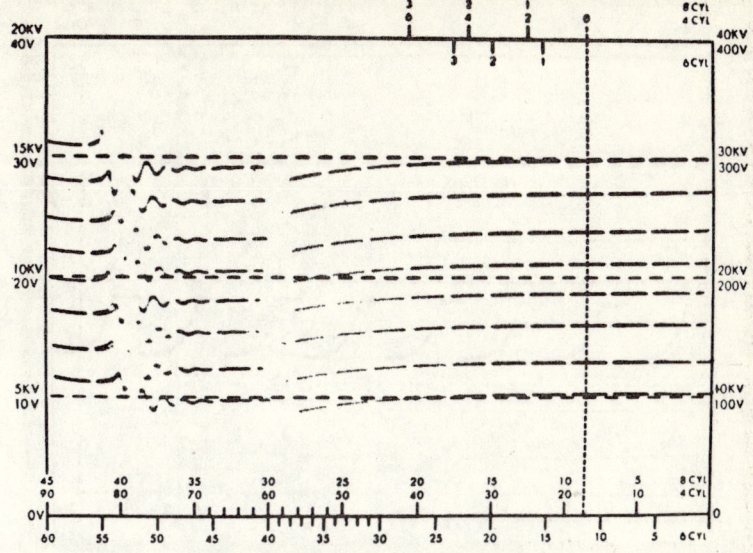

Fig. 9-29. Stacked spark patterns.

voltage to appear on the meter. The POWER BALANCE button may be held in to prevent the engine from starting during the cranking-voltage test.

To check the alternator's output voltage and view the important waveform of that voltage, the voltmeter leads must be connected to the alternator output and ground. Pull out the ALTERNATOR control and push in the PRIMARY 40V button. Read the alternator voltage on the meter and observe the waveform of the voltage on the screen. An alternator showing voltage spikes or alternate high and low pulses can well be the cause of troubles blamed on the ignition system.

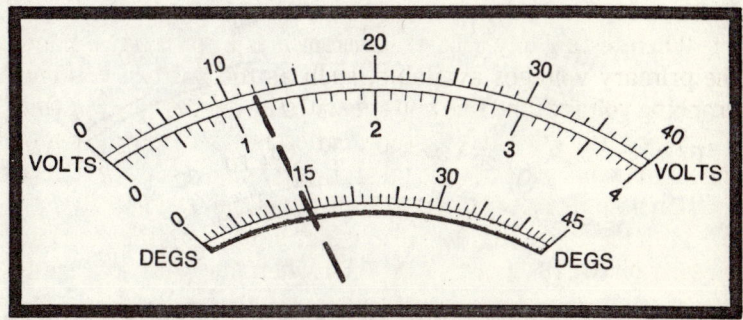

Fig. 9-30. Checking battery voltage.

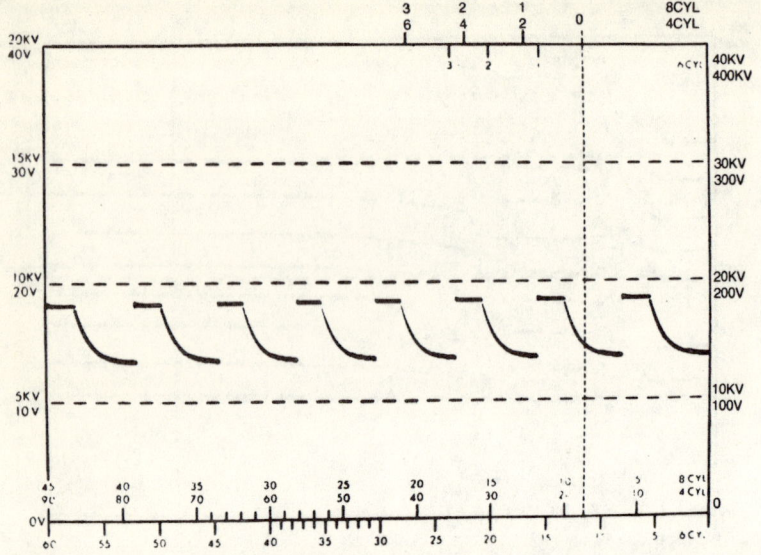

Fig. 9-31. Ballast resistor voltage waveform.

This method of checking a voltage, and the waveform of that voltage, may be used any place in the system. The ballast resistor is a frequent source of trouble that may appear to be in the transistor control box. The waveform pattern of a properly operating ballast resistor is shown in Fig. 9-31. Spikes on the waveform or varying pulses would indicate a need to replace the ballast resistor.

Dwell in degrees can be read on the tach-dwell meter by pushing in the DWELL DEG button when the engine is running. Figure 9-32 shows a dwell reading of 27°.

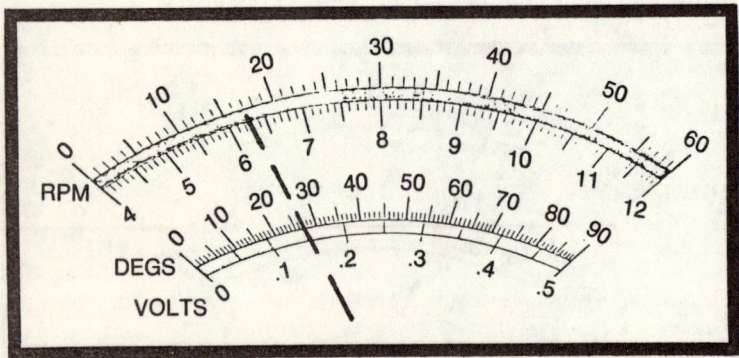

Fig. 9-32. Dwell reading in degrees.

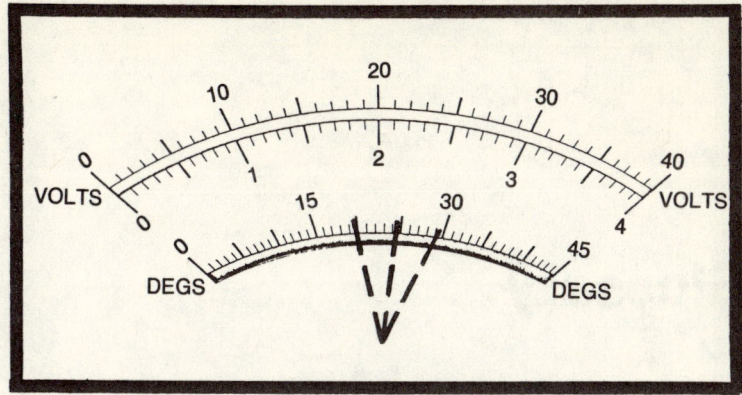

Fig. 9-33. Timing-advance indication.

If point resistance is suggested by the screen pattern, an idea of its seriousness may be obtained by reading the voltage drop across the points on the low-voltage (0V−5V) meter. Push in the DWELL DEG button. Push in and hold the POINT RES button. Read the bottom scale on the meter shown in Fig. 9-32.

Timing advance can be read on the 0°−45° meter by pushing in the DEG ADV button and rotating the TIMING-LIGHT control to align the flash with the pointer. This method can also be used to preset degrees of advance for distributor adjustment. A typical advance reading is shown in Fig. 9-33.

Glossary

ampere The unit of electrical current. A flow of electric charge at the rate of one coulomb per second.
amplifier A circuit designed to increase the strength of a signal without altering its other characteristics.
ballast resistor A resistor put in series with the battery and coil to limit the current through the coil.
bias A steady-state force, voltage, magnetic field, etc. Applied to a system or device to establish a reference level or determine the range of operation.
breaker point set A timing device used to open and close at a predetermined time to fire each plug.
capacitor condenser A device consisting essentially of two conducting surfaces separated by an insulator, or dielectric. A capacitor stores electrical energy, blocks the flow of direct current, and permits the flow of alternating current to a degree dependent upon its capacitance and the frequency of the alternating current.
coil In an ignition system, a transformer in which the battery voltage is stepped up to plug-firing voltage.
condenser See capacitor.
counter emf The voltage induced into the primary of a transformer which opposes the change in current flow.

crossfiring The firing of a cylinder other than at the proper time because of a voltage unintentionally induced at a point in the distributor or high-tension wiring.

Darlington power transistor A power transistor amplifier consisting essentially of two separate transistors connected and mounted in a single package.

diode A 2-lead semiconductor device which will allow current to flow in one direction only.

distributor cap The ignition device wherein high voltage is brought to the rotor, and from the rotor to the individual plug wires at predetermined times.

dwell The number of degrees of rotor travel for which the points are closed before each ignition spark.

electricity A movement of electrical charges, especially a movement of electrons through a conductor from negative to positive.

ground A common connecting point in a circuit. In automotive practice this is usually the chassis or body.

Hall effect The ability of a metal strip, carrying current, to produce a voltage between its two edges when perpendicular to a magnetic field.

ignition The process of igniting the compressed fuel/air mixture in an internal-combustion engine.

ignition time Time required between the moment when the electrons first jump the spark gap until the combustion front in a cylinder starts traveling away from the plug.

impedance The total opposition, in ohms, that a circuit offers to the flow of alternating current. It consists of the combined effects of resistance R, inductive reactance X_L, and capacitive reactance X_C.

inductance The ability of a magnetic field to induce a voltage in a wire when the wire is cutting through the lines of magnetic flux. Either the wire may cut the lines of flux, or the lines of flux may pass over the wire.

light-emitting diode A semiconductor diode that will glow or emit infrared radiation when a voltage is applied continuously or in pulses.

Ohm's law A fundamental law of electricity which states the voltage E of a circuit is equal to the product of the current I and the resistance R.

ohm The unit of measure of resistance, reactance and impedance.

parade pattern A pattern on a scope screen showing the voltage of each cylinder in firing order simultaneously.

photo diode A semiconductor diode in which the reverse current varies with illumination.

photo transistor A junction transistor whose base is exposed to light through a small lens in the housing, and whose collector current increases with the light intensity.

preignition Ignition occurring before top dead center, caused by an agency other than the ignition system.

primary circuit The circuit which supplies and controls the current to the primary winding of the coil. It usually consists of the battery, ignition switch, ballast resistor, primary winding of the coil, and breaker points, all in series.

primary pattern A scope pattern showing the voltage—time relationship in the ignition primary circuit.

programmable unijunction transistor A transistor that can be triggered by applying a voltage between the base terminals or by changing the bias voltage on the P-region. It is turned off by resetting the bias on the P-region. The device is also known as a double-base diode.

reluctance The opposition to magnetic lines of force in certain materials.

resistance The opposition to current, either AC or DC heat, which produces beat.

rise time The time required for the secondary voltage to change from 10% of its open-points value to that voltage required to fire the plugs.

rotor A mechanical timing device for transferring high voltage from coil to spark plug wires.

saturation time The time from the moment the points close to when the current through the coil primary has reached 90% of its eventual value.

secondary circuit The circuit which distributes the high voltage from the coil to the individual spark plugs. It usually consists of the secondary winding of the coil, rotor, distributor cap, plug wires, and spark plugs.

secondary pattern A scope pattern showing the voltage–time relationship in the ignition secondary circuit.

self-inductance The production of a voltage in a circuit by a varying current in that same circuit.

silicon controlled rectifier A 4-layer semiconductor device that normally acts as a nonconducting circuit but switches rapidly to a conducting state when an appropriate gate signal is applied to the gate terminal.

spark electrode The conductive elements on each side of a spark gap through which current flows to and from the gap.

spark energy The amount of energy dissipated between the electrodes of a spark gap. This is normally expressed as a steady-state wattage as if dissipated for a full second. Normally expressed in milliwatt-seconds or in millijoules.

spark duration The time between the moment when the electrons first jump and gap and the moment when the current ceases to flow across it.

spark gap The distance between the electrodes where the spark ionization takes place.

spark plug The device which uses the high voltage produced by the coil to ignite the fuel/air mixture in the combustion chamber.

spark plug wires Conductors of high voltage from the distributor cap to the spark plugs.

stacked pattern The oscilloscope trace of more than one cylinder, one appearing above the other on a scope screen.

superimposed pattern The oscilloscope trace of more than one cylinder, appearing one on top of another on a scope screen.

surging A continual increase and decrease in RPM.

sustaining current The current required to maintain ionization across the spark gap.

thermistor A semiconductor resistor whose resistance decreases with an increase in its temperature.

transistor A semiconductor device having three or more leads, used as amplifiers, electronic switches, control elements in voltage regulation, and for other purposes. The standard triode transistor leads are emitter, base, and collector.

voltage Electrical pressure, or EMF. The difference in electrical potential between two points.

watt The unit of measure of electrical power, abbreviated *W*. One horsepower equals approximately 746W.

zener A semiconductor diode which acts as a rectifier until the applied voltage reaches a value known as the breakdown voltage, or the zener voltage. At this point, the diode conducts with the voltage drop across the diode independent of current.

Index

A

Accel Breakerless Electronic Ignition	162
Advance	167
ignition	12
Allison Optoelectronic Ignition	187
Alternator test	241
Amperage	14
Amplifier configurations	67
Autotransformer	18

B

Ballast	
resistance	37
resistor	22
Bias stabilization	71
Borg-Warner Ignition	180

C

Capacitive-discharge ignition	86
Capacitor	21, 41
Centrifugal advance	12
Chrysler magnetically triggered ignition	92
Coil.	
ignition	18
testing	42
Common	
base	67
collector	69
emitter	68
Contact-controlled ignition	83
Control circuits	75
Conventional ignition system	15
Coupling	72
Cylinder balance	235

D

Darlington power transistor	65
Delco Remy high-energy ignition	111
Delcotronic ignition	102
Delta	
Mark Ten B	153
Mark Ten CD ignition	146
Diodes	57
Distributor	29
checks	38
Dual-point.	
dual-coil ignition	26
single-coil ignition	27
Dwell	23
extender	207
extending	26

E

Electricity. fundamentals of	14
Electromotive force	14
Emitter follower	69
Essex Elightronic Ignition	191

F

Ford magnetically triggered ignition	121
Forward-biasing	58

G

GM Delcotronic ignition	102

H

Heat ranges	45
Heatsink	59
High-Energy Ignition	111

I

Ignition patterns	223
Induction	19

J

Judson electronic magneto	143

L

Light-	
beam control disk	169
emitting diodes	61
triggering	91
Lucas	175

M

Magnetic triggering	88
Magneto, Judson electronic	143
Megaspark Optoelectronic Ignition	168

N

N-material	58
NPN	63

O

Ohm's law	14
Oscilloscope	221

P

Parade display	235
Photodiode	62
Phototransistor	64
Piranha Electronic Ignition	173
P-material	58
PNP	63
Points	41
triggered ignition	212
Pointless ignitions	87
Positive temperature coefficient	22
Power	14
Primary circuit	15

R

Rectifying devices	57
Replacement ignitions	143
Resistance	14

S

Secondary circuit	15
Self-induction	20
Sensing circuits	75
Silicon controlled rectifier	61
Sorensen Magnition Ignition	195
Spark plug	30
maintenance	44
Stevens ignition	155
Suppression devices	43
Suppressor cables	42

T

Timing circuits	72
Transistors	63
ignitions	80
Tri-Star Tiger 500 CD ignition	154
Troubleshooting	51

V

Vacuum advance	13
Voltage	
regulation circuit	77
starting	38

Z

Zeners	60